EGYPTIAN WOMAN

EGYPTIAN WOMAN

A year in the life
of a woman during the reign of
Ramesses II

HILARY WILSON

Michael O'Mara Books Limited

First published in Great Britain in 2001 by
Michael O'Mara Books Limited
9 Lion Yard, Tremadoc Road
London SW4 7NQ

Copyright © 2001 Hilary Wilson

A CIP catalogue record for this book is available from the British Library

ISBN 1-85479-800-6

1 3 5 7 9 10 8 6 4 2

Designed and typeset by Design 23

Illustrations © David Soper
Floorplan, map and chapter thirteen illustration © Hilary Wilson

www.mombooks.com

Printed and bound in Finland by WS Bookwell, Juva

Contents

This story is dedicated with love
and affection to my mother, Pat
Cawston, and my dear friend
Jean Lubbock, both of whom
know all too painfully the
disadvantages of being female.

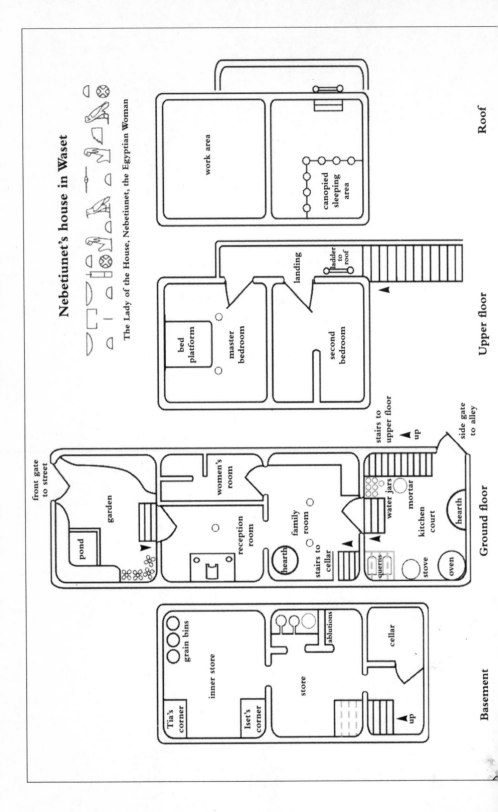

Nebetiunet's house in Waset

The Lady of the House, Nebetiunet, the Egyptian Woman

Roof

work area

canopied sleeping area

Upper floor

ladder to roof

landing

bed platform

master bedroom

second bedroom

Ground floor

front gate to street

garden

pond

women's room

reception room

family room

hearth

stairs to cellar

stairs to upper floor

up

water jars

mortar

kitchen court

querns

stove

hearth

oven

side gate to alley

Basement

grain bins

Tia's corner

inner store

Iset's corner

ablutions

store

cellar

up

Author's Note

About the Calendar

The Egyptian year consisted of twelve months of thirty days each, plus an extra five holidays added at the end of the year, bringing the total to 365 days. There was no correction made for leap years until long after the time of this story. Religious festivals were so much involved with the agricultural year that they were fixed by astronomical observation, to be celebrated in the appropriate season. For administrative purposes, scribes used the simple 365-day year, which slipped apart from the agricultural calendar by one day in every four years. For this reason dates given in contemporary documents are often very confusing, as a scribe could be writing that it was the first month of summer when all around him the fields were flooded at the height of the inundation. To avoid such anomalies I have chosen to stick to the agricultural year and to follow the sequence of the most significant festivals held in Thebes, the city of Amen-Ra.

The ancient Egyptian year started around mid-July by modern reckoning and was marked by the astronomical event known as the heliacal rising of Sirius. This is the time when Sirius, the brightest star in the northern hemisphere, appears at dawn for the first time after several months during which it rises in the daytime and so is invisible. This coincided with the start of the Nile's inundation, the single most crucial event in the agricultural calendar. New Year's Day was called Wepet Renpet, the Opening of the Year, and was the occasion of great celebration and jollification, especially at Dendera, the cult centre of the goddess Hathor, after whom my heroine is named.

People and Places

In describing family relationships I have tried to remain true to the ancient Egyptian terminology. All relationships were described by combinations of only seven words: father, mother, son, daughter, brother, sister and wife. So, for example, 'grandfather' was either 'mother's father' or 'father's father'. There was no word in common usage for 'husband', though I have used this to save unwieldy constructions. No distinction was made between half-siblings, cousins or in-laws, all being called brothers or sisters. 'Father' might also be used to mean grandfather, adoptive father, father-in-law or even master in a student-tutor relationship. Orphaned children, especially unmarried girls, were usually taken in by their nearest relative. Nebetiunet, the Egyptian Woman of this story, would have considered Paser her brother, though because of his rank she would never have addressed him as such except in private. Paser's title, Tjaty, is usually translated as 'Vizier' but no modern title encompasses the wide range of the Tjaty's duties nor his huge area of responsibility so I have chosen to use the more authentic title.

The senior priest of a temple was known as the 'First Servant' of the god. This is commonly translated as 'High Priest' and I have used both titles.

The word 'pharaoh' is a Greek corruption of the Egyptian expression meaning 'the Great House' and was not in general use as a title for the royal person until after the period of this story. I have used the simple and understandable 'King' or 'His Majesty', rather than add confusion by introducing the many euphemisms and circumlocutory nouns and pronouns that were employed in different situations. There was no single word meaning 'queen'. The King's principal consort was known as 'Great Wife of the King' or 'Great Royal Wife', and princes and princesses were simply 'King's Sons' or 'King's Daughters'.

Names were commonly shortened for everyday use or replaced by nicknames, which were known as 'beautiful names'. For example, a name compounded with the name of the god Amen, such as Amenmose, was often shortened to Ameny, and a child named after her mother might be known as Ta Sherit, 'the little one' or 'Junior'.

There is little evidence that the ancient Egyptians celebrated birthdays or even that they kept a count of age. Life expectancy in ancient times was very much lower than today, forty-five being a good span for a man and a woman being happy to reach her thirties. This meant that children grew up quickly and matured earlier than in most modern societies. Painted scenes in tombs show young boys, presumably apprentices or trainees, accompanying their masters in many trades and professions. By the age of twelve or so a girl was old enough to marry and a boy could be holding down a very responsible job, especially if he had trained as a scribe. I hope this explains why some of my characters are apparently so precocious.

The Family

Nicknames or diminutives are given in brackets. Numbers in square brackets indicate age at the start of the story and 'd' indicates deceased. Asterisks denote historical characters.

[30] **Nebetiunet (Nebet):** weaver, seamstress and Chantress of Mut
[34] **Amenmose (Ameny):** her husband, secretary to the Tjaty
[13] **Amenmose the Younger (Pakhred):** their eldest son, trainee draughtsman in the Temple of Amen
[12] **Senmut:** their second son, trainee scribe
[8] **Khaemwase (Khay):** their third son, trainee scribe
[16] ***Mutemwiya (Wiya):** their eldest daughter
[29] ***Ramose:** her husband, accountant in the Temple of Menkheperura-Thutmose
[15] **Mutnefert (Mymy):** Nebet's second daughter
*Abau: her husband, army scribe attached to the Royal Chariot Division
[11] **Nubnefert (Neferti):** Nebet's youngest daughter, apprentice weaver
Montmose: Amenmose's father
[28] **Satra:** Amenmose's sister
[36] **Nubnefert:** Nebet's sister
[41] ***Paser:** Nebet's cousin, the Tjaty
[d] ***Nebneteru:** Paser's father, High Priest of Amen
[d] **Nubnefer:** his brother, Nebet's father

The Servants

Tia: cook, formerly Amenmose's nanny
Meryt: lady's maid to Nebet
Sendji: manservant to Amenmose
Didet and **Hotepu:** housemaids
Iset: trainee maid
Gemni: houseboy
Bak and **Menna:** house servants
Ibi: washerman

Friends and Colleagues

*Nebwenenef (Weni): First Servant of Amen (High Priest)
*Huy: Chief Physician
*Hori: Chief Draughtsman
*Djehutiemheb (Djehuti): Head of the Linen Workshops
*Nedjemger: Head Gardener
*Ahmose: Chief Architect
Senetnay: his wife
Amenhotep and **Simut:** their sons
Meryra: the Tjaty's deputy

Royalty

*Ahmose-Nefertari: mother of Amenhotep I, patroness of the
  Village; deceased
*Djeserkara-Amenhotep: Amenhotep I, royal founder of the Place
  of Truth; deceased
*Isetnofre: the King's Wife
*Maatkara-Hatshepsut: the queen who became king; deceased
*Menkheperura-Thutmose: the king known as Thutmose IV;
  deceased
*Mut-Tuya: the King's Mother, widow of Sethy I, Menmaatra-Sethy
*Nefertari-Meryenmut: the King's Great Royal Wife
*Usermaatra-Ramesses: the king, Ramesses II, commonly known
  as Ramesses the Great

The Gods

Pronunciation of the Egyptian language is still very problematic, mainly
because vowels were not written. The sounds of Egyptian names have to
be guessed or deduced from the versions that appear in other languages,
so I have given the gods the names by which they have become known in
modern times. Mostly these are Hellenized (Greek) forms of the original
Egyptian names. Some will be found elsewhere with spelling variants,
particularly as regards vowels.

Amen-Ra: king of the gods, Lord of Thrones, principal deity of Thebes and personal patron of Ramesses II, who called himself Mery-Amen, 'Beloved of Amen'. Amen was shown as a king wearing a crown with two tall feathers.

Bes: ugly, scowling dwarf god, companion of Hathor and Taweret; his very appearance frightened off evil spirits. His face was often carved or painted on household furniture.

Hapi: god of the inundation, depicted as a well-fleshed man wearing a coronet of water plants and bearing the gifts of the Nile.

Hathor: also known as Gold, the Lady of the Sycomore (the wild fig tree, *Ficus sycomorous*) and Chieftainess of the West. Hathor was the goddess of women, of love and of beer, and probably the most popular deity among the ordinary people. She was commonly shown as a woman with the ears and horns of a cow but could also appear as a lioness-headed woman (like Mut or Sakhmet) or as a serpent (like Wadjet or Renenutet). Her horned sun-disc crown was also worn by Isis.

Horus: son and heir to Osiris; the falcon-headed patron of the Egyptian throne.

Isis: wife of Osiris; the goddess who taught Egyptian women the household arts including how to bring up children. She was a powerful magician and healer, known as the Mistress of Magic.

Khnum: the ram-headed potter god; controller of the River's flow.

Khonsu: the moonchild, son of Amen and Mut; a god of healing.

Maat: the personification of truth, justice and order, represented by the feather against which the heart was weighed at the final judgement; daughter of the sun god, Ra.

Meretseger: her name means 'the Lover of Silence'; she was the personification of the pyramid-shaped mountain el-Qurn, which stands above the Valley of the Kings, and protectress of the Theban necropolis. She was really a local variant of Hathor and was represented as a coiled serpent or as a snake with the head of a woman wearing Hathor's crown.

Min: the fertility god of Coptos, modern Quft; also the patron of travellers, caravaneers and miners. He was shown as a man wearing a shroud from which only his head, hands and erect phallus emerged. His skin was often black, the colour of the fertile Egyptian soil, and he wore a double-plumed crown similar to that of Amen, with whom he was closely associated.

Montju: the warrior god who had been the patron of the Theban area before being supplanted by Amen and adopted into the divine family of Karnak.

Mut: consort of Amen and so Queen of the gods; her name means 'mother'. She was shown either as a woman wearing the Double Crown of Egypt or as a woman with the head of a lioness.

Osiris: the first god-king of Egypt, who taught the Egyptians how to grow crops and tend vines; he was worshipped as a corn-god. As the deity who had overcome death to become King of the Dead, he was associated with rebirth and regeneration.

Ptah: the creator god; known as the 'Great Artificer', he was the patron of all craftsmen. His principal cult centre was at Memphis in the north of the country.

Ra: the sun god, supreme deity, worshipped in many forms but commonly as Ra-Harakhty, Horus of the Two Horizons, the sun that rules the heavens from sunrise to sunset, and shown as a soaring falcon. At Waset Ra was associated with Amen as Amen-Ra.

Renenutet: serpent goddess of the threshing floor, worshipped at harvest time as a bringer of plenty. She was sometimes shown as a woman with a cobra's head and was recognized as the nurturer of the King.

Sakhmet: wife of Ptah; an avenging deity shown with the head of a lioness. She could bring chaos, disease and destruction but she could also heal. She was patron of doctors.

Serqet: the scorpion goddess; guardian of the desert and one of the protectors of the coffin; worshipped by doctors.

Taweret: the hippopotamus goddess, who protected women during pregnancy and childbirth.

Thoth: the scribe of the gods, inventor of writing and patron of all intellectual pursuits. He was shown as a man with the head of an ibis.

Places

Abdu: the sacred city of Osiris, King of the Dead; modern Abydos
Asheru: the Temple of Mut, south of the Karnak Temple
The Beautiful Place: the Valley of the Queens

Behdet: the sacred city of Horus, consort of Hathor; modern Edfu

The Great Place: the Valley of the Kings

Gubla: Canaanite coastal port

Ipet Esut: the great temple of Amen-Ra; modern Karnak

Iunet: city of the goddess Hathor; modern Dendera

Kadesh: city on the Orontes River, in modern Lebanon

Kemet: 'the Black Land', one of the ancient names for Egypt

The Mansion Temple: the mortuary temple of Ramesses II; known as the Ramesseum

Mennefer: ancient northern capital of Egypt; called Memphis by the Greeks

Nubia: the lands south of the First Cataract, into modern Sudan and Ethiopia

Per-Ramesse: 'the House of Ramesses', northern capital and residence city; near modern Tanis

The Place of Truth: the Workmen's Village; now called Deir el-Medina

Qode: town in northern Syria, famed for its beer

Retjenu: timberlands of Lebanon and Syria

The Southern Sanctuary: the Temple of Luxor

Suan: southern border town; modern Aswan

Waset: known also as 'the City'; called Thebes by the Greeks; modern Luxor

CHAPTER ONE

First Month
of Inundation

'WILL THEY BE WAITING FOR US? WILL THEY BE ABLE TO SEE ME?'

Nebetiunet smiled at her daughter's excitement but the boat's captain frowned. The River was almost at its lowest and he was concentrating on negotiating the treacherous shallows and mudbanks just north of the city of Waset. Nubnefert, hopping up and down with anticipation of her homecoming and the news she had to share with her family, was oblivious to anything else.

'Come, sit down Neferti,' her mother said. 'It will be a little while yet before we reach the quay. The River's current may seem slow at this time of year but we still have to move against it. The sailors must be vigilant and you are likely to distract them.'

Neferti sighed and flopped down beside her mother on the sack of their belongings. 'But will they, Muti?' Clearly she was not ready to let her questions go unanswered.

'Will they what, little one?'

'Will they be waiting for us and will they be able to tell what's happened to me?'

Nebet put her arm round her daughter's thin shoulders. 'I am sure a lookout will have been arranged, and as soon as the boat is sighted someone will be sent to meet us. But you must remember that your father may not be back from his trip yet.'

'So he won't know, but will anyone else?'

'Someone may guess, I suppose, when they see you wearing your new gown.'

Neferti giggled and smoothed the white linen over her knees. The simple dress had been given to her by her namesake, her mother's sister Nubnefert. Nebetiunet had been invited with her youngest daughter to the city of Iunet to celebrate the New Year with her closest surviving relative. Neferti had complained of a pain in her midriff on the evening of the great festival, and by the next morning she was feeling so unwell that she did not even want to watch the procession of the goddess Hathor, let alone take part in it. The very thought of the open-air party with beer and sweet-cakes for allcomers made her feel queasy.

Nebet was more than a little put out when her older sister recognized the signs that she, as a mother, should have seen at once. Nubnefert had found the necessary cloths and a respectable cast-off gown which had belonged to her own daughter Hunero. 'Neferti cannot go naked now she is a woman,' Nubnefert had said, making Nebet feel even more inadequate. At least she had had time to explain what was happening before the first blood appeared, so Neferti was prepared and not frightened, but Nebet was still annoyed that she had not thought to bring a suitable grown-up garment for her daughter. Neferti was not quite twelve years old. Her older sisters had not commenced their moonflows at such an early age, and at the hottest time of the year she had not even packed one of Neferti's shifts. She could only accept Nubnefert's gift gracefully and gratefully. 'Let it be my New Year offering to our new young woman,' her sister had said, and so Neferti was the proud, if second, owner of a simple tunic dress of lightweight linen, which reached just to her ankles and was gathered at the waist by a plaited cord.

Pains forgotten in the excitement of her new status, Neferti had gone to the festival after all, and her family gave thanks to their patron goddess for her safe transition to womanhood. Later Nebet had talked everything through with Neferti and discussed the practicalities of cleanliness and laundry. There were plenty of clothes stored away at home, outgrown but not outworn by Neferti's sisters, Mutemwiya and Mutnefert. 'We shall have fun going through the linen chests to see what you can have. You can't wear that dress for ever and it's hardly practical for everyday.' Neferti was thrilled at the prospect and had talked of little else for the remainder of the holiday.

Snuggling into a comfortable position against her mother's shoulder, Neferti brushed aside a strand of Nebet's hair that had fallen across her forehead. 'What about my hair, Muti?' she asked.

'Oh yes, of course, your hair. Well, you can let it grow now as you wish.' Nebet lovingly caressed her daughter's close-cropped scalp. 'We'll have to see whether it comes out straight like mine or wavy like your father's.'

'I hope it's straight. I want to grow it long, like the Goddess, and like Iset.'

Iset was the housemaid, who was the same age as Neferti but whose mother encouraged her to dress and act older in what Nebetiunet considered to be a most unsuitable manner.

'I don't want you to think of Iset as the perfect model for your appearance or your behaviour. I hope you're too sensible to be taken in by her ways. Besides, you may find that long hair is not very comfortable, especially in the summer months, and while it's growing, before it's long enough to plait or tie back, it can be dangerous in the weaving shop. I think it would be better to keep it short and neat. Then, when the time is right, you can have a wig for special occasions.'

'A wig!' Neferti had not considered this aspect of growing up. Her contemplation of hairstyles kept her quiet for some time.

Nebetiunet leaned back against one of the crates of deck cargo and took a deep breath of morning air. The early mist had burned off and the air over the River was clear and bright with only a slight breeze from the north. Along the banks, beyond the broad stands of reeds and sedges, farmers were making their last preparations for the annual inundation, strengthening dykes, clearing out irrigation channels and dredging catch basins. Already the River was rising, though imperceptibly. Within a few days the change would be noticeable as the mudbanks disappeared beneath the rising waters, and after another month or so the River would have overflowed, bringing new life to the land beyond as the floodwaters deposited their gift of rich silt. Peasants were already saying daily prayers to Hapi, god of the inundation, and making simple offerings, begging him to send a good flood this year.

The compelling rhythm of a seasonal carol drifted over the water from a group of peasants working on a *shaduf* beside one of the major canals opening out of the River. The sight and sound brought back vivid memories of her childhood when, after the death of her father,

Nubnefer, she had been adopted by his brother, Nebneteru. Some of her happiest days had been spent on the family farm outside Iunet, where she had often watched workmen, like those on the riverbank, preparing for the inundation. The shaduf was a simple mechanism for raising water: a bucket was suspended from one end of a long pole lashed to an upright (in this case a tree stump) in such a way that it could be rocked up and down as well as swung round. The lashings needed constant attention as they stretched or frayed or became stiff with age. The counterweight on the shorter end of the pole was no more than a mass of mud, stones and other debris, and it too had to be repaired or renewed regularly.

Nebet remembered marvelling at the ease with which a lad no older than her middle son Senmut could lower the pole to dip the bucket into the canal then raise it up again, pivot it round and empty the bucketful of water into the cistern nearby. She had never tried it herself, as it was not women's work, but Nebneteru's son Paser had explained that the counterweight balanced the heavy leather bucket and made it easy for even a young boy to lift a full load of water. Nebet, who had practised carrying water jars on her head, knew just how heavy water was. She was

very glad that now she did not have to do this every day but had servants like Iset to do such work for her.

'Look, Muti, we're nearly there.'

Neferti's cry brought Nebet out of her daydream. The great temple of Ipet Esut had come into sight as the boat cleared the last bend in the River. The two massive pylons on either side of the new ceremonial gateway were still partly shrouded in scaffolding of wood and mudbrick. It would be a while before the huge bronze-clad cedarwood doors were hung in their sockets. Behind and beyond the Temple the city of Waset stretched along the riverside as far as the Southern Sanctuary, which was also undergoing radical building-works. In fact, Nebet thought, there was hardly a time when one or other of the major buildings in Waset was not being modified, renovated, rebuilt or extended, all to the glory of the god Amen-Ra and his son, the Lord of the Two Lands, Usermaatra-Ramesses.

She looked to her right, towards the opposite bank, where the houses of the Western Town clustered around the quays that served the canal and causeway linking the River to the royal mortuary temples on the edge of the cultivation. Just visible was the half-built Mansion, the new temple complex dedicated to the cult of the king, as living god and the god he would become after his death. Surrounding the temple itself were workshops, storerooms and huge mudbrick magazines, which would eventually hold the grain collected annually by the King's tax officials. Currently the tithed barley and wheat were stored in the granaries of other gods, especially at the neighbouring temple of the deified Menkheperura-Thutmose where Ramose, the husband of Nebet's eldest daughter Mutemwiya, worked as an accounting scribe. The King's grand new design included the main administrative offices for Waset, from where her kinsman Paser would conduct the affairs of the South. Paser, who had befriended the orphaned Nebetiunet and whom she had come to worship as a beloved older brother, was the Tjaty, the principal secular authority and head of the judiciary.

Nebet wondered if Paser had yet returned to Waset having attended His Majesty at Suan for the festival of the start of the Inundation. Her husband, Amenmose, as the Tjaty's secretary, had accompanied him. As far as she knew the royal barge had not passed them on its way north to Per-Ramesse and, since she could not see the great boat moored at either the eastern or western docks, she presumed that the royal party had not yet reached the City. Suan was on the southern-most border of Kemet and consequently Hapi's blessing reached that town before anywhere else in the country. Nebet looked forward to hearing her husband's report of a good forecast for this year's flood from the priests of Khnum, controller of the River. They maintained a careful watch on the water level and, by consulting the records of previous years, kept for untold generations, they could predict the extent of the Inundation with remarkable accuracy.

'I see him, I see him!' Neferti squealed in delight as she wriggled out from under her mother's encircling arm.

'Who is it you think you can see?' Nebet asked indulgently.

'The lookout. There, see, it's Gemni, at the washing place with Ibi.'

Nebet's gaze followed her daughter's pointing finger. On a stony beach on the northern edge of the town, a party of washermen had just set down their bundles of dirty linen. It was impossible to identify faces at this distance but she had to admit that the one young boy in the group had the stance of their houseboy.

'I think you're right. Gemni is just the person I would have expected Mutemwiya to send.'

Neferti began to wave and jump up and down to attract the attention of those on shore. The boy seemed not to notice at first, though he was clearly watching the boat as it began to turn towards the eastern dockside. Then suddenly he too started to wave and leap about, causing his elderly companion to look up and stare hard in their direction. The boy must have said something to the old man who turned and waved him away. Gemni needed no further bidding. He darted along the path through the reeds and was lost to sight.

'Will he reach home in time?' Neferti wondered. 'I don't want to have to wait around on the quayside too long.'

'We have legs, child,' Nebet reminded her, 'and we know our way to our own house. We can walk.'

'But it's so undignified, Muti, especially when I'm wearing this dress.'

Nebet sighed. How quickly her little girl had grown up. Almost overnight she had become a young woman and she was unlikely to let anyone forget it for a long time.

'And besides, I'm hungry,' Neferti added.

Nebet laughed.

Nebetiunet was gratified to find that her careful arrangements for the management of her household in her absence had all gone to plan. Her eldest daughter, Mutemwiya, had moved back temporarily to see that her mother's instructions were followed precisely and to make sure that the daily supplies were delivered to her younger brothers, who attended the Temple's scribe school. Amenmose's father, Montmose, had made the occasional surprise visit to ensure that the servants were not cheating his son, as he assumed all servants would do given half a chance. Though Nebet was more confident than Montmose of her employees' trustworthiness, especially that of her personal maid, Meryt, and Amenmose's manservant, Sendji, she was happy to know that the household had been kept on its toes. Meryt, as it turned out, had spent much of the holiday with her own parents, as her services were not required by Nebetiunet. Sendji, who tended to be a little officious in dealing with the household servants when his master was away, was more moderate in his behaviour when he knew that Montmose might appear at any moment.

The elderly cook, Tia, had poured out the expected string of minor complaints about the laziness and insolence of the living-out housemaids, Hotepu and Didet, and was particularly virulent in her report on the young Iset, but Mutemwiya confirmed that everything had gone as smoothly as could be expected. The servants Menna and Bak had spent their time tending the family's garden and vegetable plot along with their own, but had not neglected their other duties. Most importantly they had accompanied Mutemwiya to the Temple commissary to carry back the supplies due to both Nebet and Amenmose as employees of the state, so there was plenty of grain in the bins. Tia had kept Hotepu and Didet busy and there was a good quantity of milled flour ready for Nebet's first large baking session after her return.

First thing the next morning, after a hasty breakfast of barley porridge and dates, Mutemwiya helped her mother make up the daily ration baskets for her brothers Senmut and Khaemwase, then she called for Gemni to help her deliver them to the school gate.

'I must go home after I've seen the boys,' she said. 'I think I've done everything here but I must go and see how Ramose has been getting on without me.'

'Yes, of course. Thank you for all you've done, my dear. I couldn't have asked for a better housekeeper,' Nebet said warmly, and she kissed her daughter before letting her out through the garden gate.

In the kitchen courtyard Tia had already warmed the bake-oven and was stoking the fire with pellets of animal dung mixed with straw, and some lumps of charcoal to increase the heat and keep the smoke down. Tending the fire would keep her occupied for most of the morning. Nebet measured flour and water into the mixing vat, pleased to see that Tia had kept a decent sourdough leaven which, blended with a little beer, should make a good batch of dough. She instructed Hotepu and Didet as to the mixing and kneading and then went back to check the other kitchen stores.

Her daughter had done well. She had not been tempted to overstock by claiming too much at a time of her parents' official rations. Nebet had left the storerooms in the basement adequately stocked with jars of dried fruit and sacks of chickpeas, beans and lentils. Now there were bunches of newly harvested onions and garlic, and bundles of herbs hanging to dry. Nebet checked to see that the seal on her precious jar of honey was unbroken and that mice had not gnawed their way into her box of spices. She noticed a small new hole in the corner of the store and made a mental note to have Gemni check it out. Mice and rats were a constant menace and her cat, Tamiu, was no longer the efficient pest control she had been in her prime. If it were a snake, however, Nebet would have to find other ways to deal with it.

In the next room Nebet noted that the corner where Tia slept was as neat as ever, the mattress rolled up against the wall behind the two lidded baskets that held the old woman's worldly goods. If Tia had any living relatives, Nebet knew nothing of them. Tia had been Amenmose's wet-nurse and, having become nanny and then chaperone as her charge grew up, she had naturally followed her young master when he set up a home of his own. Her position as an old family retainer gave her more licence to speak her mind as regards the running of the household. The newly married Nebetiunet had been very grateful for Tia's guidance and advice, especially since her own mother had died long before she could teach Nebet anything of the craft of housewifery. Now Tia was crotchety and increasingly forgetful. Her back was permanently bent from years crouched over a kitchen hearth, her joints were swollen and stiff, and she rarely walked further than the well at the end of the street. But there was no question of replacing her. Amenmose was well aware of his duty to care for his foster-mother and Tia would have a home in his house as long as she lived.

Nebet next looked in Iset's corner and was equally unsurprised to find it a mess. She was supposed to be training Iset to be a lady's maid like Meryt, but first the little madam had to be taught how a proper household was run from the bottom up. She would be a good worker if only she would stop putting on airs. Her attitude was encouraged by her mother, Henut, who was constantly checking to see that her little darling was not being put upon or overworked. Nebet had no doubt that Tia's moans about Iset were more than justified.

The little ablutions room was next on her tour of inspection. The urine jar had been emptied and Menna was just replacing the sand in the dry trench. Nebet nodded her approval as he scrubbed the limestone seat and the surround of the bathing stall.

'When you've finished, Menna, I want you to go to the poultry yard. Bring back four good birds, geese for preference,' she said. 'Has Bak gone to the gardens already?'

'Yes, mistress. There should be a good basket of vegetables for the evening meal and he said he'd pick out a melon.'

Returning to the kitchen Nebet approved the kneaded dough and divided it into two batches. The first was cut and shaped into ovals, slashed to allow an even rising of the crust, and set to prove on the limestone bench along the kitchen wall. The rest was to be used for flat breads, cooked by slapping discs of dough on to the outside of the clay cylinder stove. Neferti, now wearing a simple, straight shift dress to advertise her womanly status, joined the kitchen crew as they watched to catch each loaf of bread at the moment it fell from the stove, its underside speckled brown. Quickly the loaf was turned and slapped back in place to cook its other side. They soon had a stack of bread, some of which Nebet insisted should be kept for the next few days. This meant climbing a flight of brick-built stairs and a wooden ladder up to the roof, where the loaves were laid out on reed mats to dry in the hot sun. Iset was told to stay there to turn the bread every so often and to keep away the birds.

On the roof Nebet discovered the origin of the smell she had noticed on her arrival home. Gemni had been out with his fish spear and had brought back a good string of medium-sized fish. Tia had made him and Bak gut and split them and thread them on a line to dry. This was hung on the drying frame as high up as possible, out of the reach of Tamiu and the other local cats.

'I didn't want all that good fish to go to waste and there was too much for us here to eat all at once,' Tia explained. 'I didn't like to use oil without asking so I thought to dry them.'

Nebet nodded. She would have chosen to preserve the fish in oil, because it kept the flesh moist and the richly flavoured oil could be used to season other dishes, but she understood Tia's reluctance to use precious cooking oil without permission. Tia was from a class for whom fats and oils were luxuries of substantial negotiable value.

'Next time Gemni has such luck with his fishing we shall salt some and put the rest in oil. If you had asked Mutemwiya she would have said the same,' Nebet chided Tia gently. The cook muttered something about young girls not knowing anything these days but Nebet chose to ignore this implied criticism of her daughter.

Once the bread had been set to bake Nebet decided that they had earned a little break. It would soon be time to start the midday meal but before that she sent Hotepu to fetch a jar of beer from the cellar and, as a real treat, she shared out the cakes she had brought back from the Hathor festival at Iunet. They were somewhat stale by now and needed softening by being dunked in beer, and there was only a morsel each, but the honey-sweetened bread flavoured with ground sedge-nuts was received with reverence, for it came directly from the table of the Goddess.

When their short rest was over, Nebet started to plan. 'It's the eighth day, so the boys will be home from school this evening. I think a light noon meal and something more special at sunset. I hope Menna finds some nice plump geese. With the oven properly warmed up, we can roast them.'

'The grease will be welcome,' Tia muttered. Nebet smiled again at the old woman's obsession with fats. Then all her half-made plans were thrown into confusion.

Sendji arrived back with the laundry that he had collected from the washerman Ibi. 'The Tjaty's boat was just tying up at the western quay when I was down at the River,' he announced. 'The master will be home by this evening.'

Nebetiunet took a deep breath and said, 'Sendji, you must go to invite Mutnefert and Abau, and see if Mutemwiya has got home yet. After that, call on Montmose and invite him as well – oh, and the master's sister too. Then go and find Meryt. I have much for her to do.'

And she would not have time to call in at the Temple linen-works, as she had planned to do that afternoon, to announce her return. Tomorrow would have to do. Today was a time for family.

'That was a very satisfactory homecoming,' Amenmose said as they extinguished the last of the lamps in the living room and climbed the stairs to their bedroom.

Behind them Sendji was settling down for the night on his sleeping mat unrolled on the seating platform. Meryt was already tucked away in the women's room, where she had been joined for the first time by Nubnefert. The other servants had returned to their own homes for the night, Gemni had taken up his usual sleeping place on the roof and, because it was so hot, Senmut and Khaemwase had joined him. That meant that Nebetiunet and her husband had the whole of the bedroom floor to themselves – a rare luxury.

Once they were lying comfortably side by side on the fine wooden bed that had been a wedding gift from Nebneteru, they were at last able to discuss the matter of the boys' school reports. As usual, twelve-year-old Senmut was not applying himself to his studies. His tutor complained that he had frequently missed lessons in order to go on some boyish adventure with his friends, and had occasionally turned up for school smelling more than a little of drink.

Amenmose, however, was unconcerned. 'Just typical student behaviour,' he said. 'I did the same and you know that Pakhred did too.'

Nebet admitted that they had had similar reports about Young Amenmose, known as Pakhred, the Boy. He was almost a year and a half older than Senmut and had already passed through that unruly phase so commonly experienced by boys at puberty. But Pakhred had quickly settled down to his studies and was apprenticed to Hori, the Chief Draughtsman at the Temple. Senmut's reaction to the discipline of school was proving to be far more prolonged and destructive.

'I don't remember the complaints against Pakhred being so strongly worded, or so frequent,' said Nebet, full of concern. 'You know that Senmut is not entirely set on being a scribe and he isn't happy about going on to the House of Life. I wonder if this isn't a way of drawing attention to his unhappiness?'

Amenmose snorted. 'He's got nothing to be unhappy about. I think you worry too much about him. A few beatings from his tutors will soon make him realize where his duty lies. He'll get on fine once he's worked off his youthful high spirits.'

'But what about Khay?'

Khaemwase was a different story. He was the baby of the family. Nebet had conceived him after two miscarriages and then he had been born a month early. No one had expected him to live. In fact, Nebet herself had almost died after the birth. She had not had a moonflow since, and she and Amenmose were reconciled to the fact that their family was now complete. Khay had been enrolled at the Temple scribe school, as had both his brothers and his father before him. He was a willing boy, seemingly keen to learn and to please both his tutors and his parents, but his school reports were discouraging. His penmanship was still barely legible after nearly three years of school and, though he could read tolerably well, he found it a slow, tiring business. He was forever complaining of headaches and sore eyes, which his father dismissed as excuses for his poor performance. The latest report repeated the tutor's fears that a promising lad was not working to his full potential and so was likely to be a disappointment. Coming from a scribely family herself, Nebet fully understood the implications for her son's future. Education was the key to advancement. It would not do either for Senmut to waste his talents or for Khay to waste the time and effort of his teachers.

'I think I'll speak to Huy about Khay's headaches,' Nebet said. 'He might be able to suggest something.'

Amenmose snorted again. 'If you want to go bothering the Chief Physician that's up to you. I don't think there's anything wrong with Khay, except perhaps he's a little bit slow, having been born before his time.'

Nebet bit back a defence of her youngest child and resolved to ask Huy anyway. As a friend of Paser's she had known Huy for many years. Surely a friendly chat could do no harm. She relaxed into the soft mattress supported comfortably on the bed's rope springing. There was no moon to send even a glimmer of light through the window grilles high in the wall. The darkness was all-enveloping. Amenmose started to snore gently. It had been a long day.

Early as it was when Nebetiunet rose the next morning, she found that Khay had risen even earlier. She discovered him in her tiny garden, studying the grapevine that grew in one corner with its branches trained across both the house and garden walls.

'It's coming along well this year, Muti,' he said, smiling at his mother.

'Yes, I'm rather proud of it. We shall have a nice little crop in a month or so, if we can keep the fruit from the birds.'

'What will you do with the grapes?' Khay asked. 'There won't be enough for wine, not from this one vine.'

'No, dear, but think how welcome fresh grapes will be, and if there are enough we can dry some and have our own raisins for several months.'

There followed a short, awkward silence. Nebet sensed that something was troubling her son but she knew that pressing him about it would only make him close up. Khay moved to stroke the glossy leaves of a castor-oil plant, a gesture so tender that it almost brought tears to Nebet's eyes. He was her baby for all that he was eight years old. He would always be her baby and, though she would never admit it to anyone, her favourite child. It was so obvious that Khay was deeply unhappy and she did not know how to help him. She knew he hated disappointing his father, which he did with every report that he brought home. She could only imagine what pain, physical and mental, he experienced at school, and nothing she could say or do would make it better.

To cover her own distress she asked, 'Has Senmut come down yet?'

To her surprise Khaemwase nodded. 'Yes, he's already gone out.'

'Wherever has he gone this early?' Nebet was astounded. It was usually difficult enough to rouse Senmut much before mid-morning on rest days.

'He said something about helping Abau,' Khay said.

'Oh, yes, I remember them talking about that last night.' Among the conversations at the family meal the previous evening, her daughter Mutnefert's husband, Abau, had mentioned his plans for brewing beer over the next two days. Senmut had expressed what she considered an unhealthy interest in the process, especially in the light of his recent school report. But Senmut was always a wilful boy and if he had made up his mind to spend his time off school in this way she was unlikely to be able to stop him. Only Amenmose had the authority to forbid him and Senmut had cunningly avoided that possibility by rising before both the sun and his father.

'Didn't you want to go with him? I'm sure Mymy would have been glad of your company.'

'No. I expect he'll be spending most of the time hanging around the stables while the brew is mashing, and I'd rather be in the garden or helping Bak with the vegetables.'

Nebet feared that he was right. Abau was an army scribe attached to the chariot division of Amen, and Senmut was far too interested in the army life for her liking. She was sure that it was the young soldiers and army grooms who were leading him astray, encouraging him to sneak away from his lessons and to go drinking with them. In spite of her love for her daughter, Nebet was not totally happy about the influence Mymy's husband seemed to have over her son.

Her thoughts were interrupted by a knock on the garden door. Khay opened it to admit a temple servant, who bowed to Nebetiunet and handed her a palm-sized flake of limestone on which was written a message. Though she was quite capable of reading it for herself, since she had been taught that skill in Nebneteru's house, she handed the note to Khaemwase and asked him to read it for her.

He took the note almost reluctantly and Nebet noticed that he frowned as he first brought the stone flake up close to his face, then held it down at arm's length before he began to read it out aloud. Suddenly she understood what lay at the root of his school problems. He simply could not see properly to read. It was not a complicated message but he stumbled over the words and had to correct some of them as the sense of the note became clear. It was from Djehutiemheb, head of the linen-works at the temple of Amen and Nebet's superior. It started with the friendly hope that she had enjoyed her holiday with her sister. Then Djehuti said he had some news to discuss with her and could she please pay him a visit at noon that day.

The straightforward and politely worded message took Khay a painfully long time to read out, and as soon as he had finished he handed it back to his mother and ran out of the garden before she could say anything. She was certain that there were tears in his eyes. And why not? He had just been humiliated and demoralized by his own mother. How could she have been so stupid? There was no point in chasing after him. She could not change what had just happened but she made up her mind to speak to Huy, the senior physician at the temple of Mut, as soon as possible. If there was anything she could do to help Khay she wanted to do it, though in her heart she knew that poor sight could not be rectified. Khay's career as a scribe was probably over before it had properly begun.

Amenmose would be extremely disappointed but it was Khaemwase that they had to consider now. Nebet had to find a way to help her son regain his confidence and to give him hope for the future.

Nebet entered the temple precinct as usual by the side-gate in the huge mudbrick enclosure wall, which gave access to the gardens. She was acknowledged by the gatekeepers as she passed into and out of the southernmost court of the temple on her way to the linen workshops. The weaving sheds and sewing rooms, which served both the temple of Amen-Ra and that of his consort, the goddess Mut, were situated to the south of the sacred lake in the same area as the priests' quarters. The lake provided all the water necessary for purification rituals and libations, as well as being home to a large flock of geese, birds sacred to Amen-Ra himself. A little further to the south, Mut's sacred precinct of Asheru occupied a smaller site around a crescent-shaped lake. As a Chantress of Mut, Nebetiunet had a great affection for the Lady of Heaven, whom she recognized as another manifestation of her own personal goddess, Hathor. Both deities could be portrayed as a regal woman with the head of a lioness. Indeed, there were hundreds of statues in this form surrounding the Asheru Lake, each given a title relating to one of the goddess's many attributes.

The aspect of the goddess that was uppermost in Nebet's mind at present was that of Sakhmet the Healer. It was said that Hathor had healed the Eye of Horus when he had lost it in a battle with the god Seth. Hathor was also known as the Eye of Ra, protector, defender and avenger of the supreme sun god. Nebet had great faith in the meaning and significance of names and titles. Mut, Hathor and Sakhmet. Mother, Eye and Healer. If there was any hope at all for improvement in Khay's sight, it would be found at Asheru where many of the priests of Mut were skilled doctors.

But first she had business to discuss with Djehutiemheb. She found him in one of the rooms where bolts of woven cloth and spools of spun thread were stored. Djehuti kept careful records of all the products of the linen-works, listing and storing them by quality, and insisted that his storerooms were kept immaculately clean to prevent contamination of the fabric, which might be destined to clothe the god. His was only one department of the temple administration but to hear him speak anyone would have thought that it was by far the most important. Nebet had long ago become accustomed to Djehuti's overblown opinion of his own significance.

'Ah, there you are, my dear. I trust you made the most of your time off, because things are about to get quite busy around here.' Djehuti's smile implied that he would share his news with her as a mark of his favour.

'It was very pleasant in Iunet, thank you,' she said. 'I think I am suitably refreshed to take on any new task you may have for me.'

'That's my good girl,' Djehuti said, patting her hand as if she were a child. Such a gesture could so easily be misconstrued by any who did not know Djehuti as she did. He would often stand over a weaver, leaning his face just that bit too close to hers, or rest his hand on a spinner's shoulder while he talked to her. He thought he was being friendly and fatherly calling his staff 'my girls', and he was totally oblivious to the inappropriateness of his actions. The parents of some of the younger girls saw Nebet as something of a chaperone and were happier knowing that she was there to look out for their daughters.

Of course, if the girls stayed for any length of time they soon came to realize how harmless Djehuti was. He had never married, which was unusual for a man in his position, and he still lived with his widowed mother, a redoubtable lady who had reached the remarkable age of seventy. The girls sometimes mimicked his actions and imitated his manner of speech but all in good spirit. They never teased him to his face and they never said anything cruel about him behind his back because they knew him to be genuinely concerned about them.

'Well, now. I received a message myself last evening from the Tjaty. He informs me that His Majesty has requested new vestments for the Opet Festival this year and, of course, we are to make them. That means priestly garments for the King, a festival gown for the King's Great Wife, and robes for the First Servant Nebwenenef and for the Tjaty himself. I want you to help me select the cloth and to oversee the cutting, because I would trust no one else with such an important task. I will also require you to recommend those seamstresses whose stitches are finest and who can work under pressure. This commission is to take priority over everything else.' The look on Djehuti's face was a mixture of pride, anticipation and anxiety. 'Do you think it can be done in time?'

'It will be a challenge but we've worked to tighter deadlines in the past. I see no reason why we should let down the reputation of the linen workers of Amen on this occasion.' Nebet smiled to put him at his ease. That he was willing to put his complete trust in the work of his girls showed how much he appreciated their worth. To Djehuti it mattered not what other workshops might have been asked to prepare for the Opet Festival; the clothing of the royal couple was the greatest honour.

'Of course,' he said, 'you will have the royal likenesses to work on. We can't expect the licence of being allowed to conduct fittings on the Royal Person. But it is a great honour nonetheless.'

Nebetiunet agreed and then suggested that they pick out some of the necessary linens while they were there to hand. It was mid-afternoon before she left the temple precinct and made her way to Asheru to seek out her friend Huy.

'My dear Nebetiunet, what brings you to my office? You're not ill I hope?'

'No, dear friend, but I have a medical problem I would like to discuss with you.' She poured out the story of Khay's school reports and her own observations, finishing by saying, 'I know you probably can't do anything for his eyes but I must do something to help him. I can't bear to see him so unhappy and school is just making him more miserable.' She was embarrassed to feel the pricking of tears in her eyes and lowered her head to hide her discomfort.

Huy said gently, 'You would not be the good mother I know you to be if you were not worried. It sounds to me as if you are right. Khay does have a problem with his sight, but without examining him myself I can't tell what sort of problem, nor how serious it is. Rather than make him feel uncomfortable by seeing him at home, I think it would be better if I visited the school. I can use the excuse of giving some of my students practice in the examination of eyes. That way I can examine several boys at the same time and Khay won't feel he's being singled out. I think you'll find he'll be relieved to have this problem out in the open. Once it's identified, you'll be able to discuss his options freely.'

'Oh, I'd be so grateful if you could do that. It wouldn't put you to any trouble?'

'Not at all,' Huy reassured her. 'As I said, it will be good experience for my apprentices. Leave it with me. I can't say exactly when I'll be able to arrange it but I will see Khay, that I promise you.'

'Thank you, thank you so much.'

On her way home Nebet walked with a lighter step. It was as if voicing her fears had gone some way towards allaying them. Her talk with Huy had eased the burden of worry. All she had to do now was to explain the situation to Amenmose. She knew her husband would not be so easily convinced of Khay's difficulty. He would consider acceptance of his son's disability an admission of weakness. No matter how many people told him that no one was at fault, or that there was nothing anyone could have done about it, Amenmose would seek to place blame on someone or something for Khay's imperfection. Nebet knew that she would have to shoulder the responsibility. That was what a mother was expected to do. Amenmose was not unkind; he loved his wife and, though he did not always show it, he loved his children. Undoubtedly there were trying days ahead but she knew that it would all be well in the end.

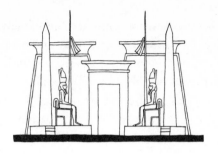

CHAPTER TWO

Second Month
of Inundation

NEBET FROWNED AS SHE STUDIED THE FALL OF THE SLEEVES ON THE High Priest's gown. She twitched the pleats over his left shoulder and stood back to take a better look.

'Don't fret at it, Nebetiunet,' the High Priest said. 'I'm sure it's just fine. You are striving for impossible perfection.'

She was not convinced. Nebet took a fishbone pin from the reed tube hanging at her waist, but then she could not decide where to place it to best effect. 'I don't understand why the sleeves are so uneven. I've measured them again and again, but as soon as you tried it on I could see they were wrong.'

'Well, there's your answer. It's not your excellent sewing, it's my old and crooked body.' Nebwenenef shrugged the offending shoulders and smiled a wry smile. 'There's nothing you can do about that – no pins or tucks will even up my ancient frame. And besides, the first time I raise my arms, the lie of the sleeves will be disturbed and no one will notice, so stop worrying.'

She had been reluctant to suggest that the fault lay with the wearer rather than the garment so she was quite relieved to hear Nebwenenef's words. She could hardly criticize the posture of the First Servant of Amen, even if he was an old and dear family friend. 'I suppose you're right,' she said without conviction.

'Of course he's right,' a voice said from the shadows behind her.

'Paser,' the priest said, waving a welcome to his friend, 'you arrive at a very opportune moment. I cannot convince our little Nebetiunet that this gown is finished. As Chief Justice you have all the veracity of Maat and the wisdom of Thoth. She has to believe you. Tell her that it is perfect so that I may be released from this torture.'

Nebet felt her cheeks redden as she turned to see her kinsman, the Tjaty, in the doorway. She bowed as he entered the room.

'You look very smart, Weni, very stylish, as you would see for yourself if there was a mirror big enough,' Paser said.

'Are you suggesting I'm fat?' the High Priest asked with mock indignation.

'Oh, I'm sure not,' said Nebet, flustered. 'The Tjaty means that a mirror which is held in the hand can only show a small part of the figure at a time. You would not be able to see the full effect.' She realized that this statement had not made things any better and her blush deepened.

'We are embarrassing this charming lady, Weni,' Paser said. ' I think we owe her an apology.'

'Oh, don't. You are quite as bad as each other,' she snapped.

'That's the little Nebetiunet I remember,' the High Priest said with a grin. 'You are too strict with yourself and tend to take yourself too seriously at times, but we wouldn't want to change you.'

She knew he meant it and she felt an overwhelming warmth as she accepted this good-natured teasing from two of the most powerful men in all the Two Lands. She had known Nebwenenef as a friend of her father for many years and she had grown up in the same house as Paser. She had seen how differently they behaved in private in comparison with the aloof, formal appearance they presented to the public. It would not do for either of them to be seen smiling, for fear of being accused of showing undue favour. As for joking and laughing, that was unthinkable. Nebet had to admit that Nebwenenef was somewhat plump around the midriff but she would not dream of voicing her observation. Plumpness was a sign of prosperity, almost of rank, so the High Priest deserved to be a little overweight, though Paser was as slim as ever.

'Have you come for a fitting too?' Nebwenenef asked his friend.

'No, my official robe is of a far simpler design than yours. I caused Nebet much less trouble. It was finished days ago.' Paser tipped his head to one side to appraise the priest's garment and then asked Nebet, 'Have you considered that the cheetah skin will probably disguise any problems there might be with Weni's gown? And by that I am not implying that there are any problems with it.'

'There speaks the lawyer,' Nebwenenef laughed.

Nebetiunet had forgotten the ceremonial animal-skin cape that the High Priest would be wearing as officiant for the Opet rituals. She put a hand to her face, which was colouring again, 'Of course! Why am I worrying? No one will be able to see the sleeves anyway.'

'You're worrying because you have pride in your work, which is just as it should be.' Paser took her hand between his and gave it an affectionate squeeze. 'Put the pins away now.'

'What are you here for?' Nebet asked as she collected up her sewing things.

'I want your professional opinion on some of the festival preparations at the Southern Sanctuary. Would you be able to meet me there tomorrow morning?'

'So you're running your own errands now, are you? What's all this about? You could have sent a message through Amenmose. You're being very mysterious,' said Nebet, suspiciously.

'If you're worried about wagging tongues, have no fear. I have festival business to discuss with our esteemed First Servant and I was told he was here. I've given the message to Amenmose as well, so wait until tomorrow. You'll see then.'

'Can I please change out of this now?' Nebwenenef wailed, plucking at the folds of his festival gown. They laughed at his comical expression.

'The River is rising well,' Amenmose said as they stood beside the docking basin in front of the Southern Sanctuary.

'This morning Tia claimed that the level in the well has risen by a hand's-breadth since yesterday,' said Nebet.

'I can believe it, even though I usually take little notice of the old dear's rantings.'

'Ameny! That's very bad of you. You shouldn't talk of Tia like that.'

'I know, but *you* know that I don't mean anything by it. I've known Tia all my life and by now I'm well acquainted with her views on everything – and believe me, she has strong views on *everything*. I wouldn't dare contradict her to her face, even if she told me the River had dried up altogether.'

'I think I might question such an outrageous statement, even from Tia,' Nebet smiled. 'Not that she would ever say anything so blasphemous.'

Amenmose took her arm and they turned to walk towards the Sanctuary's impressive new pylon gateway.

'Why have we been asked here?' Nebetiunet asked again, but Amenmose was no more forthcoming than when she had first asked the question the previous evening. He just looked unbearably smug.

There was a great deal of activity around the temple entrance. The wooden shuttering that protected the obelisks on their pedestals to left and right of the central gateway was being lowered. Workmen were stacking the planks neatly behind the eastern wing of the pylon. The last of the scaffolding was being removed from the pylon towers and would not be replaced until after the Opet Festival. The outer face of the pylon would eventually be carved and painted with scenes of the King's military achievements, but at present it was a blank expanse of mellow sandstone against which the red granite of the obelisks was a pleasing contrast. The only other adornment was four flagstaffs set in niches, two on either side of the gate. Each was a single tree trunk, taller, straighter

and more slender than any tree that grew in Kemet. They were pine trees that had been brought all the way from the land of Retjenu, far to the north. The decision had been made to erect them in time for the King's visit to Waset and Nebet had overseen the weaving and dyeing of the banners that would soon flutter from their gold-plated tops.

Workmen were clearing the debris of broken mudbricks and scaffolding ties from the ceremonial road that linked the Southern Sanctuary with the temples of Amen and Mut. Nebet suspected that much of the rubbish was being swept behind the sphinxes or into the depressions edged with mudbrick, in which were planted the persea trees that flanked the paved way. None of this, however, was visible from the quayside road, which was the approach that would be taken by the procession in a few days' time. She wondered if there was a temple housekeeper who would discipline these lazy workers, but she rather thought not. Clearly they believed in the same principle of 'out of sight, out of mind' as Iset, whom she had caught, only that morning, hiding the sweepings from the kitchen court behind the water jars in the corner. Inspection of the area had shown that this was not the first time she had done so. Nebet had told Iset precisely what she thought of her and had left the girl in a sulk. She was beginning to despair of teaching the child even the rudiments of household management, let alone the niceties required of a lady's maid.

The temple gates had not yet been hung and the entrance to the colonnaded court was simply barred with woven reed panels and guarded by two ancient gatekeepers, who were already dozing at their posts in spite of the hubbub around them. It would be some time yet before the King's works were ready for the dedication ceremony, and access to this area was not as restricted as it would be once the temple was fully functioning. Nebet realized how impractical it would be to insist on the usual purification rituals for everyone entering the sacred precinct.

'Come,' Amenmose said. 'The Tjaty said we were to gain entrance to the court through the western door.'

Picking their way carefully across the rubble-strewn ground and avoiding the porters with their unwieldy burdens of scaffolding planks and ropes, they walked past the western end of the pylon and found the gateway halfway along the outer wall of the court. The gatekeeper here was much more alert and asked Amenmose's name and business, mentally checking his identity against a memorized list of today's visitors.

In the shelter of the colonnade it was noticeably cooler than outside. It was also dark after the brilliant morning sunshine, and to Nebet's dazzled gaze the small group of people standing in the south-western corner were no more than silhouettes. As her eyes became accustomed to the shade she saw Paser deep in conversation with a man whom she recognized with pleasant surprise as her daughter's husband, Ramose. It would have been unforgivably rude for even Amenmose to interrupt the Tjaty's discussion, so the couple remained a little way off in the dappled light of the colonnade until Paser should acknowledge them.

Nebet wondered what Ramose's presence might signify. Amenmose had told her that the Tjaty had recently shown great interest in Ramose, having heard good reports of his work in the accounting department of the temple of the Divine Menkheperura-Thutmose. 'Paser as good as asked me for a character reference, so I think Ramose might be in line for a promotion quite soon,' Amenmose had said. Nebet hoped this was so. Mutemwiya deserved some good news.

When her eldest daughter had married Ramose, Nebet had had some fears about the difference in their ages and their rank. Ramose's father, Amenemhab, was of a minor noble house and still bore the title King's Messenger, though he was no longer active in the royal service. Recently widowed, he lived in a comfortable house on the family farm, which was run by Ramose's older brother. Ramose had made his own way in the world, owing little to his father's influence although undoubtedly helped by his social position. Consequently he had made his own choice of wife. Ramose and Mutemwiya had met when she was delivering a message to her father and he was visiting the Tjaty's office. They had literally bumped into each other in the reception hall. Nebet liked to think that it was love at first sight.

Ramose was almost twice as old as Mutemwiya, more of an age with Nebetiunet herself. It was unusual for a man, especially one of Ramose's rank and situation, to remain unmarried for so long. Nebet had heard rumours of casual romances in his early years but there was nothing to complain about in the way he had treated Wiya since their marriage. He had become a devoted husband and Wiya was perfectly happy. It was clear that in concentrating on his career he had had no time for wife-hunting and he had obstinately refused to comply with his parents' attempts to see him settled. Ramose's mother had not approved of Mutemwiya, and to her dying day she blamed the poor girl for stealing her son away, even though Ramose had severed his maternal ties long before his marriage. The one thing that everyone regretted was that Wiya had not given Ramose a child before his mother died. A new generation might have softened her attitude towards her son's wife.

While these thoughts passed through her mind Nebet became aware that another of the Tjaty's group was not only looking at her but trying to catch her eye. She realized, with even greater surprise, that it was her son Young Amenmose. She turned to her husband and whispered, 'What's Pakhred doing here? Why didn't you tell me?'

Amenmose whispered back, 'It would have spoilt the surprise.'

At last Paser finished speaking and turned to beckon them forward. They approached and bowed respectfully. 'I'm glad you were able to come,' he said, as if they had had any choice. When the Tjaty issued an invitation, no matter how friendly, it was understood as a command. 'Amenmose, you know all these gentlemen so I leave you to make the introductions. I have something more to check up on but I'll see you again before I go back to my office.' Everyone in the group bowed as the Tjaty took his leave. Followed by his manservant, he walked across the open-roofed court, through the door in the eastern wall and then out of sight.

Amenmose took Nebet's hand and led her forward. 'Master Hori, I present my wife, Nebetiunet, daughter of Nubnefer. Nebet, this worthy is Hori, Chief Draughtsman of Amen.'

Nebet bowed her head to the man who was her son's boss in the temple design department. 'I greet you, sir,' she said formally.

'And I greet you, Nebetiunet. I am delighted at last to meet the mother of my most promising student.'

Nebet felt her face warming again, only with pride this time rather than embarrassment.

Hori appeared not to notice her flushed cheeks and was too much of a gentleman to have said anything if he had. He went on, 'The Tjaty and I have been inspecting the latest phase of the decoration in this fine court, and he was most interested to know that this particular scene was drafted by your son. We both thought you might like to see it.'

They were standing to the right of the gateway that gave access through a high-roofed corridor to the older parts of the temple. Hori indicated a section of the wall which was quite deeply shaded and there, drawn in clear black lines but not yet carved, was the image of the new temple entrance. Nebet recognized at once the towering pylon blocks, the obelisks and the flag-poles, but there was more. Six statues of the King were shown, one seated and two standing to each side of the gate, although she knew there were no such statues in place yet. This was a picture of what would be when the temple improvements were complete.

It was not an elaborate design compared with some of the vivid battle scenes that decorated the exterior walls of the Great Columned Hall at Ipet Esut, but it was the first commission entrusted to her son, who was grinning broadly and almost bursting with pride.

Pakhred, at a nod from his master, started to explain the picture to his mother. 'There are the obelisks and there are the images of His Majesty, which are even now being sculpted in the temple yards. Do you see, Muti, I've drawn the flagstaffs with your banners flying from them. Your work, too, is recorded in stone for all time.'

Nebet was too full of emotion to be offended by his rather patronizing tone. She knew she was highly favoured to have been allowed to see this work. Once the court was consecrated, only temple personnel would be permitted to enter here, and very few women, even on special festival occasions. There was just a chance that she might be admitted as one of the Chantresses of Mut, but during a ritual she would have no opportunity to stop and admire her son's work, let alone point it out to her companions. She was grateful to Paser for allowing her this honour and she would make sure Pakhred showed his own gratitude for the Tjaty's condescension.

Ramose spoke for the first time. 'The Tjaty asked me to escort you back to the main gate once you had seen this. If Master Hori will allow.'

The Chief Draughtsman nodded his permission and Nebet's family bowed in farewell. Ramose took them back the way they had entered the temple court and round the western wing of the pylon to the ceremonial avenue. 'I think we need to be a little further back,' he said mysteriously.

'I wish someone would tell me what's going on,' Nebet said in frustration.

Her menfolk simply smiled indulgently. When Ramose was satisfied that they were in the right place he indicated that they should turn to face the magnificent gateway and watch.

'Watch what?' Nebet asked plaintively. Ramose pointed. A man's head had appeared in the window behind the easternmost flagstaff and he was tugging at a string hanging from a neat bundle secured to the top of the pole. Nebet suddenly realized what was about to happen and she found she was holding her breath, only to sigh with satisfaction as the broad streamers unfurled and began to ripple in the morning breeze. The yellow safflower dye would soon fade in the heat and the sunlight, but it would last for the duration of the Opet Festival. The temple servant moved across to the next flagpole and soon a second set of streamers was fluttering gold against the brilliant blue sky. Nebet looked instinctively towards the western poles and saw that their banners were already flying, loosened by another servant. The effect was complete.

While she had been looking up, her hand shading her eyes from the bright sunshine, Paser had approached unnoticed, and she was startled to hear his voice. 'It's only a little thing in the whole scheme of the festival, but I knew you'd like to see the results of your work. These are the first banners to decorate the King's temple. You should be very proud.'

'Oh, I am, I am,' Nebet said, breathlessly. He was right. Her small contribution to the most important event of the year in Waset was unique because it was the first occasion of the flag-raising. More than that, her own son had commemorated the occasion in a lasting monument. Nebet's involvement in the event might not be recorded in words but the gods would know the heart of the artist and would therefore understand the part she had played. This was a gift indeed, beyond her ability to express. The people around her knew what it meant and allowed Nebet her moment of glowing satisfaction.

On the morning of the first day of Opet the family gathered in the kitchen courtyard. The sun had not yet cleared the eastern horizon but already noise and laughter could be heard from the houses all around as their occupants prepared for a long day of celebration. Tia was serving date cakes and the special honeyed beer that had become a family tradition for Opet. Amenmose and Pakhred had stayed overnight with their respective masters, so it was Senmut's duty to welcome the other members of his family as they arrived, a duty he had been less than eager to perform.

'Do I have to, Muti? I said I'd help Abau.'

'There are more than enough servants at the stables, especially with the King's guard in residence. You'd only get in the way. Your brother can do without your help, and I need you here.'

Senmut knew better than to argue with his mother, especially when she took that tone. He reluctantly took up his post at the garden gate, ready to offer bread and beer to the visitors gathering for the family party. First to arrive was Amenmose's father, Montmose, accompanied as always by his unmarried daughter Satra. Nebet had given instructions that they were to be entertained in the garden and not brought through to the kitchen. She would give Satra no excuse to criticize her housekeeping.

Amenmose's sister had kept house for her father since her mother died. This was the excuse she gave for never having married, but everyone who knew her suspected that either she had not found a man who reached her exacting standards or, more probably, she had never been asked.

Each guest was given a festival collar which Nubnefert, Didet and Hotepu had made from leaves and flowers sewn on to a linen background. Satra inspected the workmanship of her collar carefully before she allowed Meryt to fasten the flaxen cords at the back of her neck. She accepted the beer served in one of Nebet's finest glazed-ware bowls and sipped it tentatively. As Nebet said to Amenmose later that day, 'You'd think I was trying to poison her. Why does she have to be so ungracious?' to which Amenmose had no reply.

Mutemwiya arrived next with Ramose who was quite content to join the younger members of the family in the kitchen and to drink his beer from a plain pottery cup.

Khay presented the floral collars to his sister and her husband saying, 'You won't see better than this at the festival, despite what Satra may say. Many of these flowers came from the temple gardens.'

'I heard you'd been spending more of your time there,' Ramose said. 'How do you manage that with your studies?'

Khay answered easily, for he had had time to come to terms with the Chief Physician's verdict on his eyesight. Huy had done as he promised and had suggested that Khay would be better off working outdoors, in the brighter light of day, than indoors by the flickering light of oil lamps. This meant that his school studies had effectively stopped, but by now he had acquired enough scribely skills to be of use to any of the outdoor departments of the temple administration.

His love of plants made the gardens the obvious choice and he had been apprenticed to Nedjemger, the Chief Gardener of the Divine Offerings at Ipet Esut. He had spent the last two days filling orders for cut flowers and herbs to decorate the temple, the temporary way-stations along the processional route and the sacred barques in which the deities would travel. He had proved to have such a light touch with the plants that he had been asked to select the flowers for the presentation bouquets for the King and the Great Royal Wife, Nefertari. As reward for this special task he had been given two baskets full of surplus flowers, which he had brought home to present to his mother as his contribution to the festival celebrations.

Nebet had received the flowers with tears in her eyes. Less than a month ago she had feared that Khaemwase was doomed to a life of failure. Now, not yet nine years of age, he was already being entrusted with royal commissions. Amenmose would always regret that his son had not completed his education, and Nebetiunet knew that he secretly made offerings to Thoth, the patron god of scribes, in the hope that Khay's sight would improve enough to allow him to resume his studies. Nebet herself had prayed and made offerings to Sakhmet the Healer but, seeing how Khay had found a situation where he was happy and where others appreciated his worth, she was content.

Mutnefert arrived at the last moment, as usual, her festival gown poorly draped and her wig askew. Nebet sent her daughter up to her own bedroom with Meryt to help her dress properly but not before Mymy's wild appearance had been seen and frowned upon by Satra. Nebet was very glad that she had given Iset leave to return home to her mother for the festival. The girl could be truculent at the best of times and her resentment at being forced to work during Opet did not bear thinking about. Her surly face and defiant attitude would not be missed and Satra would have no cause to complain about Nebet's household discipline.

At last all were ready. Satra was particularly eager to leave early in order to find a good vantage point on the riverside path from which to watch the sacred flotilla but, as always, everyone else in Waset had had the same idea. Nebet smiled to herself because she had anticipated this problem and she remained perfectly calm in the face of her sister's complaints that they should have left earlier to avoid the unseemly crush.

The narrow streets were already thronged with people, all dressed in their finest clothes, making their way to the River. They called greetings to their neighbours and friends, and family groups mingled into one happy crowd. Nebet found herself walking beside Senetnay, wife of Ahmose, the Chief Architect of the Estates of Amen-Ra. Senetnay's two young sons, Amenhotep and Simut, and her baby daughter were in the charge of their nurse so she had time to chat.

'I see she hasn't mellowed,' she commented, tipping her head towards Satra, who was holding her skirts close as if the mere brushing of the linen folds against a stranger would defile her.

'Not at all,' Nebet sighed. 'She's so objectionable that I wonder Montmose hasn't said something to her about it. She cannot hope to win a husband if she treats every man she meets like dirt.'

'Montmose is the typical doting father. He doesn't see her as we do. In his eyes, no doubt she's perfect,' Senetnay said.

'I know,' Nebet replied, 'and today is not the day to disillusion him, even if he'd listen. I shall enjoy myself, no matter what my sister thinks of me.'

Nebet was pleased to see how well her plan had worked. The previous day Amenmose had gone with Menna and Bak to pick out the family's roost for Opet.

They had chosen a point about halfway between the two way-stations, the tented shrines marking the places on the riverbank where the sacred barges would be moored while offerings were made to the divine family. The areas immediately around the way-stations had been cordoned off from the ordinary public for the use of priests, royal courtiers and their families.

Amenmose had fetched a donkey from the temple stables to carry the heavy jars of beer and the wineskins. Four large water jars had been set up on jar stands and filled so that the water would cool overnight, and Amenmose had left the two servants there to guard the pitch. First thing in the morning Hotepu, Didet and Gemni had brought down the baskets containing the festival picnic which Tia had spent days preparing. On the embankment against the town wall Menna and Bak had set up awnings of coarse linen sailcloth over reed poles and there were leather-covered cushions strewn over the rush mats covering the bare earth. The whole arrangement was very comfortable and even Satra could not find fault.

Each member of the family found a place to sit and the first of the food was handed out, small dishes of salted lupine seeds, bean rissoles and sedge-nuts, washed down with more honey-beer.

When Nebet had discovered that Senetnay had made no firm plans to meet either family or friends, she insisted that room be found for her, the two little boys and the baby with her nurse. 'I won't hear of you sitting out in the sun all day. It will do the little ones no good at all.'

Senetnay thanked her warmly and said, 'The very least I can do is to make my small contribution towards the food.' She indicated to her houseboy that the baskets he was carrying on a yoke across his shoulders should be added to the pile of picnic containers.

Released from his duty, the lad asked and was granted permission to go with Gemni to look out for the flotilla. The two boys ran down the slope and across the waterside path to the River's edge, where they were quickly joined by Senmut, Khay and little Amenhotep. They were soon indulging in the usual pushing and shoving and general horseplay enjoyed by young boys everywhere.

'How long before one of them falls into the River, do you think?' Senetnay asked.

'I fully expect all of them to be soaked through by midday. It's the festival tradition,' Nebet said lightly, ignoring the frowning Satra, who clearly disapproved of children.

This was made even more obvious when Senetnay's daughter started crying and was promptly put to her nurse's breast. Satra pointedly turned her back and stared determinedly across the River. Nebetiunet was at first amused and then a little angry on her friend's behalf. It was at least impolite of Satra to behave so, and at worst insulting to Senetnay who, although younger than Satra herself, was of higher status, being a respectable married woman. Then, as Nebet observed Satra casting surreptitious glances over her shoulder at the nurse and her charge, she realized that in fact her sister was envious. Perhaps there was hope for her yet.

Shortly Khay darted back to report that the sacred barges had been spotted and that they were currently anchored before the first way-station. The rituals to be performed were quite lengthy and it would be some while before the gods, borne on their gilded and bronze-plated barques, recommenced their voyage upstream, towed by their escort vessels. There was time to catch up with the latest gossip and to comment on the clothes and deportment of the other festival-goers as they passed by.

Ramose was engaged in polite conversation with Montmose. The old man was always complaining that he had no one of sense to talk to and he heartily approved of Mutemwiya's husband. Ramose had an easy manner which made people like him, and he was an excellent listener, a valuable talent when dealing with Montmose. Neferti had taken charge of Senetnay's younger son, four-year-old Simut, and took him off to hunt for lizards along the town wall.

'Will Ahmose be joining you later?' Nebet asked her guest.

'I doubt it,' Senetnay sighed. 'There's been so much going on at the Mansion that he's away from home for days at a time. He sent a message to say he'd try to be back for today but it looks as if he won't make it. All traffic across the River will have been stopped now to clear the way for the sacred barges.'

'What a shame,' Nebet commiserated. 'Ameny came back yesterday morning to help set up our tent so he knows exactly where to find us. I hope he'll be here before the procession passes.'

Amenmose arrived just in time. Having been prevented from using the tow-path by the soldiers and men of the local medjay police force stationed along its length to keep back the crowds, he had had to fight his way through the mass of spectators. He acknowledged Senetnay, and his father and sister, then called for a drink.

Hardly had he taken the first gulp of pomegranate wine when a shout went up from the youngsters by the River. The barges were on the move again. Everything began to happen at once. The boys scrambled up the bank, wriggled between the honour guard and reached the family viewpoint just as the Nubian archers marched into view.

The feathers in their hair, the heavy ivory earrings and bracelets and the animal-skin loincloths showed brightly against their dark skin. Some carried regimental standards, others held palm fronds as a sign that this was a peaceful event. A cheer from the crowd a little to the north indicated that some of the Nubians were treating the spectators to a display of acrobatic dancing. The rhythm of drums accompanying their lively performance could be clearly heard. To the glee of all the children, the troupe chose to repeat their vigorous dance right in front of the family gathering.

Next came the chariots bearing the King's sons. Senmut eagerly described the finer points of the horses and their trappings to anyone who would listen.

'He sounds just like Abau,' Mymy laughed.

To Nebetiunet the comparison was unwelcome. It confirmed her opinion that Senmut was spending far too much time in the company of

Mymy's husband. It was little wonder that his school reports had not improved.

Her attention, however, was drawn to the princes. Amenhirkhopshef, the oldest, was younger than both Pakhred and Senmut, but he stood proudly beside his charioteer and waved to the crowds. The youngest prince in the parade was the son of the King's second wife, the Lady Isetnofre. This was Prince Khaemwase, who had been born in Waset only a month before Khay. When the physician had said that her baby was unlikely to survive, Nebet had insisted that he be given the same name as the young prince. Names were important. Surely Amen-Ra, who protected the child of his son the King would extend his care to any child bearing the same name. Nebetiunet had been proved right. Khaemwase was a lucky name.

After the chariots came the solemn procession of the temple singers. Over and over they chanted the Opet hymn in praise of Amen-Ra and his wife, Mut, who were being escorted to their private residence at the Southern Sanctuary to celebrate the festival of their union. The words of the hymn spoke of Amen's love for his wife, and of the gods' love for the King and his wife. His Majesty was praised as a true son of Amen-Ra, brother to the divine child Khonsu. The Great Royal Wife was praised as Beloved of Mut, the epithet she had added to her name at the King's coronation. The men of the sacred choir marked the beat with ivory clappers. The chantresses shook their sistra, adding a gentle tinkling sound to the rhythm. Over the heads of the procession the first of the escort boats could now be seen, rowed as close to the shore as its draught would permit so that the crowds had the best possible view of its occupants.

Enthroned under a canopy sat the King in all his royal splendour. Upon his head he wore the Double Crown of the Two Lands, composed of the White Crown of the South set inside the Red Crown of the North. About his neck was a jewelled collar, and golden bracelets encircled his wrists. At his side stood Paser.

Shielding her eyes against the glare of sunlight reflected from the water, Nebet dared to cast a critical gaze over the royal person, to see how well the new gown fitted his athletic frame. She had to declare herself satisfied and more than a little proud that it had turned out so well. Paser, as always, looked immaculate.

Her attention was distracted by the sudden rushing forward of the younger spectators as they vied to lay hands on the tow-rope attached to the god's barque. The tow-rope was only a token gesture, for the barge could not be held safely on course by a raggle-taggle crowd on shore, but it was considered an honour, indeed a right, for any citizen of Waset to offer his assistance to his god on this festival occasion. Khay came back disappointed, for he had been elbowed out of the way by some larger boys.

'You must try again when the goddess reaches us,' Nebet said.

Amenmose put his hand on Khay's shoulder and said, 'You did well to try. You got closer than I did when I was your age.'

Nebet was amazed and greatly touched by this demonstration of affection from her husband for his youngest child. Amenmose, gazing out towards the flotilla, missed the beaming smile on Khaemwase's face.

The barge bearing the Great Royal Wife now came into view. In the shelter of its brightly coloured awning sat Her Majesty, as gaily attired as her royal husband, and attended by her eldest daughter, Merytamen, a child younger than Khay. Nebet, inspecting the folds of Nefertari's gown, was not so pleased with the effect. She had become used to fitting garments to a wooden dummy but the results were rarely as perfect when seen on the living wearer. Her experience told her how differently fabric hung over warm flesh. Nevertheless, she had been happy enough with the simple shape of the gown ordered for the Royal Wife to have delegated the task to one of her younger seamstresses. Even at a distance she could see something was not quite right. Perhaps it was the way the Lady's dresser had folded it, or perhaps it was because Her Majesty was sitting down that it looked wrong.

Then Mutemwiya leaned over to whisper in her ear, 'Is Her Majesty pregnant again, do you think?'

Of course, that explained everything. 'It would appear so,' she said. 'This will be her sixth or is it seventh child?'

'Some of us would be happy with one,' Wiya said with feeling.

Nebet struck by the bitterness in her daughter's voice took her hand. 'Your time will come. Let's pray to the goddess as she passes. She'll see how much you deserve to be a mother.'

Hand in hand, mother and daughter stood in silent prayer as the barque of Mut was towed past. Nebet had not realized until that moment just how much Wiya's childless state had been preying on the girl's mind. All around her were happy, laughing children, mothers and nurses with babies, every one reminding her of the empty place in her life. Nebetiunet prayed harder, beseeching the goddess to allow Mutemwiya to know the joy of motherhood.

Suddenly a small body squirmed between them and threatened to tumble down the slope and under the feet of the crowd tugging at the tow-rope. Mutemwiya deftly scooped up little Simut and set him on her hip. 'We don't want you squashed, young man. Come with me and I'll find you some dates.' Any hint of regret or sadness was instantly forgotten.

'I think it's time we all had something to eat,' Nebet said. 'Let the party begin!'

CHAPTER THREE

Third Month
of Inundation

IN THE GOLDEN SHADOWS OF EARLY MORNING NEBET APPRAISED THE grapes on her vine. There were fewer bunches than she had hoped but each cluster of blue-black fruit was heavy enough to need support. Khay had helped her prop up the branches with sturdy reeds as he had been taught by Nedjemger in the temple gardens. The little pomegranate tree in the opposite corner had produced fruit for the first time this year, six shiny globes whose leathery skin was just acquiring the blush of ripeness. Nebet hoped that this was a good omen, since the pomegranate fruit, packed with seeds and therefore with the potential for life, was a symbol of fertility. She planned to give the first fruit she picked to Mutemwiya.

Amenmose found her sitting on the brick bench beside the tiny pool. The water was contained in a limestone basin sunk into the ground and it was barely deep enough to support the blue water-lily and the clump of flowering rushes that Nebet had planted in it. She had so wanted a pool that Amenmose had bargained energetically with a stonemason over the carving of the trough. She would never know just how expensive it had been or that Amenmose had taken on commissions outside his work for the Tjaty to pay for it. He considered it was worth the effort because Nebet always found contentment in her garden. It was a luxury in terms of the space it occupied but Amenmose was repaid by the obvious pleasure his wife derived from it.

'I thought I'd find you here. I'll have to leave soon to take the ferry across the River and I won't be back for a few days, so is there anything I can do before I go?'

'I can't think of anything at the moment but no doubt I'll have a list before you're halfway across.' She smiled at him.

He sat down beside her and put his arm round her shoulders. It was rare, these days, to find a few moments when they could simply enjoy each other's company. It was the first day of the month, an important time for the collection of taxes and tithes. Amenmose would soon be busy at Paser's side, receiving the produce of the temple estates, inspecting the royal workshops and preparing reports. He said very little about his work but the permanent ink-stain on the middle finger of his right hand was eloquent proof of his profession. She had noticed that Ramose was similarly marked by the education, which raised all scribes above the common mass of the population.

It was education which allowed a scribe to earn a decent living, to put regular meals before his wife and children, and clothes upon their backs. It was education that saved the scribe from dangerous and unhealthy occupations and gave him exemption from certain taxes and obligations. A scribe would not be called up for military service. Even a humble inventory clerk would not be required to serve as a common labourer on the royal building works.

Nebet stroked the inky black callus. Better that than the broken and twisted fingers of a boatman or a fisherman or the disfiguring scars of a worker in stone. She could not imagine how awful life must be for the field workers and diggers of ditches, who lived a hand-to-mouth existence, never sure whether they would have food for the next day, let alone the next month. The peasant women of Kemet lived an even more uncertain life, often cut short by death in childbirth, and made miserable by hunger and disease. Nebetiunet could only count herself fortunate that the gods had caused her to be born into a family which prized and encouraged education for that was the only pathway out of poverty.

Amenmose reluctantly released her from his encircling arm. 'I really have to go.' Nebet nodded. He kissed her cheek and stood up. 'Are you seeing Wiya today?'

'Probably,' Nebet said. 'This morning I must go to the stores to put in my order for the grain supply and a few other things Tia says we need. Wiya might well be there at the same time, it being the first of the month.

If she isn't, I'm more likely to see her this afternoon. The Choir Mistress wants a rehearsal of the Chantresses before the goddess returns from the Southern Sanctuary. Apparently she wasn't too pleased with their performance on the first day of Opet so she's summoned some of her more mature singers, as she puts it, to show the youngsters how it should be done.'

Amenmose laughed. 'What a wonderful excuse for a gossip,' he said.

'Oh, go away with you,' she replied, in mock indignation.

'Yes, dear. I only meant that you might find something rather interesting to gossip about today,' Amenmose said casually.

'What? What do you know? Is it about Wiya?'

But Amenmose would not be drawn. He planted a farewell kiss on her forehead and said, 'I've no time. The Tjaty will be waiting for me. Enjoy your rehearsal.'

He went back into the house to collect his bag, with Nebet following close behind. She knew him well enough not to press for further information but her mind was buzzing with possibilities.

As she waved him off from the street door he turned and winked, saying, 'Give my love to Wiya and that excellent husband of hers,' and then he was gone round the corner of the street, heading towards the ferry landing.

Nebet had to contain her curiosity and tell herself that whatever was going to happen would happen when the gods allowed and not before. She could not believe, wonderful as the notion might be, that Mutemwiya was pregnant. It was unthinkable that her daughter would have confided in Amenmose or even her own husband before speaking to her mother. No, the news that Ameny was hinting at must be something more in the public domain. In all likelihood it concerned Ramose's job. Still pondering the nature of that news, Nebet returned to the kitchen to see how the girls were getting on with their chores.

Hotepu and Didet were hard at work grinding barley. The greater portion of the previous month's ration had been parched by being soaked in water to soften the outer husks, then dried on mats in the sun. Menna had spent much of the previous morning pounding the grain in the big mortar set in the kitchen floor. This had broken up the barley to make the girls' job easier when it was transferred to the quern stones. The baskets at the foot of each quern already held a satisfying amount of barley meal. Nebet intended to use some for meal-cakes but the bulk would go towards a new brew of beer. She had opted to take part of Amenmose's monthly grain allocation in malted barley and she was very pleased with its quality. The beer should have a good, deep flavour as well as being quite strong.

Tia was preparing a stack of bread pots to be heated over the hearth. When the barley dough was placed in them, the heat retained by their thick pottery walls would set the mixture without cooking it too much. There was a great art to judging when the pots were hot enough. If the dough burned or cooked right through, the yeast would be destroyed and the mash would not ferment. If the pots were too cool, the dough remained sticky in the centre and its flavour would not develop. If all went well, the malt loaves would be broken up in the big brewing crock, covered with hot water and left to soak overnight.

Nebet had not yet decided what flavouring agent to use. Amenmose liked the bitter tang of coriander seed but the rest of the family preferred a sweeter beer. The smell of the crushed malt indicated that the brew would be quite sweet anyway, sweet enough to disguise any aromatic flavour she might add, so she settled for the usual dates. The first of the new season's date crop was appearing in the marketplace, and beer always tasted better when flavoured with fresh rather than dried fruit. She must remember to set aside some of the meal to make the cakes.

'Has Bak already gone to the garden plots?' she asked.

'Yes, mistress, and Menna with him,' Hotepu answered, without looking up from her work.

Nebetiunet was glad the men had remembered her instructions. The domestic gardens on higher ground at the edge of the town would soon become an unreachable island in the inundated surrounding fields. Any remaining fruit or vegetables had to be harvested within the next few days or left to rot. She was particularly keen that the marrows and melons should not go to waste. They would not store easily but they would be welcome in the marketplace. Tia had demanded that they leave the late melokia crop until the last moment. The older leaves would be rather tough but they were always tastier fresh than dried. When stewed in a good flavoured meat or vegetable stock, melokia produced a glutinous broth which Tia swore was the most nourishing and sustaining dish for the cooler months. What was not used immediately would be hung in bunches to dry and kept to thicken stews and soups throughout the winter. The herbs, too. It had been a good year for garden produce.

Nebet's thoughts were rudely disturbed by the eruption of a very unladylike argument between Iset and Neferti. The two girls almost tumbled into the little kitchen courtyard, their fingers twisted in each other's hair, their voices raised to a pitch that set teeth on edge. Not wanting to discipline her daughter in front of the servants, Nebet caught each girl firmly by an arm and steered them back into the house. Her own arms were soon aching with the effort of keeping the spitting cats apart. In desperation she slapped first Iset's face and then, much as it hurt her to do so, Nubnefert's. The noise stopped instantly. The two girls stood shocked into silence by her uncharacteristic action.

In the lull before the shock wore off Nebet said in a firm but quiet voice, 'That's better. If you start screaming again I shall hit you again. You are supposed to be young ladies. You do not squabble like quarrelsome children. You will now explain yourselves, one at a time, Neferti first, since you're the one who should know better.'

Nubnefert at least had the decency to hang her head in shame, while Iset held her head high and stuck out her chin in defiance.

'I'm waiting,' Nebet said in a calm tone, which nevertheless indicated that she was not prepared to wait long.

Neferti looked up at her mother and said, 'Iset asked to use my comb. She has such long hair and it gets so tangled that I was afraid she would break the teeth of the comb so I said no and . . .'

'Let me guess,' her mother said. 'You said no but Iset went and borrowed it anyway.'

Neferti nodded.

'I didn't do any harm to it,' Iset said defiantly. 'You'd never have known if you hadn't come spying on me.'

'That, my girl, is beside the point. You are the servant in this house and Nubnefert is of the family. Don't impose on the friendship she has chosen to show you. If you ever hope to have a reference from me as a lady's maid you will mind your behaviour and learn to conduct yourself in a more fitting manner. Now go and help Tia.'

Nebet's stern face made Iset think twice about responding to this rebuke. She slouched off to the kitchen without another word.

Nubnefert stood with her head down, unable to look into her mother's eyes, and sniffed. 'I'm sorry Muti, it was all my fault. I shouldn't have let her annoy me like that, but it was the ivory comb Father brought back from Suan. She was dragging it through her hair so hard that I was sure she'd break its teeth. I'm certain she was doing it deliberately to upset me.'

Nebet remembered the comb which was carved from a hippopotamus tooth with a handle in the shape of a bird's head. Amenmose had brought it back as a New Year's gift for his wife but, when he heard that his youngest daughter had passed into womanhood, and so would be growing her hair, he had given the comb to her instead. The gesture had made Nebet happier than if she had received the gift herself. Amenmose rarely showed his affection for his children in such an obvious way. It was no wonder that Neferti had risen to Iset's teasing.

'Iset has an unhappy knack of annoying people,' Nebet said, taking her daughter in her arms. 'It does seem as if she was goading you but I'm surprised that you reacted so violently, especially as the comb survived.'

Neferti sniffed again.

Her mother sensed there was something more at the heart of the argument. 'What is the real problem?'

Neferti suddenly burst into tears, and through her sobs she spluttered, 'Why is my hair still so short? Iset says I look like a boy. Her hair is down below her shoulders. She says mine will never be as long as hers.'

Nebet had to stop herself smiling. The matter was a very serious one for a twelve-year-old. 'You've only been growing your hair for two months. Iset has had long hair since the day she arrived here. Don't you remember the arguments we had over it? She's still very lax about tying it back for work and she doesn't keep it anywhere near clean enough for my liking. I've given her a nit preparation on several occasions but I'll swear she never uses it. Be thankful that your hair is short enough to be manageable and to be kept clean. You'll always look nicer than Iset.'

'Really?' Neferti asked in a tiny, childlike voice.

'Really,' Nebetiunet said. 'And never compare yourself with her again. She's beneath your notice. Now go and wash your face.'

Neferti gave her mother a kiss to show that the slap was forgiven and forgotten and then went to do as she had been told.

Nebetiunet sighed. Would there ever be a time when her children were no longer a worry to her? At least she and Amenmose had brought them up to respect their parents and adults in general. The same could not be said for Iset. But for all the love, the care and the heartache they had expended on their family the children had grown up so differently.

Neferti's problem was a fleeting one that would be quickly forgotten.

Senmut's rebellion was proving more than a boyish whim and his teachers still complained that he appeared unmoved by the passages of good advice that were used as handwriting practice. She remembered hearing and reading some of the texts that student scribes were set to copy. Admittedly they included some very old-fashioned ideas, but the advice about family life and duty was timeless. One author wrote that a dutiful son would follow the good example set by his father. Sons, when grown, would repay their parents for their loving upbringing by caring for them in their old age. Senmut was not a bad boy but Nebet feared he would never qualify as a scribe at a level acceptable to his father. In fact, she began to doubt that he would qualify at all. With Khaemwase no longer in school, that left only Pakhred to follow his father's example, which was only fitting for the eldest son but a heavy responsibility for him nonetheless.

The ancient sage had also written that a son should remember what a burden he had been to his mother as she carried him in her womb and after she had given him birth. He recommended that the son should recompense his mother twofold for her unselfishness and sacrifice. Nebet could only look forward to that luxury. At present, though the physical load had been eased, the emotional burden seemed to grow heavier every day, and it had become no lighter since two of her daughters had left home. As far as she knew, the writers of the books of wisdom had nothing to say about the relationship between a mother and her daughters. What could a man know about that?

Mutemwiya was not among the crowd of women and servants queuing at the stores that morning but she was waiting for her mother at the Asheru Temple gate in the afternoon. They linked arms as the gatekeeper nodded them through into the garden area beside the sacred lake. Between the persea and sycamore trees that bordered the crescent-shaped lake were statues, images of Mut, Lady of Heaven, Mistress of the Two Lands, whose divine spirit touched all who came into her presence. It was always peaceful there. Nebet slowed her pace so that they might linger in the mottled shade of the sacred grove, giving Wiya the chance to share the news at which Amenmose had hinted that morning.

The young woman clung to her mother's arm in excitement as she announced, 'Ramose has been promoted.'

'Oh, my dear, I am glad. He's worked so hard he deserves recognition. What's his new job?'

'He's to be Scribe of the Tomb in the Place of Truth, answerable only to the Tjaty and in charge of administering all the work on His Majesty's resting place. It's a very responsible position.' Mutemwiya's voice was eager, almost too eager.

Her mother sensed her uncertainty and frowned slightly. This was not quite the promotion she had imagined, though, now she thought about it, she remembered Amenmose mentioning that Paser had been directed to reorganize the establishment known as the Place of Truth. It was a tiny walled village hidden away in a fold of the hills on the edge of the royal cemetery and home to the elite group of craftsmen who built and decorated the royal tombs. The villagers were entirely supported by the King. Their food, their clothing and all their domestic needs were provided from the treasuries and storerooms of the mansion temples. The houses they lived in and even the tools they worked with belonged to the King. Ramose had already had some experience of dealing with these Royal Servants in the course of his work at the Mansion of the divine Menkheperura-Thutmose. Though not one to criticize others without reason, Ramose had admitted that the Servants in the Place of Truth were a close-knit community, very conscious of their own status and suspicious of outsiders. As chief administrator of the village, he would have to live among them and Mutemwiya would, of course, go with him. No wonder she was apprehensive.

Putting as much enthusiasm into her voice as possible Nebet said, 'That's wonderful news. It shows how highly the Tjaty regards Ramose. How soon will he be taking up his post?'

'His appointment is from the start of this month so we shall be moving within the next few days.' Mutemwiya sounded worried.

It was no small thing that she was being asked to do. It was a wife's duty to follow her husband wherever his work might take him but it was still a daunting prospect for her to move into a community which was known to resent newcomers. Although Nebet had never visited the Place of Truth, she had heard tales of the cramped conditions, the discomforts of heat and dust and sand, and the uncertainty of life on the desert's edge without a permanent water supply.

'So, when will you want me to help you pack?'

Mutemwiya stopped in mid-stride and said, 'Oh, Muti, I hoped you'd offer but I didn't like to ask.'

'You silly girl! Did you honestly think that I'd leave you to move house on your own? There'll be far too much for you to do alone. This is a time for the family to help. Come home with me after the rehearsal and we'll start to make plans.'

Wiya gave her mother a quick hug of gratitude and walked on with a lighter step towards the courtyard where the other Chantresses were gathering.

The house looked very empty now. Mutemwiya had spent last night with her parents, as all the furniture she was taking to the Place of Truth had been dismantled, bundled up and shipped across the River. Ramose had gone ahead to receive the goods from the donkey train that wound its way daily through the cultivation, along the well-trodden path beside the King's Mansion Temple and into the northern end of the little valley where the Place of Truth nestled, shimmering in the desert heat. Their personal possessions, clothing, household linens and the remaining food supplies from the storeroom had been packed into baskets and sacks, and sent down to the quayside to await Mutemwiya's instructions. As Nebet looked around the house it seemed strangely larger than she remembered it.

She put her hand on her daughter's shoulder and asked, 'Is that all now?'

'Yes, that's all. Ramose's father will take back the bed he gave us. It's far too big to fit in the new house.'

'It was always too big even for this house,' Nebet said, to make Wiya feel better.

'I know' – Wiya forced a smile – 'and it was never very comfortable.'

'New house, new start. It will all be for the best. Do you know who'll have this house now?'

'Ramose has sold it to a clerk of the Temple Granary. He got a very good price for it, and as we haven't got to buy a new place it's all profit. He would have sold the bed, too, but he felt he had to offer it to his father first as a matter of courtesy. We were astounded when the old man took it. What he wants with another bed, when he has houses full of furniture already, I hate to think.'

'Come, then, it's time to leave. You have a new life waiting for you on the other side of the River.'

Having lived all her life in Waset, Mutemwiya was not used to walking so far in one day. Nebet had often walked such distances in her childhood on Nebneteru's country estate, but now she was older and less energetic. To protect their feet they wore strong leather sandals with straps around the heels, but they had not perfected the art of walking on the rough, stony surface of a desert path. They were constantly shaking out small stones and sand, and so found it very difficult to keep a steady pace. The donkey driver was not unsympathetic and, when he realized how uncomfortable they were finding the journey, he rearranged the packs on one of his animals so that they could take turns at riding.

As Wiya walked beside her mother, her hand resting on the donkey's rump, she poured out her increasing apprehension at the prospect of meeting the other Village wives. 'Of course, Ramose doesn't see what I'm worried about. He says everyone is very friendly and he's looking forward to working with them. But he can't tell me anything about what life's like for the women in the Village, because that's an entirely different matter. It wouldn't occur to him to ask about the everyday things like laundry and storage facilities. And I'm sure he's not told me the whole truth about the house. You hear such tales about how tiny they are and how close together. I don't know how I'm going to fit everything in.'

'You're worrying unnecessarily,' Nebet said. 'If Ramose is happy, you should be, too. If the house is as poky as you fear, you'll have to make good use of the roof space. You have plenty of baskets and boxes and I believe each house in the Place of Truth has at least one cellar, so storage won't be a problem if you're sensible. As to the washing, I know from Ibi that there are men employed specially to do the Village laundry so you won't have that to deal with.'

'I hope you're right, Muti. I really want to be a good wife to Ramose, and as Scribe of the Tomb he's going to be the most important man in the Village. That will put me above the wives of the Workmen, even those who are much older than I am. I don't know how they'll take to having someone so young, and an in-comer at that, as their social superior.'

Nebet had been having similar thoughts. The status of a woman in the Place of Truth was determined by her husband's rank within the community. Wiya was still very young, especially in comparison with the wives of the chief Workmen, and Amenmose had mentioned that there was a senior scribe, already in residence at the Village, whose wife might well feel that her position was being usurped by Mutemwiya. She had to reassure her daughter.

'Trust Ramose when he says everyone is friendly. If you go in expecting them to be stand-offish, your manner will make them think the same way about you. You'll see. It'll be like any village anywhere in Kemet. There will be friendly folk and unfriendly, people who will welcome you with open arms and others who will keep their distance. Just be yourself. You'll soon make new friends.'

'I really hope so,' Wiya said plaintively.

'It must be your turn to ride now,' Nebet said to change the subject.

Happily, Wiya's fears proved to be unfounded. In the open space outside the northern gate of the Village they were met by Ramose and a smiling welcoming committee of Village ladies accompanied by some of their children. Most of the men, of course, were at work in the Great Place, busy excavating the King's tomb. Mutemwiya was introduced first to Tuy, wife of the Foreman, Kaha, and so one of the most senior female citizens of the Place of Truth, though she was probably only five years or so older than Wiya. Tuy was tiny; Wiya was taller by a head and shoulders.

Tuy smiled broadly and waved her hands about as she said, 'You and I are to be neighbours, but then we're all neighbours here, with the houses so packed together.' She giggled. 'We have a custom, too. We all get together to help each other on moving day, so of course we've done the same for you. We've had a good clean-out of the house and your furniture has been delivered and put back together again, though obviously we've left the arranging of it to you. Are these the last of your packages?' She waved at the loaded donkeys.

Mutemwiya, hardly able to conceal her relief at this cheerful if rather overwhelming welcome, nodded.

'Good. We can get the boys to unload them and deliver the luggage while I show you the house. I'm afraid you'll find it rather small after your lovely town house but I'm sure you'll settle in fine. Follow me and I'll show you to your new front door.'

Tuy preceded Mutemwiya through the gate into the narrow main street, which was barely wide enough for two people to walk side by side. The single-storey houses forming solid blocks to east and west had red-painted wooden doors fronting on to the street, but Nebet deduced from the many rooftop shelters and screens that most of the daily comings and goings were conducted above ground level.

Ramose stepped up to greet Nebet and said, 'Thank you so much for bringing her. I know how nervous she was.'

'She still is,' Nebet warned him. 'She's going to need a lot of support for a while.'

'I can help there,' said an older woman, coming forward to join them.

'Nebetiunet, may I present Kanefert, wife of the scribe Huya,' Ramose said with a warmth in his voice which told Nebet that he already considered this woman a friend.

Kanefert was much the same age as Nebet but looked older because her skin was quite brown and wrinkled, a consequence of living for twelve months of the year in the arid heat of the desert.

'I am very pleased to meet you, lady,' Nebet said, bowing.

Kanefert smiled and bowed in return. The formalities over, she said, 'Ramose has told us all about your lovely daughter. We know what a wrench it must be for her to leave her family like this, but be assured that we'll look after her.'

'Kanefert and Huya have been kind enough to give me shelter while our house was being put to rights,' said Ramose. 'They could not have been more helpful.'

'And we invite you and your daughter to stay with us also, while the last details are seen to,' Kanefert said. 'It may be a little crowded but we can always find sleeping space for a friend or two.'

'That's very kind of you,' Nebet said with genuine feeling. She liked Kanefert at once and was much relieved to think that Ramose and Wiya had found such a friend.

'So what's Wiya's new place like?' Mymy asked.

Nebet had been back in Waset for only half a day before Mutnefert called on her to hear all about her sister's move. They were sitting by the pond in the garden, sipping the first of the new brew.

'It's not as small as we thought it might be,' Nebet admitted. 'In fact, it looks as if two houses have been made into one. She has quite a large kitchen yard but being on the east of the Village it's in the shade of the hill for most of the morning.'

'That means things will stay cooler,' Mymy observed. 'I should think she'd be pleased about that.'

'That's true,' her mother agreed, 'and the large cellars under the house were noticeably cooler than any other room. I was surprised at how well fresh food will keep there, in spite of the desert heat and the flies. Wiya was more concerned about how dark it seemed first thing in the morning, but I told her to forget how we do things here and to follow the example of the other Village women. Everything is done on the roofs there. They fence off their own property with woven reed screens but leave paths and alleyways so they can get from one end of the Village to the other without touching the ground.'

'I don't think I'd like being that close to my neighbours,' Mymy said.

'Nor I, but it's unavoidable in the Place of Truth and Wiya will have to adapt to it. She'll miss the gardens most, I think.' Nebet ran her finger around the edge of a lily pad. 'She's asked me to send her some seeds and cuttings so she can start her own herb garden in pots. I saw some very healthy plants there, despite the difficulties they must have with watering them. There's no well there, you see. They've tried to dig one but all there is to show for their efforts is a deep, dry hole. Water is delivered in skins and jars twice a day, and the villagers have to be very careful about how much they use. People have priority, of course, so they can't keep animals there permanently. That means Ramose will have to keep his donkeys at the Mansion stables. Wasting water is seen as an offence against the community. The sun just sucks the moisture out of everything – plants, animals and people. It was a very exhausting three days, I can tell you. I only hope Wiya adjusts quickly to the new way of life.'

'Well, I think she's extraordinarily lucky,' Mymy said with just a hint of envy in her voice.

Nebet realized that Wiya's new home, though small in comparison with her old house, was probably still larger than Mutnefert's ground-floor apartment in the administration block of the stable compound. When she married, Abau had seen no need to move from his lodging which, while suitable for a single man, was little better than army barracks accommodation. Nebet suspected that Abau had not considered finding a more suitable family home simply because he intended to move on in the not too distant future.

Nebet felt uneasy about this change in Mymy's circumstances. She had had no doubts about Abau's affection for her daughter at the time but, having come to know him better in the last year, she could not honestly say that she trusted him with her daughter's happiness. She was certainly unimpressed by the influence he appeared to have over Senmut. She hoped that Abau's plans would continue to include Mutnefert and that she would not wake up one day to find her daughter crying on her doorstep, having been deserted by her husband.

Mymy herself steered the conversation in another direction, asking, 'Was the house blessed before they moved in?'

'Oh yes, that was very interesting. The people of the Village respect many gods as particular patrons of the Place of Truth but, as there is no permanent priestly position at any of the local shrines, they act as their own priests and acolytes. Kanefert is the principal servant of the divine Ahmose-Nefertari, and her husband serves the divine Djeserkara-Amenhotep. It seems these two royal gods were the founders of the Place of Truth and are still involved in all aspects of Village life. They were brought out of their sanctuaries to inspect and approve the house and to bless its occupants. I know Mutemwiya was very touched when she realized what a special honour this was. Many of the houses have a little statue or carving in stone of these royal gods to keep watch over them.

Ramose said he intended to have a suitable image made for their home as soon as possible.

'Then there were the more practical considerations. Among the Workmen are some who have the power to charm snakes and scorpions. They wove their spells over the house and declared it free of pests, though Wiya was given a lot of advice as to how she should keep them away. Scorpions are particularly worrying and that's something that Wiya hadn't anticipated, but as a house-warming gift Kanefert gave her an ivory wand, just like Tia's, inscribed with lots of magical symbols which should help to keep them safe.'

'How very kind. It sounds as if Wiya has made a good friend there,' Mymy said, 'but what about the Goddess? Surely, living so close to the Sacred Land they must revere her as the Lady of the West?'

'Of course. There's a sweet little chapel for Hathor, and they recognize her presence in the mountain that guards the Village. They call her Meretseger, 'Lover of Silence', and the Peak, as the mountain is known, is named after her. The people of the Place of Truth recognize the Goddess in her serpent form and I must say the Peak looks uncommonly like a coiled snake guarding the skyline. Kanefert was so pleased when she discovered that Mutemwiya has some experience as a chantress. I expect she'll be asked to take part in the rituals, and she may become chief servitor in time.'

'I'm glad for her, though I'll miss her.' Mymy sighed. 'It's a shame she's so far away. Do you think she'll come back very often?'

'There seems to be a lot more coming and going from the Village than I thought. Ramose will have to report regularly to the Tjaty, and I'm sure Wiya will take every opportunity to accompany him. We'll probably see quite a lot of them still.'

Nebet hoped that this would be so. She glanced across to the pomegranate tree and remembered that she had meant to give Mutemwiya one of the fruit. If Wiya did not come back to Waset soon, the fruit would be overripe. Nebet believed that, to increase her chances of conceiving, Wiya would have to eat the fruit, taking its magical life-potential into her body. But then, with the Goddess looking after her in the Place of Truth, perhaps this little charm would prove unnecessary.

Ramose did not say much but he was inordinately proud of the way Mutemwiya fitted in to Village society so easily. He was also quietly proud of the trust shown in him by Paser. Though he was not the sort to put on airs on account of his position, he could not resist trying out his new title. On a limestone flake he wrote a little memorandum of the promotion that had brought him to live in this unusual place:

'I became Scribe in the Place of Truth in year five, third month of inundation, day ten of the Lord of the Two Lands, Usermaatra-Ramesses.'

CHAPTER FOUR

Fourth Month
of Inundation

NEBET LOOKED IN DISMAY AT SENMUT'S BEST KILT. SHE HAD FOUND IT
screwed into a bundle and stuffed behind the clothes press in the boys'
bedroom. It had clearly been damp when Senmut tried to hide it, and the
creases he had caused would probably be permanent. But that was not
the worst of it. The front overlap, which she had lovingly shaped and
hemmed, was now irretrievably stained. Senmut had tried to rinse out
the livid purplish mark but had succeeded only in spreading it further. It
was wine, or at least deep-red grape juice, and leaving it to dry had fixed
the stain. The grape harvest was well under way and the vintners were
already busy pressing their precious fruit to have the first of the new
vintage ready for the Feast of Osiris. Nebet decided that she would rather
not know how Senmut had come to spill wine on his kilt. She was certain
he had been playing truant again to go and watch the grape-treading, but
even he would not wear his best clothes for such an occasion. He had
probably been out sampling the raw young wine with some of his less
reputable friends.

If she had been told about it at once, Nebet could have spread salt
over the linen to soak up the worst of the colour and then Ibi might have
been able to reduce the damage by repeated immersion in a strong
natron soak. Now it was far too late. Senmut's festival kilt was ruined. She
had no time to make him another, and she resented the idea of having

to pay someone else to do what she herself could do so much better. She felt somewhat less angry when she looked at the size of the kilt and realized that it would probably not have fitted Senmut for much longer anyway. He was shooting up like a weed and was nearly the same height as his father. However, he would need another kilt to look respectable for the Osiris Festival. Perhaps she could alter one of Amenmose's. She held the kilt up to the light wondering if she could save anything of it, maybe as a work kilt for Khay. Then she saw that the stain had soaked right through the double thickness of the overlap into the underlayer. It was made of good-quality cloth which she was loath to waste, but she would be able to rescue barely enough material for baby clouts and there was no sign yet of a baby for Wiya.

Nebetiunet was trying not to think too much about Wiya's desperate yearning for a child. After all the prayers and offerings they had made, there must be a reason why the gods had not seen fit to grant that wish, and to question their decision was close to blasphemy.

Amenmose had said, in his usual sensible way, 'A child will come when the gods allow. Wiya's young and healthy and there's plenty of time.'

Nebet knew he was right. She also knew in her heart of hearts that it was much better for a woman to delay childbearing until she was fully grown. So often a young wife died giving birth to her first child simply because the baby was too big for the mother's childish body. In such a case the baby almost always died as well, a double tragedy that was all too common. In that way Nebet had lost several friends from her early days in the temple weaving sheds, and death in childbirth was her greatest fear for all her daughters. She knew how lucky she had been to have six healthy children, despite the miscarriages and the problems with Khay. She had to admit that the gods had already been kind to her family. To ask them for more might seem ungrateful.

She put the ruined kilt into the sack with the other dirty laundry and carried it downstairs. Gemni was waiting to take the bundle to the washerman Ibi, who had set up his tubs on the raised embankment of one of the canals because his usual mudbank had not yet emerged from the inundation. She gave Gemni special instructions about the kilt and had him repeat them back to her to be sure he understood. Gemni was a bright boy and messages taken by him rarely went astray.

Nebet returned to her chores but, as Gemni was leaving, there was a knock at the back gate, which he opened to reveal an odd-looking figure standing in the alleyway between the houses. Gemni hurried back to Nebet and announced, 'It's Tjeti, Mistress.' Even if she had not seen him Nebet would have recognized her visitor by the pungent smell of goat that accompanied him.

'As long as he hasn't got the animals with him, you can tell him to come into the kitchen. Then you'd better be on your way with the laundry.'

'Yes, Lady.' Gemni gave her a hasty bow and went to usher in the goatherd.

Tjeti was a scrawny stick of a man with such weathered features that it was impossible to guess his age. His crown was completely bald but round the back of his head he had an uneven fringe of dirty greying hair hanging down to his shoulders. His kilt was no more than an unhemmed length of coarse cloth wrapped round his waist and secured with a rope belt. He wore another, narrower strip of linen about his neck, with its two ends crossed over his chest and tucked into his belt to protect him from the cold, which his spare body felt sorely. In the coldest part of the year he wore a goatskin cape, which made him even more fragrant. From a leather strap worn diagonally across his body hung a variety of tools and pouches. Nebet had learned not to inquire as to the contents of Tjeti's 'kit', as he called it, because if he once started on his pet subject of goats he was difficult to stop. He had lived with and for goats all his life, following in the footsteps of his father, and his father before him, probably for more generations than he knew how to count. He was also totally unaware of the unpleasant odour that emanated from all he possessed. At least he knew well enough not to enter the house, and there was a chance that Nebet would be able to rid the kitchen court of his smell in a day or so.

Tia, however, from her position crouched by the hearth where she was tending a stew-pot, scowled at this unwelcome intrusion into her space. Though she was now a cook, as Amenmose's nurse Tia had been a servant of some social standing. Nebet had never discovered what Tia's background was, but her antipathy to Tjeti made her think that the cook's efforts to dissociate herself from people of his class were meant to divert attention from her own humble origins.

'Welcome, Tjeti,' Nebet said loudly and with a smile. 'What news have you?'

'Good news, Lady, good news. Your little Hedjet has done you proud. Twins she had, both females, and her udders are brimming over,' Tjeti said in a booming monotone.

'That is good news,' Nebet said, indicating that the goatherd should sit down on the bottom of the staircase. The cat, Tamiu, who had been sunning herself on a lower step, suddenly roused, nose twitching at the rank smell that had disturbed her rest. Despite her age she performed a very nimble avoiding action as Tjeti threw down his kit. Deciding that her favourite position within easy reach of any titbits that might be forthcoming from the kitchen was no longer so attractive, Tamiu made a hasty escape up the stairs to find refuge on the upper landing.

'Tia, fetch some beer for Tjeti so we can drink to Hedjet and her young,' Nebet said.

Tia slowly and painfully got to her feet saying, 'Lot of nonsense. Anyone would think it was a child he was talking about. What's to celebrate about the birth of a goat? Animals do it every day, it's the way of life, nothing special . . .' And she continued her muttering all the way to the cellar and back.

Nebetiunet ignored her bad manners. Although Tjeti was of a much lower social class than Tia, he had been invited into the house by her mistress and so should have been accorded guest status. But Tjeti was also as deaf as a stone and had not heard a word of Tia's monologue, and, whatever she might think about him personally, Tjeti's information was of great value to the family.

Tjeti looked after the goats owned by several households in Waset. He took them out daily to forage among the thorn bushes on the desert's edge and returned them along the causeway across the fields to the animal pens close to Ipet Esut in the evening. He had given each animal a name and could identify a goat at a glance, which was more than many of their owners could do.

Nebet had two goats in Tjeti's flock. The white nanny goat Hedjet was a good milker, and the birth of two more females who were likely to take after their mother was welcome news indeed. If both survived, Tjeti would keep one with his flock to breed from and the other would be sold on, either as a milch-goat or for meat. The male, which Tjeti had named Sethy, was a black and white yearling, Hedjet's kid of last season. Nebet was saving him for the Harvest Festival Feast.

Tia, with very poor grace, served Tjeti with beer and a flat loaf, which

he proceeded to crumble into his bowl until the brew resembled a thick soup. As he slurped up this treat, Nebet started to consider how to make best use of Hedjet's increased milk yield. Her mind flitted over the luxurious possibilities of butter-oil and cream, but then settled on cheeses. Small balls of white cheese rolled in herbs kept well if preserved in oil, especially if the oil itself had a good flavour. There was a small quantity of precious olive oil left in her store, which she had been saving for just such a project.

This year's olive pressing would not start until the middle of the next season, and there was never enough oil produced locally to satisfy demand. Foreign vessels laden with huge jars of olive oil were regular visitors to Waset, where the traders from lands as distant as Retjenu in the north found a ready market among the wealthier citizens. But, even though Amenmose's allocation from the commissaries was generous in comparison with that of other state employees, olive oil was a luxury that the family rarely enjoyed. For cooking, Nebet mostly relied on duck or goose grease or the cheaper oils of safflower and sesame, and if Tia had

had her way the olive oil would have been hoarded for ever. But it had such a delicate flavour, and everyone in the family enjoyed her herb cheeses so much, that Nebet felt justified in setting the jar aside for that purpose. That would account for only a small part of Hedjet's milk.

A regular delivery of milk over the next months could be put to many uses, but fresh, sharp-tasting cheeses were always popular and could be bartered in the marketplace at any time, so cheese-making would soon become another important household chore. Hotepu had already shown some skill at this craft and Nebet looked forward to teaching Neferti how to separate the milk, strain off the whey through a cloth and then mould the brilliantly white curd. Young Amenmose, like his father, was fond of a soft, spreadable cheese, a delicious accompaniment to malted bread. Tia liked to spoil him by putting a thickly slathered loaf in his daily food basket whenever the cheese was available. Just thinking about the possibilities made Nebet's mouth water.

Tjeti finished his bread and beer, unfolded himself from the step and shouldered his kit. 'I'll bring along the first milk in a few days, once the youngsters have settled down,' he boomed. 'That little Hedjet, she'll have no trouble feeding both of them, and I dare say you'll have more trouble knowing what to do with it all.' His lips parted in a toothless grin.

'Thank you, Tjeti,' Nebet said, mouthing her words carefully as it seemed that he could fill in some of the gaps in his hearing by following the word-shapes formed by her lips. He shuffled out of the gate and was gone without a backward glance.

'Comes in here, stinks the place out, and then goes off without so much as a thank you. Some people have no gratitude,' Tia remarked darkly.

'Oh, Tia, do you ever think kindly of anyone?' Nebet asked in exasperation.

As soon as she had spoken she regretted her words. Tia gave her a hurt look before returning to her hunched pose beside the fire. Nebet considered apologizing, but one look at Tia's accusing back, indignation surrounding her like a cloud, and she decided against it. Tia was Tia and there was no changing her. She went to find some sweet-smelling herbs to disguise Tjeti's lingering presence.

Neferti had been busy working at the little handloom on which her mother was teaching her to weave a continuous narrow strip of cloth. She had been at pains to keep a very even tension and there was hardly any perceptible variation in the width of the strip.

Nebet was pleased with the result. 'This is excellent work, Neferti. I think we can move on to a fancy weave now, and when you have mastered that we might see how you fare in making a sash.'

'A full-length sash?' Neferti asked. 'One that I could sell?'

'You have to make one first before you can think of selling it,' her mother laughed, 'but I don't see why you shouldn't find a buyer for your work if you maintain this quality. You have a good feel for the loom. If you continue to improve I might be able to find you a place in the linen shop at the Temple.'

Nubnefert hugged herself with excitement. Ever since becoming a woman she had been trying hard to prove she could make a proper adult contribution to the family. Her older brothers still treated her like a baby, especially Senmut, who was less than a year older than Neferti, and now Khay, who was *much* younger than she, was in paid employment. The suggestion that she might become an apprentice under her mother's direction made her feel very grown-up.

'But now you must put away your weaving. I want you to collect the basket of cheeses from the cellar and go with Meryt and Iset to the marketplace. There should be Osiris beds for sale by now,' Nebet said.

She was referring to the small pottery saucers or carved wooden trays, shaped in the likeness of the Great God, Lord of Abdu, Osiris, King of the Dead. Osiris beds, sprinkled with a mixture of earth and seed corn, played an essential part in the annual ritual in which people sought the god's blessing on the cereal crops that would soon be planted. The bed would be buried to the accompaniment of invocation prayers, just as the god himself had been buried at Abdu. The first green shoots to emerge from the ground were seen as a sign of his regeneration and rebirth and so as a promise of a good growing season to come.

The speed with which the corn germinated and the number of shoots produced were also thought to predict the fortune of the suppliant's household, particularly with respect to fertility, both human and animal. Nebetiunet, still hoping that Wiya would become a mother very soon, planned to make special prayers for her daughter this year.

'How many Osiris beds will you want?' Neferti asked.

'If they aren't too expensive I'd like to buy one each for Wiya and Mymy, as well as one for us. You might be able to exchange cheeses for them but, if not, Meryt is very good at working out a bargain. Watch what she does and learn from her.'

'Do we have to take Iset?' Neferti whined.

'Yes, I'm afraid you must. I'm beginning to think she'll never learn to do anything well because she's such a hollow, vain creature, but I promised her mother I'd teach her the sort of things a lady's maid needs to know, and marketing is good experience. It will be good practice for you, too.

'I suppose so,' Neferti said in the sullen tone of a spoilt child.

Nebet tried to look severe. 'I thought we had agreed that Iset isn't worthy of your envy.'

'Mmm' was Neferti's only response.

'Someone will have to see to it,' Montmose complained for the third time. 'I'm not as steady on my legs as I was and I can't go clambering over that hillside. I'd break my neck.' Amenmose's father, accompanied as always by the sour-faced Satra, had arrived unannounced at the crack of dawn.

Apparently he had been awake all night worrying about the Festival of the Dead that was part of the Osiris celebrations. Amenmose normally made the appropriate offerings at his mother's tomb, which was tucked away in a fold of the cliffs to the north of the great temple of Maatkara-Hatshepsut, but he had gone with the Tjaty to Abdu, where the King would preside over the most sacred of all the Osiris rituals. Usually it fell to the eldest son to perform the offerings in his father's place but Montmose considered Pakhred too young for such an important duty. Nebet was at a loss to know how to mollify the old man, who had now reached a very unreasonable state of indignation. Satra, predictably, was taking no part in the discussion, even though it was her mother's mortuary rites they were discussing.

Then Nebetiunet was struck with inspiration. 'I'm sure Ramose would be only too glad to make the offerings. He's bringing Wiya here to stay for a few days over the festival period. Would you like me to ask him, or perhaps you could ask him yourself?'

Montmose grunted, the wind taken out of his sail. 'I suppose that would be in order,' he said grudgingly. 'Ramose is a sensible man, polite, well spoken. He'd not make a mess of it. Yes. Ask him.'

'Of course, my father,' Nebet said through gritted teeth. It was quite clear that Satra was not the only ungracious member of the family.

Nebet put the suggestion to Ramose when he and Mutemwiya arrived later that day.

'I shall be happy to carry out the duty,' he said with genuine feeling. 'I shall go to Montmose's house and tell him.'

As soon as he was gone, Nebet was rather startled to have Wiya fling her arms about her neck and burst into tears. When the sobs had subsided a little, she said, 'What is it, my dear? I can't believe that Ramose has made you unhappy.'

'No, no, Muti, of course not. He is the dearest and kindest of men. I am so lucky to have him for my husband.'

'Then it must be about children – am I right?'

'As always, Muti. What am I doing wrong? Why can't I bear him a child? He deserves that much from me at least.'

'There's been no sign of a pregnancy?'

'None. My moonflows have always been so predictable. I hoped the move to the Place of Truth would be a fresh start in all respects, but the bleeding came upon me exactly when I expected it. Now it will be another month before I know, and probably another month after that, and another. How long must I endure this terrible waiting?'

Nebet had eased her daughter into a chair and was kneeling at her feet holding Wiya's hands in hers. 'There is no answer I can give you. I have prayed to the Goddess in all her forms. We can only hope she hears me. Did you eat the pomegranate?'

'Yes, and thank you, it was very sweet. But it did no good.'

'I'm not sure the effect would be immediate,' Nebet said, in an attempt to give Wiya hope. 'Are you wearing my amulet?'

In answer, Wiya showed her mother the blue moulded charm she wore about her neck on a flaxen cord. It was shaped like the counterpoise of the *menyt*, the sacred necklace of Hathor, and bore the face of the Goddess surmounting a short inscription, which Amenmose had told them read, 'May Gold protect you every day'. Gold was one of the Lady's beautiful names. Nebet had started wearing the very same amulet after her miscarriages, and she was sure it had helped her to conceive and bear Khaemwase. She had hoped it would work for Wiya, too.

'I know it's hard but you must have patience. The Goddess will grant you a child when she knows you're ready. We must pray all the harder over the Osiris beds. I have one for you, too. We'll prepare them this evening.'

They were already quite tired when they returned home from the festival. The Sacred Mysteries of Osiris had culminated in a re-enactment of the god's triumphal resurrection as King of the Dead. Bands of local boatmen and hunters had performed carefully choreographed stick-fights to represent the battle between the followers of Horus, Osiris's son, and the followers of Seth, the god's brother and murderer.

Senmut was particularly interested in this aspect of the ritual. On the way home he tried to persuade Abau to teach him how to fence, a request which, Nebet was glad to see, Abau refused, saying, 'Those men have been acting out the same fight for years. They learn the moves from their fathers and have generations of experience to guide them. You and I would only get hurt if we tried it.'

Senmut knew it was a lost cause so he contented himself with picking a sturdy reed from the ditch beside the path and using it to swish the heads off other plants as they walked towards the River. It had been a long day and for some it was not yet over.

Ramose had left them after the public ceremonies at the King's Mansion Temple and had gone with Pakhred and Wiya to perform the rites for the deceased at the tomb of Montmose's wife. In the morning, before Montmose had arrived to travel with them across the River, Ramose had told the rest of the family how the people of the Place of Truth celebrated the occasion.

'They believe that everyone, even the dead, should be given the opportunity to perform the pilgrimage to Abdu to pay homage to the Great God in person. They set up little boats on the offering tables before the tombs and point them towards the north, showing the spirits of the deceased which way they should travel. It is said that sometimes at Abdu you can hear the voices of the dead calling out to each other in joy as they draw near the goal of their pilgrimage. Then, when they have had time to celebrate the god's festival, the boats are turned round and their sails are set so that the deceased may travel back to their own resting places.'

'I think that's a lovely custom,' Nebet said, 'but I suggest you don't tell Montmose about it or he'll want you to do it today.'

'I'd be glad to,' Ramose said seriously, 'but it really needs to be done sooner to give the dead time to reach Abdu for today's festival.'

'My dear son,' Nebet said, patting his arm, 'don't put yourself out. I wasn't suggesting that we should adopt this custom, especially since Amenmose isn't here to approve it. The simple, straightforward rites will suffice.'

Nebet sent them off with two baskets packed with festival food which they would share as a family feast after the offerings had been made to the spirits of the deceased. They would be in good company, because there were many family groups making their way along the causeway towards the western cliffs. As daylight waned, tiny points of light appearing all over the hillside showed where lamps and torches were being lit before the tombs. The living relatives of the dead would keep vigil until the sun had set and they could be sure that their loved ones had gone to join Osiris in the Land of the West. Later the celebrants would form a cheerful torchlight procession back through the cultivation towards the River and then home to continue the party for as long as they had the energy to do so. Most would not reach their homes before the next sunrise.

As the senior member of the family Montmose was acting as host for the celebrations and Satra was in charge of preparing the food and drink. This was the one part of the Osiris Festival that Nebet dreaded because Satra's obsession with economy made for a rather plain meal and dampened everyone's high spirits. This was supposed to be a hopeful time, looking forward to a season of new growth and fruitfulness. After months of flooding, the land was emerging from the waters, and very soon the fields would be covered in the delicate green haze of new life, the life promised by Osiris. It was a time to stop worrying about whether the stores would last until the next harvest. It was a time to rejoice in the god's blessing by eating and drinking the bounty he had bestowed on Kemet.

In particular it was a time to enjoy the first of that year's vintage, to compare the taste of the young wine with memories of vintages of years past. Satra seemed to go out of her way to choose the sourest, least palatable wines she could find, probably because they were the cheapest and because she knew no one would want to drink very much of them. Nebet had always been surprised that Montmose put up with this, since in most things he had a very discerning nature, but apparently his palate for wine was not so well developed. He had always preferred beer and liked the strongest and darkest of brews.

Nebet was also disappointed to see that Satra was serving dates which were so dry and hard that they could have been left over from the year before last. When there were fresh, newly harvested dates in the marketplace this seemed an insult to her guests. Nebet had long ago learned to hold her tongue and had instructed her children to do the same. They all knew to mind their manners and were reassured by the knowledge that there was better food at home.

When they felt that their duty was done, Nebet and her children took their leave of Montmose and walked home through streets lit by pools of golden lamplight falling from the many open doors of houses where people were celebrating. It was not until they reached their own door that Nebet realized Senmut was missing. He had been muttering complaints about the food, and more particularly about the wine, all through the evening. Abau had tried his best to keep him quiet but Nebet had seen Satra frowning in their direction more than once. When they left Montmose's house, Mymy and Abau had gone their own way, leaving just the three youngest children to accompany their mother home. Nebet had been chatting so happily with Neferti and Khay, all of them relieved to have survived Satra's hospitality without a major upset, that she had not noticed Senmut's disappearance. He had simply lagged further and further behind until he just blended into the darkness and vanished. There was nothing she could do about it now. Pakhred and Ramose were not back yet, so she could not ask them to go looking for him. Menna, Bak and Sendji were all celebrating with their own families, and Gemni was too young to have any hope of bringing back a reluctant Senmut. She could only suppose that he had back-tracked and gone home with Abau, as on many occasions before. If that were the case, Mymy would see to it that he came to no harm and would find him a place to sleep.

Just before dawn the family was awakened by a hammering on the side-gate and someone shouting. Hastily pulling a shawl about her shoulders Nebet went out on to the bedroom landing and looked over the wall into the alleyway below. In the dim shadows she could make out two figures, one leaning heavily against the other.

'Who is it?' she called softly.

The answering voice was not one she recognized and it was far too loud for her liking.

'Lady, I have your son here. For the love of the gods, open up and let me bring him in.'

Ramose appeared on the landing. He had barely dozed off after his return from the West Bank, and Mutemwiya was still asleep. He called down to the man in the alley, 'Wait there and I'll come down, but please lower your voice.' He turned to Nebet. 'You stay up here until I discover what this is all about.'

'But it's Senmut. I must go to him. What if he's hurt?'

'If he is, I suspect it's all of his own doing. I won't be long.'

Ramose made his way down the unfamiliar staircase into the kitchen court and unbarred the gate. Senmut, who had been leaning against the doorpost, almost fell into his arms. The man who had delivered him home handed Ramose a small fold of papyrus and said, 'My mistress said to give you this,' and then disappeared into the pre-dawn gloom.

Nebetiunet flew down the stairs as Ramose allowed Senmut to slide down the wall into a slumped sitting position. 'What's wrong with him? Is he injured?'

'We won't know until we get some light,' Ramose said sensibly.

He found a rushlight on a shelf against the wall and thrust it into the banked-up embers of the cooking hearth. By its smoky orange flame they examined Senmut from head to toe. He was a mess. His face, arms and legs were filthy, caked with mud and worse. There was a bruise beginning to show on his cheek and a small cut on his forehead, but whether these had been acquired during a fight or as a result of his falling down they could not tell. The kilt that Nebet had made to replace the wine-stained one was torn and so dirty that she could have wept then and there. She was also conscious of several smells, all of them unpleasant, hanging about her son.

Senmut opened his eyes and with a remarkably silly smile he said, 'Hallo Muti,' before bending forward and being violently sick over Ramose's feet.

The note was from Senetnay. Her husband, the architect Ahmose, returning from making the offerings at his family tomb, had found Senmut asleep in his doorway. The boy had obviously been drinking and was cradling a jar in which only the lees remained. No one would ever know whether Senmut had been drinking alone or in company nor how he had come by his injuries, since he could remember nothing about his adventures. One of Ahmose's neighbours claimed to have been woken by a party of drunken louts singing crude songs beneath his bedroom window, but no one could swear that Senmut had been one of them. He could not, or would not, say where he had been, who he had been with or how he had come by the wine. Nebet immediately suspected Abau but later inquiries proved that, on this occasion at least, Abau was innocent.

To save making too much of a mess in the bathing stall, Ramose and

Pakhred dragged Senmut down to an irrigation channel and made sure that he washed thoroughly, then they marched him back to the house before too many people should see him. Luckily, everyone in Waset tended to rise later than usual after a long day and night of celebration. By that time he had sobered up a little and was complaining of a headache. To his obvious surprise no one expressed any sympathy for him. He was told to take himself up to the roof and sleep it off. As he went, head hung dejectedly, Nebet felt a surge of motherly concern. Was he in any fit state to climb the stairs, let alone the ladder that led from the landing to the roof?

She was about to call him back when Pakhred said, in a voice that was disconcertingly like his father's, 'Leave him, Muti. He has only himself to blame. If you help him any more he'll think you forgive him. He must learn that wine turns people away from a drunkard, and even the drinker's own family will desert him if he doesn't mend his ways.'

Nebetiunet was surprised to hear such sentiments from her son, even though she knew he was paraphrasing one of his student exercise texts. She looked at Young Amenmose with new eyes. He had grown up. All her children were growing up so quickly, or, in Senmut's case, trying to act grown-up. All too soon they would be living their own lives in their own homes with their own families, and what would her role be then, when her children no longer needed her help and guidance? She realized quite suddenly that she was old.

Nebet inspected the garden plot where her Osiris bed had been buried. She studied with great satisfaction the patch of tiny green shoots, each as fine as a hair and just peeping through the earth. She could make out the outline of the god's body, blurred by the unevenness of the grain's germination, to be sure, but still the familiar shape of the mummified Osiris, complete with feathered crown. This early promise of the Osiris bed was a good sign. She hoped to hear news from Wiya at any time now. However, the next person to enter the garden was Mutnefert, and Nebet knew at once that Mymy had exciting news of her own.

'Muti, I'm pregnant,' Mymy announced without preamble.

Unable to speak, Nebetiunet took her daughter in her arms and hugged her tightly. It was such a little time before that she had done much the same for Wiya, and yet how different the circumstances.

'Are you sure?' she asked at last.

'Oh yes. My last moonflow was nearly two months ago, and I've done the test.'

Mymy was referring to the practice of moistening grain with a woman's urine to discover whether or not she was carrying a child: if the grain germinated she was pregnant. Both wheat and barley were used. If the wheat grew better the child would be a girl, and if the barley was stronger it would be a boy.

'What was the result?' Nebet asked. She had used the test herself only once, and it had predicted that Mutemwiya would be a boy, so she had no great faith in it. Others, however, swore by its accuracy.

'It's a girl,' Mymy said with a little disappointment in her voice.

'That's wonderful. Little girls are so much easier to deal with than boys,' Nebet said with feeling, her experiences with Senmut a catalogue of sore memories.

'I'd have liked a son for Abau,' Mutnefert said, 'but there's always next time.'

'So you want a big family then?' Nebet forced herself to laugh. She could not help wondering how Mutemwiya would take the news of her sister's pregnancy.

CHAPTER FIVE

First Month
of Winter

THE INUNDATION WAS RECEDING RAPIDLY. SOME OF THE CORNFIELDS were already dry enough to be ploughed, and the marginal lands, along the banks of the canals and irrigation basins, were ready to be sown with other less demanding crops.

Nebet was conducting the yearly ritual of checking the supplies of dyestuffs kept in the Temple linen stores. She found madder root, safflowers and acacia pods, which would provide red, yellow and blue dyes, but the older the dried plants were, the less reliable the colours that could be produced from them. Woad gave a deeper blue when used as fresh as possible, but it was not as easily obtainable as acacia, and she feared the brittle woad leaves from the store had lost their potency. She needed fresh supplies. The seeds saved from last season's dye crops, and those painstakingly gathered from the wild, had to be planted soon to supply the needs of the temples. Since the linen-works of Amen-Ra also supplied the royal household when the King was resident in Waset, she had to estimate what demands might come from that direction as well.

Nedjemger, the Chief Gardener, had sent a message by Khay to say that he needed to know how much land to set aside this year for the dye crops. As always Nebet found it difficult to work it out, as she had not Nedjemger's instinctive understanding of the yield to be expected from a particular sized plot of a certain quality soil.

Khaemwase, on the other hand, seemed to be able to grasp such details very quickly. His youth and lack of height were no hindrance to his chosen profession. He was a natural gardener, with such a feel for the soil and the seasons that Nedjemger, recognizing his talent, had started to give him more and more interesting and challenging tasks. Khay was now known to be the Chief Gardener's personal apprentice. Nebetiunet was very proud of her youngest son, and even Amenmose agreed that Khay's career change was probably for the best, which was the closest he had come to giving the boy his blessing. If only he would admit his change of heart to Khay himself, Nebet thought; their son would so like to have his father's approval.

Djehutiemheb bustled in to the store. 'How are things coming along?' he asked.

'The stocks are good but I'm sure some of these bundles are too desiccated to be of much use now. I'm trying to work out what commissions might come in over the next year but, apart from the regular festival needs, things are so unpredictable. You know how much coloured cloth is needed for decorating the temples, especially for the inauguration ceremonies. Also, I heard a whisper from one of the Ladies of the Royal Wardrobe that the King's Mother might have some work for us. Have you heard anything? Will any more of His Majesty's new works be dedicated this year?'

'I have not been informed of any such plans,' he said, as if he would naturally be the first to be told, 'but I wouldn't be surprised if the King's Mother and the Great Royal Wife were to pay us a visit very soon.'

Nebet knew that Djehuti was only stating the obvious. The Festival of Mut was due later in the month and, as both royal ladies claimed the goddess as their patron, they had adopted the custom not only of attending the celebration but also of joining the other chantresses in the ritual. Their annual visit had given rise to the custom of presenting gifts of fine linen cloth suitable for royal gowns. The weaving of this gauzy fabric had been Nebet's principal concern since the end of the Osiris holiday. But the cloth was pure white linen and her contact within the royal household, the wife of one of Paser's friends, had implied that the King's Mother in particular was interested in something coloured.

Nebet hoped Her Majesty wanted some embroidery work, since the necessary materials were already to hand. She had just checked the baskets full of balls of coloured thread, each wrapped in a square of linen to protect it against fading. But if the Lady wanted a self-coloured garment the fabric would have to be dyed to order and probably double-dyed at least to achieve the depth of colour she preferred. Nebet could hope that the King's Mother wanted red but blue was known to be her favourite colour and that posed more of a problem, and if she wanted it before she returned to Per-Ramesse it would be well-nigh impossible.

'I like to have enough dyestuffs to cover all eventualities,' she said, 'but I hate to see anything wasted.'

'Of course you do, because you are an excellent manager,' Djehutiemheb cooed. 'However, you must remember that the temple of Amen-Ra is the richest of all establishments and the god will not weep over a few discarded leaves and roots. As to planning for the year ahead, it's better to have too much than too little. What did we do last year?'

Nebetiunet had to admit that she had left the decision to Nedjemger. She did not say, however, that she had resorted to the same tactics every year of the King's reign so far.

Djehuti said cheerfully, 'Then why not do the same again? Don't go worrying your little head about such matters.'

'I suppose that would be the sensible plan. Thank you, Djehutiemheb, you have eased my mind,' she said with the sweetest smile she could muster. Flattery went a long way with her boss, and a little insincerity made life in the linen-works more bearable for everyone.

'That's my good girl,' he said, patting her shoulder in his familiar way.

A short while later she went to seek out Nedjemger in his 'office', a little brick-built pavilion tucked away in one corner of the formal garden to the north of the temple entrance. Its lime-washed, plastered exterior was totally in keeping with the regal architecture of the religious buildings and could have been mistaken for a small shrine, but once inside visitors were confronted by an untidy, overcrowded glory-hole from which the Chief Gardener dispensed orders and horticultural advice to all and sundry.

Nedjemger was unmarried, as any woman who saw his office would have known instantly. He and Djehutiemheb were two of a kind in their dedication to their work and their single-minded belief that Waset, and probably all Kemet, would be thrown into confusion if either of them took a day off. Nebet had been told that the gardener had had a wife once but that she had died within the first year of their marriage and he had never wanted to marry again. That explained why he had never

acquired domestic habits. He was also, if the evidence of the
accumulated bags and baskets, buckets and brooms and other garden
paraphernalia was to be believed, a hoarder. There were corners of his
storeroom where only a very brave or determined person would venture,
and then only if armed with a stout stick to fend off rats and the
occasional snake.

Nedjemger was not in. She found him, eventually, in the 'nursery'
behind the vine trellises, where he was directing the sowing of seeds in
specially prepared beds and wooden troughs. Among the garden workers
Nebet saw Khay, listening intently to his master's wise words and
following his instructions precisely. They were planting onions and garlic,
which reminded Nebet that it was time to start planting her allotment.

As soon as the vegetable plots became accessible Bak had started
working manure into the soil, since the rich silt brought by the
inundation had not been spread as far as the domestic gardens. He would
next give the plot a good soaking, carrying water from the nearest cistern
in two jars hanging from a yoke over his shoulders, then he would reduce
the surface to a good tilth for sowing. He had saved some seed from last
year but more would be welcome and, if Khay continued to please his
master, he would very likely bring home some of this high-quality seed
as a bonus payment. The nursery beds were edged with pots in which
seedlings of coriander, cumin and dill were beginning to show. Nebet had
similar potherbs in her own garden and when the plants were strong
enough they would be transplanted into the allotment. Even Wiya had
been successful in starting a herb garden on her roof.

Nebet could see that Nedjemger would not appreciate being
disturbed, so she decided her message could wait until the next day. As
she retraced her steps to the linen-works, her thoughts were once more
with Wiya. Her eldest daughter had seemed to take the news of her
sister's pregnancy very calmly. Mutemwiya had such a pleasant nature
that she could not but rejoice for Mymy's sake, but Nebet knew that she
was hiding a deep anguish. Both mother and daughter were beginning to
fear that Wiya was barren, though neither had as yet voiced that fear, for
speaking of it would make it so. All the while this worry went unspoken
there was hope that it would prove groundless, and there were still many
things that could be done to promote a woman's fertility. Nebet intended
to make special supplication to the Goddess at the Festival of Mut.
Mutemwiya and her mother, as Chantresses of Mut, would be in the

company of the Royal Wife and the King's Mother. With the two senior royal ladies in attendance, surely the Goddess would be even more amenable to granting the prayers of her worshippers? Then Nebet remembered that the Great Royal Wife, Nefertari, was herself pregnant. She wondered how close to term she was. Perhaps there would be even more cause for rejoicing at Mut's festival this year.

The Chantresses of Mut met at the Asheru Temple, where they received their sacred instruments from Iny, the controller of the temple stores. The sistra used for special occasions were made of gold or silver mounted on handles of smooth, black ebony with gilded decoration, and were kept in secure storerooms together with the sacred vessels used in temple rituals. The arching hoop of a sistrum emerged from the distinctive image of the face of the Goddess, whose eyes were inlaid with obsidian. Each hollow head contained pellets, which added a gentle rattle to the rhythmic, metallic jingle of the chimes threaded on wires across the hoop.

The choir had gathered to practise their stately walk round the Asheru Lake, because the Choir Mistress was worried that they might let her down in front of the Great Wife and the King's Mother. The respectable ladies of Waset, including Mutemwiya, Nebetiunet and several of their friends, were enjoying some good-humoured, girlish giggling, and their director was horrified that they seemed not to be taking their duty seriously. The rehearsal, she said, would take up as much of the afternoon as was necessary and the Chantresses would not be released until their performance came up to her exacting standards.

'I can't understand why she's so worried about it,' Senetnay said, as the Choir Mistress called them to order once again in a voice which was becoming increasingly exasperated.

'No, no, no!' she snapped. She snatched the sistrum from the hand of one of the younger Chantresses and waved it to and fro saying, 'Like this, like this! Why do you make it look so difficult?' The young girl blushed furiously at this public admonition.

Senetnay clicked her tongue in disapproval. 'She's picking on that poor girl for no good reason. What does she expect? Perfection? This is only the rehearsal after all.'

'Yes, it's not as if we haven't done this before, and with Their Majesties, too. I wonder that she didn't ask them to join in the rehearsal,' Nebet said wickedly.

'Have you seen the Royal Ladies since they arrived in the City?' Senetnay asked while the procession was reforming yet again.

'No. The boats docked late in the afternoon and I only caught a glimpse of their chairs being carried towards the Residence at Ipet Esut. My friend told me that rooms have been made ready for some of the Royal Children too.'

The Choir Mistress clapped her hands for silence and, having satisfied herself that they were all in their correct places, gave the signal to start the parade again. Walking in step, two by two, the Chantresses of Mut waved their instruments from side to side in unison, producing a delicate percussion accompaniment to their sacred chant. This time their efforts were almost acceptable, and the Choir Mistress required only two more repetitions before she felt ready to dismiss them. The Chantresses were reminded to return their sistra to the stores overnight for safe-keeping. They were to collect the instruments again at dawn the following day.

Mutemwiya and Nebet walked home with Senetnay, who wanted to know the latest news about Senmut. 'I was so worried when I realized it was your brother,' she said to Wiya. 'Of course, Ahmose didn't recognize him but I remembered him from the Opet Festival. He was in such a dreadful state that I wanted to bring him in and clean him up a bit before sending him home, but Ahmose insisted that he should go home at once.'

'And quite right too,' Nebet said. 'Amenmose was extremely angry that Senmut had put you to so much inconvenience.' She did not add that, when Amenmose had returned from Abdu and had been told about Senmut's escapade, for the first time he had seen fit to give his son a beating. His heart had not been in it and Senmut suffered more humiliation than pain, but he had been considerably more tractable since then. Nebet's main concern now was that Senmut showed even less eagerness for his studies than before, and no beating was going to make school seem any more attractive.

'He's a typical, thoughtless boy,' Wiya said. 'He should have apologized to you in person.'

'Oh he did,' Senetnay said, to the surprise of Senmut's mother and sister. 'He came round the very next day and he even offered to clean up the step . . .' She stopped as she saw the disbelief in her friends' eyes. 'You didn't know?'

'No,' Nebet said shortly, 'but I suppose it makes it better that he did it on his own initiative rather than being dragged to your house by his father.'

'He looked very sorry for himself but then I suppose he was suffering from a hangover. There didn't seem to be much else wrong with him,' Senetnay remarked.

'He was very lucky,' Nebet said, grateful that they had reached Senetnay's door. They said goodbye until tomorrow, then Wiya linked arms with her mother and they walked on.

Senmut had been at school when Mutemwiya arrived that morning so she had not seen him since the day after the Osiris Festival. She knew from her mother's tone that something was wrong.

'Did Senmut have any trouble with his injuries?' she asked. 'I thought they looked quite trivial.'

'That's what we all thought,' Nebet said. 'I'll tell you about it when we get home.'

Sitting in the garden, sipping pomegranate wine, Nebet at last was able to unburden herself of some frightening memories. Wiya was right. The wound on Senmut's head had looked like a mere scratch. There was little blood and it healed over quickly. Amenmose would never have beaten his son if he had thought the boy was ill, but the day after his punishment Senmut developed a fever. The wound began to swell and turned an angry red. Nebet had at once applied to his forehead a poultice of acacia leaves pounded with oil, and had dosed him with an infusion of unripe berries from the sidder tree to bring down his fever.

When these remedies failed she begged Chief Physician Huy to send one of the Sakhmet priests to help her son. The doctor had immediately pierced the wound with a small flint blade to let out the noxious fluid that had accumulated under the skin. He packed the incision with beer-moistened bread, covered it with a strip of mandrake leaf and bound it in place with a linen bandage. He instructed Nebet to change the dressing each day.

'When the swelling has reduced you should mix incense and the pulp of carob pods into a salve with animal fat. Smear this over the wound to keep it sealed. For the fever I recommend dill weed steeped in wine and bread made with dom palm fruit. You should pray to Sakhmet the Healer to take away this evil and to Serqet of the Hot Breath to reduce the heat of his body. Then you should make an offering at the Temple of Asheru.'

In order to follow these instructions Nebet had bartered a pot of her preserved cheese for a minute quantity of incense resin and Amenmose arranged for an offering to be made at the temple in Senmut's name. He had been badly frightened by his son's sudden decline and had blamed himself for being too harsh on the boy. Nebet never discovered the exact nature of the gifts he had provided but she knew they were expensive because Amenmose had asked his own father to contribute to the offerings. Whatever the expense, it was worth it. Senmut's wound healed quite quickly, though the new scar above his left eye was longer and more jagged than the original cut, giving him a rakish air of which he became unnecessarily proud.

'So, has he learned his lesson, do you think?' Wiya asked.

'Only until the next time, I fear. It certainly gave him a great shock. The doctor said he could have died. Of course, that made your father even more upset because he thought he might have killed him.'

'But it wasn't Father's fault. The wound would have turned poisonous anyway. It was just coincidence that it happened after the beating which, I must say, was thoroughly deserved,' Mutemwiya said severely.

'There's no question about that,' Nebet agreed, 'and Senmut knows he's his own worst enemy. But the young forget very quickly and, whatever the squalid circumstances in which he came by the injury, he'll remember this only as a great adventure. By next month he'll be out carousing with his old friends and neglecting his studies just as badly as ever.'

The next morning, as the sun was rising, the Chantresses of Mut made their way to the ceremonial enclosure of the Goddess. The Festival of Mut was a celebration dear to the hearts of the women of Waset, for the Lady of Asheru was their own personal protector. In her many aspects the Great Goddess was honoured in shrines and temples throughout the Two Lands, but only in Waset was she worshipped as Mut, Lady of Heaven, Mistress of the Gods. Only in Waset was she recognized under her simplest name, Mother.

The royal party arrived at the last possible moment to take up their positions at the head of the procession. The ladies of Waset were honoured to see that the King's Great Wife was attended by her daughter Merytamen, while the King's Mother was accompanied by the King's eldest daughter, Bint-Anath, the child of the Lady Isetnofre. The little girls had clearly been schooled in how to walk and how to rattle the sistrum and they took their role very seriously. The Choir Mistress gushed with praise for their poise and timing, but then she would not have dared to find fault with their performance, not when they had clearly received instruction from the King's Mother herself. Mut-Tuya was a tall, elegant woman, whose height and striking if not beautiful features had been inherited by her son, the King, and by his daughter Bint-Anath. The Royal Daughter Merytamen, dressed in a flowing gown which was a miniature version of that worn by the Great Royal Wife, was the image of her beautiful mother, Nefertari.

At dawn the cult statue of Mut had been lifted from the stone shrine in the innermost recess of the temple. Washed and anointed, dressed in fine linen and adorned with jewels, the goddess had been placed in the portable shrine that became the cabin of the sacred barque, the miniature boat in which she was to be carried in procession. The barque had been brought into the open court and set down on a block of stone decorated with flowers and streamers. The Chief Servitor of Asheru, Penashefi, presented the libations of wine, water and milk, and offerings of food. Incense was burned in saucers and censing spoons, and flowers were offered in bouquets and garlands. Standing in a crescent formation before the bark of the goddess, the royal ladies in the front row, the Chantresses recited the verses in praise of the Goddess.

'We praise the Lady of the Thrones of the Two Lands,
The Lady of Heaven, the Mistress of All the Gods.
The Wise One who cares for Kemet,
Who keeps the Two Lands in her protection.
With Mut as protector, no harm can befall,
With Mut as protector, no evil will prosper,
With Mut as protector, no sadness prevails,
With Mut as protector, all life is joyful.
She is Mut, the Lady of Waset, the Great Mother,
She is Hathor, Flame of Gold, beloved of Horus.
She is Sakhmet, the Powerful One, the Eye of Ra.
Give praise to her, the Most Beautiful One.
Extol her Majesty with songs of praise.'

The words subsided and the rhythm of the sistra was now augmented by the music of pipes and harps as the temple dancers entered the courtyard in front of the sanctuary. At first slow and stately, the dancers became more and more animated until they were high-stepping and tossing their heads so that their unbound hair swung wildly from side to side. The Chantresses kept pace with the increasing tempo by watching closely the musical director's clapping hands. When the dancers had performed their last spectacular movement, a series of back-flips, the music ceased abruptly.

In the silence that followed Nebet was sure she could sense the presence of the Goddess smiling her approval of their worship. She offered up her own silent prayer for Mutemwiya, 'Please, Lady, Mother of All, in your goodness, grant my daughter the joy of motherhood.' She knew Wiya would be making a similar plea.

Then she heard a gasp and a low moan. She frowned at this unwelcome intrusion into the holy silence, but dared not look around to discover who was responsible. Suddenly it was all too clear who had made the sound and why. The King's Wife sank to her knees, clutching her hands to her swollen stomach and emitting a groan of pain.

The priest Penashefi turned to admonish the woman who had interrupted the ritual but was struck dumb by the scene of Nefertari being tended by those of her ladies who were among the Chantresses. The King's Mother, Mut-Tuya, stepped forward to say a few quiet words to him and he bowed his agreement. He recited an abbreviated closing prayer, bowed to the Goddess and declared that part of the ritual over.

In the meantime the King's Wife had been escorted out of the temple court. Her Majesty's labour, it seemed, was progressing too quickly and too painfully for her to walk as far as the King's House at Ipet Esut so it had been decided that she should be taken to Huy's residence in the nearby physicians' college.

The dowager Royal Wife surveyed the stunned faces of the choir, her gaze coming to rest on Nebetiunet. 'You look like a sensible woman. You will escort the Royal Daughters back to the Residence and deliver them to their nurses while I attend Her Majesty.'

'Yes, Lady.' Nebet bowed low.

Before she could think of anything else to say, Mut-Tuya signalled that she should go with her. Nebet gave her sistrum to Senetnay, who nodded her understanding. She followed the King's Mother to where the little Royal Daughters were standing and bowed to them.

Mut-Tuya said, 'This lady will take you back to the palace. Obey her for she is doing my bidding.'

The elder child bowed stiffly and said in a tiny voice, 'We will obey.'

Mut-Tuya turned to Nebet, said 'They are good girls,' and then swept away to attend the birth of her son's latest child.

The festival of the Going Forth of Mut would have to continue without half the usual complement of Chantresses. The Goddess's sacred barque was lifted on the shoulders of the servants of Mut and then carried from the sanctuary court to begin a circuit of the Asheru Lake. The remaining Chantresses followed the attendant priests, shaking their sistra and repeating the hymn again and again. Outside the temple precinct the sacred barque would be paraded round the enclosure wall to allow the people of the City, especially the women, to greet their patroness. Somewhere out there Neferti and Mymy were waiting to pay their respects to the Mother of All, and proudly to point out their mother and sister among the choir. But having left the sacred court Nebet would take no further part in the festival. Instead she found herself in the company of two frightened children.

The King's Daughters were still very young. Bint-Anath was about nine and her half-sister was just seven. They had both been slightly overawed to be included in this ceremony in the first place. Now they looked totally bewildered and Merytamen was close to tears.

'What is wrong with Mother?' she asked Nebet.

'She's having a baby, you silly goose,' said the more grown-up Bint-Anath.

'Yes, Highness, your lady mother is about to give birth. There is nothing to be afraid of.' Nebet prayed that this was the truth. Childbirth might be natural but it was not necessarily safe. She had no wish to lie to the Royal Daughter, but the little girl needed reassurance. 'The Royal Wife has had many children already – Your Highness is living proof of that. Now, come, I must take you to your nurses as the King's Mother commanded.'

'What is your name?' Bint-Anath asked.

'I am Nebetiunet, daughter of Nubnefer and wife of the Tjaty's scribe Amenmose,' she answered.

'My sister and I thank you for your kindness, Nebetiunet. The little one would be afraid to be left on her own.'

Nebet kept a straight face as she said, 'I am honoured to be of help, Highness.' In fact she was surprised that none of the ladies-in-waiting had stayed to attend the Royal Daughters. She was even more surprised, as they walked along her usual short cut between Asheru and Ipet Esut, to find a small hand slipped into each of hers.

'The King's Mother asked me to bring you her thanks and this token in recognition of recent events,' Paser said as he handed Nebet a small, linen-wrapped parcel.

Nebet was stunned. To have the Tjaty turn up at her door unannounced was honour enough. That he bore a message and gift from the Lady Mut-Tuya was recognition beyond her wildest dreams. 'I don't know what to say. Should I reply to Her Majesty's favour or would that be presumptuous?'

Paser smiled. 'The Lady expects no reply. Her Majesty rarely lets a good deed go unrewarded. She asked me to seek you out, not knowing you were my sister. I asked the Choir Mistress to identify the Chantress to whom the King's Mother had entrusted the Royal Daughters, and I was very proud when I heard that it was you. That's why I wanted to deliver the Lady's gift in person.'

'Open the package, Muti,' Neferti said, eager to see what her mother had received from the King's Mother.

'Before I do, we must know if the Great Royal Wife delivered her child safely.'

'Of course – how stupid of me to forget. Her Majesty gave birth to a girl child before sunset on the day of the Coming Forth of Mut. In honour of the Goddess the Royal Daughter has been named Nebet-tawy, Mistress of the Two Lands. Both mother and child are in good health.'

Paser's announcement was greeted with joy by the whole family. 'I think this calls for wine,' Amenmose said, and he went with Sendji to choose the best from his limited cellar so that they might drink to the health of the King's Wife and her new daughter.

When wine had been poured for everyone, Paser lifted his cup and said, 'To the spirits of the Great Royal Wife Nefertari-Meryenmut and her daughter Nebet-tawy. May the Goddess continue to smile upon them.'

All present raised their cups and said, 'To their spirits!' before drinking the toast.

'Open the package, Muti,' Neferti begged again.

Nebet unwrapped the linen to reveal a kidskin pouch from which she pulled a small pendant amulet. The charm was in the shape of the sacred

bird of Mut, a vulture, with a royal sceptre tucked under one wing and perched on the basket symbol for 'Lady'. What made everyone gasp was that it was made of gold, inlaid with dark-blue glass, pale-blue turquoise and red carnelian, and it hung from a fine flaxen cord threaded with gold wire for strength. The jewel was so delicate that Nebet could hardly feel its weight on her palm. The quantity of gold was small by royal standards but for the wife of a middle-ranking scribe it was of enormous value. Nebet had never in her life owned anything made of gold. She stood staring down at the amulet in disbelief.

'There's something else here,' said Neferti who had rescued the linen wrapping, for anything that came from the royal hand was special. She had found an even smaller packet made from a fold of papyrus.

When Nebet opened it she found a tiny blue-glazed amulet of Taweret, the hippopotamus goddess, shown standing upright with pendulous breasts and distended belly, her front feet resting on the symbol for 'protection'. It was the sort of amulet that could be found in any marketplace, that any woman of any class might wear to invoke the protection of the goddess of pregnancy and childbirth. Its workmanship could not be compared with that of Mut-Tuya's gift but Nebet had a feeling that the sentiment behind it was more heartfelt. Looking at the scrap of papyrus she found written on it the words 'With gratitude' in a childish scrawl. There was no name but she knew it was from one of the Royal Daughters, perhaps from both of them, and that knowledge gave her a warm feeling. The golden jewel would be kept as an eminently saleable asset, but this little trinket would be stored away in a place of honour and would go to the grave with her.

Djehutiemheb was worried. 'I am surprised there has been no word from the King's Mother,' he said, 'when she seemed so eager to sample our coloured wares.'

Nebet never ceased to be amazed at how Djehuti could turn an idea round and round until he had convinced himself that his daydreams and wishful thinking were reality. *She* had told *him* that she had heard a rumour, no more, that Mut-Tuya was interested in having something made from coloured cloth. Now he was certain that the King's Mother had actually placed an order or, at the very least, made an appointment to discuss the matter, although Nebet knew that such things would normally be dealt with through the Mistress of the Royal Wardrobe. Djehuti also seemed to have forgotten that Mut-Tuya had other, more important, matters to consider.

It had been announced that the Great Royal Wife would remain in Waset for the duration of her purification period, while the King's Mother was to escort the Royal Daughters back to Per-Ramesse. They would be leaving within the next few days. It was the news of their departure that had caused Djehutiemheb to become so agitated.

'Her Majesty has much to occupy her thoughts at present. I wouldn't take her apparent lack of interest as a snub or criticism,' Nebet said in an attempt to placate her boss.

'Oh, I'm sure there's no question of *your* work being criticized,' Djehuti said, proving how far he had misread the whole situation, 'but a great lady should always honour her promises, even in the most trying of circumstances. After all, it wasn't the King's Mother who gave birth.'

How typical of a man, and an unmarried man at that, Nebet thought, but she decided not to point out that the only promises made by the King's Mother were entirely of Djehuti's imagination.

There was a knock at Djehuti's office door and one of the weavers poked his head round it to say, 'There's a messenger come for you, Mistress. He's waiting in the courtyard.'

The way he said it told Nebet at once that this was no bringer of good news. She made her excuses to Djehutiemheb and hurried to meet the messenger.

It was Sendji and he looked uncharacteristically flustered. At once all sorts of horrible visions flashed across her mind. Senmut dead in a common street brawl, Mymy dead of a miscarriage.

'Whatever has happened, Sendji?'

'It's Master Montmose, Mistress. My master says to come at once.'

It seemed to take twice as long as usual to make their way through the streets of Waset to Montmose's house. Nebet knew before they reached the door that the worst had happened, because she could hear the keening of mourners. In a moment of detachment she marvelled that Satra had thought to employ mourners so quickly. The wailing women were proclaiming the family's grief in the small courtyard in front of the house.

To justify their fee, their cries became louder as she passed between them, but they were not loud enough to drown out the voices of Amenmose and his sister. Their argument was in danger of becoming audible to everyone in the street. She found them in the principal reception room and, to her horror, they were almost screaming at each other over the body of their father.

'Husband!' she said, almost shouting to make herself heard. 'Sister! Think of the servants. Think of the neighbours. Think of your father.'

They stopped in mid-yell.

When everyone had calmed down enough to make sense, Nebet was able to work out what had happened. Satra had discovered Montmose dead in his bed but she had not told anyone of his death immediately. The cook, Kheti, had become suspicious when her master had failed to call for his morning meal. Montmose was a creature of habit and had a healthy appetite, so he rarely missed an opportunity to eat. Kheti had found Satra going through her father's personal belongings, even his document box. When the old woman asked Satra what was going on, she had flown into a rage and ordered her out of the house. Kheti had made her way at once to Amenmose's house, only to find that he was at work on the other side of the River. In the time it took for a message to reach him and for Amenmose to return to the eastern shore, Satra had tidied up the house so that there was no evidence of her search, and she had called in the professional mourners.

Amenmose was doubly in shock at the suddenness of his father's death and at his sister's callous behaviour. It was clear to everyone that Satra had been looking for Montmose's will. All she was interested in was knowing how big her inheritance would be. Any daughterly feeling she might have had gave way to greed.

At last everyone was silent. Satra had given up trying to justify her actions, Amenmose had stopped accusing her of disrespect for their father, and the truth was sinking in. Montmose was dead. There were many things to be done and quickly. Nebetiunet took her husband's hand and as she looked into his eyes the tears began to flow.

CHAPTER SIX

Second Month
of Winter

'THE TJATY HAS BEEN SUMMONED TO PER-RAMESSE,' AMENMOSE
announced.

Nebetiunet felt a chill of apprehension. Usually Amenmose followed
his master wherever Paser went and she had learned to cope with all
family matters in his absence. But this time it was different.

There was much to be done following Montmose's death. It was
Amenmose's duty, as the eldest son, to preside over the last rituals at his
parents' tomb. These rites could not be performed by a woman, not even
by Satra, the daughter of the deceased, and, though they might help him
with the preparations leading up to the funeral, neither Nebet nor Satra
could direct the ceremony itself. The actual funeral would not take place
for almost a month, since even the simplest embalming process took up
to forty days, but something in her husband's voice told Nebet that this
summons was out of the ordinary.

'Will you have to go with him?' she asked. 'How long will you be
away? You'll be back for the funeral, surely?'

'Oh, don't worry about that,' Amenmose was quick to reassure her.
'The Tjaty wants me to stay here. The royal summons was quite urgent
and he'll leave as soon as his boat can be prepared. He hopes that this
will be only a short visit to the north, but in the meantime I'm to take
care of his regular business while he is away.'

She sighed with relief. 'For a moment I feared we might have to delay the funeral.'

'Thankfully, no,' Amenmose said, equally relieved, 'but it does mean I shall be very busy. He said I could be of invaluable assistance to his deputy, Meryra, and that he would commend me to Lord Tjia.'

This was better news. Lord Tjia was husband to the King's Sister and recently he had been appointed Superintendent of the Treasury at the King's Mansion Temple. He was a very demanding man but fair, Nebet had heard from Ramose, and he would treat a recommendation from the Tjaty with respect. Amenmose would be moving in very influential circles.

'I'm glad for you,' she said, kissing him on the cheek.

'You may not be so glad to know that I shall be spending a lot more time at the Tjaty's new offices at the Mansion. He has arranged rooms for me there and I shall have to take Sendji and another servant to keep house for me. I'm afraid you and Satra will have to deal with most of the funeral preparations by yourselves.'

'If that's how it must be, we shall cope,' she replied, 'but I think you must do something about Satra before you move across the River. That household is in complete turmoil. Most of the servants have already found other employment. There's just the cook, Kheti, left and she only stays because she's so deaf that she can't hear what her mistress is saying. And when I gave some sisterly advice, Satra told me in very blunt language not to interfere in her affairs.'

'You're right, as always,' Amenmose said. 'Satra cannot stay in that house alone. It will have to be sold.'

With a sinking heart, because she already knew the answer, Nebet asked, 'And where will Satra live?'

'She'll have to come here.' Amenmose's matter-of-fact voice indicated that this was the only acceptable solution, but Nebet knew that he had given very little thought to the practicalities of his suggestion. She held her tongue.

Ever since Montmose's death Nebet had known that Satra would have to move into her brother's house. It was unthinkable that she should live alone without the protection and respectability offered by the presence of a male relative. Even though the conditions of Montmose's will required the sale of his house and most of its contents, his daughter had been vociferous in her objections to the very idea of moving out. Nebetiunet had some sympathy with her sister in this respect, as she could not bear the thought of having to leave her own comfortable home, but Montmose's house was of medium size and in a very desirable part of the city. It would sell quickly and Satra knew it had to be sold. However, it would have to be a brave person who broached the subject with her, and Amenmose was no more eager for the task than his wife. For once Nebet was determined to take no part in the negotiations. Amenmose would have to deal with Satra, and the Tjaty's unexpected summons to Per-Ramesse had made the matter more pressing.

After an uncomfortably long silence she said, 'You'll have to tell her, then, before you go back across the River. The sooner the better.'

Amenmose looked at her with a mute appeal.

'No,' she said firmly. 'Satra is *your* sister. I can't say I like the idea of living with her but it's your duty to bring her here, especially now. If it came to the ears of the Lord Tjia that your unmarried sister was living unchaperoned, what would he think of you?'

'You're absolutely right, my dear. I've left it too long already. I'll go to Satra now and tell her.'

Nebet felt most uncomfortable checking the inventory of Montmose's house. As she moved from room to room, Satra stayed close by her side, scrutinizing over her shoulder every entry on the papyrus scroll. The list of Montmose's belongings had been kept together with his will. Satra had almost torn the house apart looking for them in vain and was beside herself with anger when Amenmose calmly announced that both documents had been in his keeping for some years, ever since their mother had died. At that time Montmose had sensibly made a new will to take account of the property inherited from his wife and to make provision for his daughter.

Both parents had hoped that they would see Satra married in their lifetime but her mother had died disappointed. Montmose had continued to talk about finding Satra a suitable husband for a year or so until he had realized how much he had come to rely on her in running the household. Once he had recognized this dependence he had ceased pushing her in the way of eligible young men and had tied her even closer to him with unrealistic promises of what she would inherit when he died. But to Satra such promises were not unreasonable, and she had fully expected to be heiress to the bulk of her father's estate.

When at last she heard the details of the will Satra had turned pale with anger, stormed out of the room and was soon to be heard breaking things in her bedroom. Having calmed her down enough not to fear that she would injure anyone, or herself, Nebet had talked her through the implications of the will as Amenmose had explained it to her. For the first time she felt genuinely sorry for Satra. She had given up twelve years of her life to look after her father, who had rewarded her with scant gratitude. All this could have been borne if the division of his property had been assigned as he had promised, in particular if the house had been left to her outright.

But it was not. Montmose had stipulated that his house and such furnishings as were not needed for his burial were to be sold. He had specified that a substantial share of the proceeds should be set aside for Satra, but only if she was married. In the unlikely event, as Montmose saw it at the time of writing his will, that Satra was unmarried at his death, this inheritance was to be her dowry. In any other circumstances this would have been seen as more than generous, but twelve years later Satra still had no husband and no prospect of marriage. Even the promise of the inheritance was unlikely to bring a flock of suitors to her door at her age. She had become orphaned, homeless and poor at a single stroke. Little wonder that she was upset.

Nebet tried to engage her in the selection of items for the tomb. 'Would your father want his favourite chair, do you think? And what about the leather-covered footstool?'

'Not that chair,' Satra said quickly. 'It's too valuable. Take the other one, the one with the shorter legs.'

Nebet looked at the smaller chair. It was of sycomore wood painted white to cover the unevenness of the grain. The curving planked seat required a cushion for the sitter to be at all comfortable and the back was simply slatted. Montmose's preferred chair was painted black in imitation of ebony and had armrests and a comfortable seat of woven rushwork. There was no doubt as to which chair was the more saleable but Nebet was horrified at Satra's callous attitude. She was totally uninterested in what her father might have wanted to take with him into eternity, and saw the furniture only as commodities which would increase the value of her inheritance. They had had similar arguments over his other possessions.

Nebet decided she would not ask Satra's opinion again but made a mark against the black chair on the inventory. Of course, the final choice would depend on how much could be packed into the tiny tomb, which already contained the burial goods provided for Amenmose's mother. Nebet had never been into the tomb but she knew it would be quite a squeeze to find space for Montmose's body, let alone large pieces of furniture. Perhaps Satra had the right idea, though with entirely the wrong motives.

The reception room was the last to be checked. Nebet rolled up the papyrus before Satra could argue further and said, 'That's done now. Are you sure you've removed all your own belongings?'

Like a sullen child, Satra nodded. Bak and Menna had collected her pitifully small bundles earlier in the day. All that was left was a small painted box containing the few pieces of jewellery inherited from her mother, which Satra had not trusted to the servants.

Nebetiunet with a rush of sympathy looked directly into Satra's eyes where tears were forming, and said gently, 'It will be all right, you know. You'll have a home with us for as long as you want.'

Satra nodded again but kept her head bowed as tears began to fall unchecked. Nebet could not hug her as she would have done her own child, because the jewellery box clutched to Satra's chest was in the way, but she put her arm round her sister's shoulders in the first gesture of genuine affection she could remember showing her.

'Come home, sister. There's nothing to stay for now. Come home.'

The embalmers' workshop was on the very southern edge of Waset, close to one of the communal refuse heaps. It was hard to say which of the two was responsible for the worse smell. Most people avoided the area if at all possible, but there were always some scavengers picking over the rubbish and fighting with the local dogs for choice scraps from the kitchens of the more fortunate citizens. Those who had business in that unsavoury vicinity were usually dealing, like Nebetiunet, with the sad and expensive business of a funeral.

On the evening after his death Montmose's body had been collected from the house and carried in a litter, borne on the shoulders of the embalmers' servants, accompanied by Amenmose and Pakhred, and followed by a small group of professional mourners.

Satra had complained about the ostentation and expense of this parade through the streets but, as Nebet pointed out sharply, the cost of the funeral was to be borne by Montmose's estate and his wishes would

be followed exactly, as far as it was within the family's power to do so. If all their careful preparations were successful, as regards both his funeral and their own in future years, they would eventually be reunited in the Realm of Osiris. No newly dead soul would want to face the wrath of a father harbouring grudges about the way in which he had been consigned to the Afterlife. Whatever Satra might think about making economies, Amenmose was not prepared to compromise. Montmose's funeral would be just as he had wanted it to be.

Amenmose was at present engaged in the Tjaty's business at the Mansion, so he had left instructions for Nebet to check on the progress with the embalming so that they might set a date for the funeral itself. She took no pleasure in the task and was comforted only by the presence of Young Amenmose acting as his father's spokesman. The embalmers were among the most conservative people in all Kemet and they would not take kindly to receiving instructions from a woman.

There were many stories told about these men, craftsmen in their own right but excluded from the rank and social position that attached to a craftsman's skills. Some of the tales were horrific and, Nebet told herself, almost certainly untrue – almost. Tales of how the embalmers, who were shunned by women of sensibility, used the dead bodies of females for their own gratification. As the stench of this unpleasant place reached her nostrils, taking her breath away for an instant, she could believe even the most lurid of stories. All the most distasteful of human odours were concentrated here, permeating the fabric of the workshop and all those who worked in it. What living woman would willingly submit to the attentions of an embalmer whose very flesh reeked of death?

In front of the tented workshop area, there was a small 'office', a simple reed shelter, where a scribe sat cross-legged on the ground, surrounded by the boxes and jars that contained his records. It looked chaotic, but as soon as Pakhred mentioned Montmose's name the scribe reached into an open box and brought out the limestone flake on which the family's instructions had been written.

'You have further instructions?' the scribe asked hopefully.

'No,' Pakhred said, in his most authoritative tone. 'My father wishes to know how much longer it will be before he can lay his father to rest.'

Nebet was glad his voice had broken already. It would not have helped her son's confidence to have delivered his words in something between a squeak and a growl. Senmut was finding this aspect of growing up very trying.

The scribe turned over the scrap of limestone to read the notes he had added. 'Looks like it'll not be before the beginning of next month. The drying-out process has barely begun. You can't hurry these things, you know.'

Pakhred nodded. This was what Amenmose had expected. 'We need to know what size coffin will be needed.'

'Have you engaged a coffin-maker?' the scribe asked, 'because if you haven't I can recommend a good man.'

'There's no need,' Pakhred said. 'My sister's husband, the Scribe in the Place of Truth, Ramose, is seeing to that. But the coffin-maker will need to know the size.'

The scribe's eyebrows twitched at the mention of Ramose's title. 'Oh well, if you're employing one of *those* people,' he said with a sneer in his voice, 'he won't need to be told more than the height of the deceased. *Those* people are the experts, or so they like to think. Do you want to come through and measure him yourself?'

Pakhred, who was too young to recognize the man's twisted sense of humour, blanched at the thought.

Knowing the scribe would expect squeamishness in a woman, Nebet put her hand on her son's arm and said, in a breathy voice, 'Oh no, please. Couldn't someone just bring us the measurement?'

The scribe chuckled. He had had his fun with this pair. He called over his shoulder and a scrawny boy of about Khay's age scuttled out from the embalmers' tent. The child was blank-faced, with scabby knees and elbows and the tell-tale skin lesions of ringworm. He epitomized grime and disease, which, for an apprentice in what was euphemistically called the Place of Purity, was not a high recommendation. The scribe grabbed him firmly by one grubby ankle to make him stand still while he pulled out a measuring rod from the basket containing all the tools of his trade. Then he said, slowly and precisely, 'Take this to Ipuy and tell him to measure the Montmose body, and then come back at once and tell me what the height is.' The boy scampered back into the tent.

Not wanting to be shown up in front of the embalmers' clerk, Pakhred asked his mother, 'Are you feeling all right, Muti? You look very pale.'

'I'm fine, dear, but thank you for asking.' She smiled at her eldest boy, who was a boy no longer. He looked more like his father every day and was taking new responsibilities like this in his stride.

The urchin emerged from the embalming booth and ran to the scribe's side. He handed back the measuring stick and bent down to whisper his message into the clerk's ear before returning to whatever gruesome task he had been set by his master.

'There you are, then,' the scribe said. 'Your body is a finger's-breadth over three cubits. That should be enough for your coffin man as long as he remembers what sort of cubit to use. Anything else you need to know?'

'Thank you, no,' Pakhred said with dignity.

The scribe bent forward to shake a pottery dish, then looked up expectantly. Young Amenmose flushed at this unsubtle reminder but recovered his composure immediately. He drew a small black object from a leather pouch at his belt and dropped it into the saucer saying, 'For your trouble.'

Then he offered his mother his arm to lean on as they turned and walked away from the noisome place as quickly as decency allowed. A final glance behind showed the clerk turning the token over in his hand before dropping it into his tool basket.

'What was that you gave him?' Nebet asked.

'A cake of black ink. I thought it was an appropriate offering for a scribe's services, not that he did much to earn it.'

'It was very suitable. Well thought, my son.'

Amenmose had solved the problem of Kheti by taking her with him as his housekeeper during his stay at the Mansion. Satra posed a far more difficult problem. She had been running her own household for twelve years. She had her own ways of doing things and was used to being obeyed unquestioningly by everyone in the house. However, she was not mistress of her brother's house. She had to share the women's room with Nubnefert and, to her obvious distaste, with Meryt. She had to lend a hand with those ordinary household tasks which she was accustomed to delegating to servants. Most galling of all, she had to fit into a well-established family order of precedence, giving way not only to her brother's wife but also to his young sons and, when they visited, to his married daughters. Her self-esteem had been dealt a harsh blow and her reaction was to become even more sharp-tongued and critical than before. Since it would have been ungrateful to display her resentment in front of the family, the servants bore the brunt of her anger.

Within days of Satra's moving in Meryt appealed to Nebetiunet, in tears, to let her return to her mother. 'I'll come in every day, Mistress. I don't want to leave you, but nothing I do or say seems to please Lady Satra. I don't think I can hold my tongue much longer and I don't want to say something I'll regret.'

'I understand, Meryt,' Nebet said soothingly. 'The death of Master Montmose came as a great shock to Satra and I can only hope that she will mellow once the funeral is over. Perhaps after a month or so you'll feel able to come back to stay. Meanwhile, of course you may go home to your mother and I shall send her a message to explain that you are not dismissed or in any sort of disgrace. I don't want to lose you.'

Unfortunately Satra saw Meryt's capitulation as a minor victory, confirming her authority in the house, and she started to boss the other servants about in her high-handed way, though never in Nebetiunet's presence or hearing. The atmosphere became tense and unhappy. Nebet refrained from speaking to Satra herself and instead took aside each of the servants in turn and asked them to be patient and understanding. She felt very awkward doing this, almost as if she was betraying their trust, but with Amenmose away so much and the worry of the funeral preparations, she was in no mood for a confrontation with Satra.

Tia, as always, had a comment to make. As Amenmose's nanny, she had known Satra since birth. 'She was always a wilful child. She could net the Master in her smile like a fowler nets a bird. She had her parents' every indulgence while my lovely Ameny had only me. She won't ever change. Spoiled she is, spoiled rotten.'

Tia should not have spoken so, even if no one else was there to hear, but Nebet had not the heart to reprimand her. For once she tended to believe that Tia was not exaggerating.

Ramose, true to his word, had arranged for one of the carpenters in the Place of Truth to make Montmose's coffin, and for a painter to decorate it. As a skilled scribe himself he would compose the necessary texts and make sure that they were inscribed correctly. There remained only the matter of its price. They chose a simple design, in the shape of a mummy wrapped in a white shroud held in place by red straps, but it would still be the most costly item of Montmose's funerary furniture. The carpenter and painter proposed an all-in price of twenty-five *deben* of copper, to which Amenmose agreed. Nebet was left to assemble goods to that value to pay for the coffin before the funeral.

She took some of the unsold bronze and copper kitchen equipment from Montmose's house to be weighed by the local customs officer, who was a friend of Amenmose. His scales could be trusted and the coffin-makers would not dispute his valuations. She was pleasantly surprised when the total weight of a dented bowl, a leaking ewer and assorted broken or worn pieces came to nine and a half *deben*. To this substantial contribution to the cost of the coffin she added two lengths of linen which she had found in Montmose's storeroom. She recognized the first, by the sealed cords tied round it, as being of her own making. She remembered Amenmose, so proud of his wife's skill, having given this sample of her work to his father as a festival gift.

At the time she had hoped that Montmose might ask her to make him a gown from the fine linen but, now she knew Satra better, she understood why the cloth had never been used. Satra was useless with a needle but she would have died rather than admit that, in any respect, she was inferior to her brother's wife. The bolt of linen had stayed on the shelf in the storeroom for at least six years. The outer folds were a little discoloured but the best part of it was still good and, in Nebet's professional estimation, worth about three *deben*.

The second length was of a coarser weave and a width suitable for bed linen. It was newer than the other and had probably been purchased in anticipation of renewing some worn sheets, the very sheets that had been given to the embalmers to be used for mummy bandages. Nebet valued the bolt of linen at three and a half *deben*. That left nine *deben* still to find.

While she was puzzling over what else she could use to pay for the coffin, Tjeti called to deliver a skin of milk. As he slurped his customary bread-and-beer soup, Nebet had a sudden thought.

'Tjeti,' she said loudly, waving her hand to catch his eye so that he might understand what she was saying, 'did Master Montmose have goats in your flock?'

'Master Montmose? Oh, yes. A fine little nanny goat, I calls her Blossom, and her kid of last year, a male called Djed. He was the offspring of the old grey male who was also the father of your Hedjet . . .' Tjeti would have gone on about the genealogical details of his charges indefinitely had not Nebet interrupted him.

'My husband needs to know the value of all of his father's possessions. What price would you put on those two beasts?'

'Well, now, for the nanny I'd say three, maybe three and a half. For the male, seeing as he's not full-grown yet, though there'd be sweet meat on him even now, I'd say two. Do you want I should look for to sell 'em for you?'

'No, Tjeti, not just yet, but I think at least one of them will have to go.'

''Tis always the way with a death,' the goatherd nodded sagely. Some might say that his animals were like his children, especially if they had heard him raging about a kid lost to jackals, but they had not seen the sanguine way in which he accepted the sale or even the slaughter of one of his flock. Tjeti was a realist and goats were just about the most real thing in his narrow world. There was no place in that world for sentiment.

Her thoughts having been turned in the direction of animals, Nebet asked Satra later that day, 'Was Montmose keeping a pig somewhere?'

Most well-to-do households in Waset kept a pig or two each year. Some of the poorer houses on the outskirts of the town had ramshackle sties where pigs were reared for the table. The animals thrived on a diet of kitchen scraps provided by their owners and on other domestic garbage scavenged from the rubbish dumps. As payment for their services, the pig-breeders took one or two piglets from any litter to rear for their own consumption or for sale, and at least twice yearly the owners received a fresh-killed carcass. Nebet had been reminded by her conversation with Tjeti that it was nearing the time for the first pig-kill of the year.

'Of course,' her sister replied in a tone as acid as vinegar. 'Father was fond of pork and we always had meat.'

Satra's remark was an implied criticism of Nebet's housekeeping, for only the previous day she had complained about the lack of meat in a very tasty bean stew.

Nebet bit back the reproof she would have delivered if spoken to in that manner by one of her children. 'I only ask because we might have to sell the pig to help pay for the coffin,' she said quietly.

Even Satra knew enough to recognize that when Nebet spoke firmly in that low, patient tone there would be no arguing with her. She nodded her understanding. 'I suppose we shall. I'll send Bak to find out how things are.' With that, she left the room in search of the said Bak.

Nebet was stunned by Satra's casual assumption that she could give orders to servants in another woman's house. How she wished Amenmose was there to speak to his sister. There were limits even to Nebet's forbearance, and those limits were close to being reached.

Bak had the great sense to check discreetly with his mistress that he was allowed to go on Satra's errand and, when he returned, he reported directly to Nebet before giving the message to Satra herself. It appeared that Montmose had owned an elderly sow whose only litter this year had been two runtish piglets. The rearer suggested that the sow's breeding days were over and it was best to sell her and her latest young for slaughter.

'He reckoned they'd fetch about seven *deben* between them,' Bak reported, 'maybe eight if someone could be persuaded that the sow had another litter in her.'

That was more than ample to complete the coffin purchase, if the carpenter and the painter would accept the valuations of these goods and animals. There was likely to be enough left over to pay for a painted wooden stela to set at the tomb entrance.

Nebet was perfectly satisfied. She could only hope that Satra would be happy too, but Nebetiunet, like Tjeti, was a realist.

Amenmose tried to get home as often as his duties allowed, and such visits were usually unheralded. On this occasion, after working through a rest-day, he had felt the need for familiar faces in familiar surroundings, so he had taken the last ferry across the River at dusk.

He arrived in time to witness the latest of the ever more frequent and heated disagreements between his wife and his sister. He knew all was not well as soon as he heard Nebet's raised voice. In all the years he had known her he had rarely heard her shout except in warning, as when she had urged him to scoop Senmut away from the quayside just as the toddler was about to fall into the River. To hear Nebetiunet almost screaming to make herself heard above his sister's incoherent shrieking was to have his world upturned like a spilled wine jar. He could only hope that they had not come to blows, for he remembered of old Satra's cruel fingers searching out and pinching his most sensitive spots and her sharp teeth drawing blood from his hand as he tried to fend her off. He entered the room to find his wife being restrained by Neferti and Pakhred, while Satra was struggling in the arms of Menna and Bak. Most worrying of all was the sight of Senmut sitting in the middle of the floor, his head in his hands and a trickle of blood oozing between his fingers. Khay was kneeling beside him, his arm round his brother's shoulders.

Amenmose's appearance at Nebet's side had an immediate calming effect. He took her gently by the arm and nodded to his children that they should let her go. Neferti at once ducked behind him to attend to Senmut, and Pakhred turned to speak to the men. Satra's rage, too, had somewhat subsided at her brother's entrance but she was still incensed at having been manhandled by mere servants. Pakhred muttered something to Menna and Bak, who were only too pleased to retreat to the safety of the kitchen.

Amenmose looked at each member of his family in turn, taking in their anguished, frightened and defiant faces, and said, 'Someone had better tell me what this is all about, at once.'

Nebet was the first to find her voice. 'Let me see to Senmut first.'

'I'm all right, Muti,' he said. 'It's nothing.'

'That's what we thought last time,' she said prising his hand away from his forehead. As she feared, the wound had opened again. 'Neferti, take him to Tia. She knows where the salve is kept. She must treat this quickly before the evil has a chance to return.'

Khay and Nubnefert helped their brother to his feet and led him through the living room and out to the kitchen court.

Amenmose turned to Pakhred, from whom he thought he was likely to receive the most sensible answer. 'How did Senmut come by his injury?'

But before Pakhred could answer, Satra flung herself at her brother's feet, wailing, 'I didn't mean it, Ameny, I didn't mean it!' She looked up at him, tears glinting on her cheeks, though whether they were tears of true regret or plain fury he could not tell.

He asked again, 'What happened here?'

As if a sluice gate had been opened in an irrigation channel, words began pouring from the mouths of all in the room. Amenmose had no power to control the flood, so he tried to make sense of everyone at once. The story he pieced together from their different points of view was one of mounting resentment, jealousy, grief and pride, culminating in a petty argument which had flared out of hand until Senmut had stepped in front of Satra and taken on his head the blow she had meant for Nebetiunet. The original bone of contention was completely forgotten, buried beneath the landslide of bitter feelings let loose by Satra's ill-judged action.

Wisely Amenmose decided that all concerned had been punished enough, one way or another. Standing hand in hand with his wife to demonstrate where his first loyalty lay, he ordered everyone off to bed and even Satra, though she was a full-grown woman, accepted his authority without question.

Nebet's first reaction was to run to the kitchen to see to Senmut. Tia had washed the wound and applied the precious salve on a pad of clean linen, as the physician had directed. She was bandaging the pad in place, to the annoyance of Senmut, who protested that she was making a fuss about nothing.

'Be still and let Tia finish,' his mother ordered, and to her surprise he obeyed.

Amenmose dismissed Bak and Menna, telling them that they could come to work late the next day. Gemni and Iset were found huddled together on the roof. They must have heard the whole sorry affair but were too frightened to move for fear of becoming involved. Iset was especially fearful of Satra and would not come down until she was sure that the lady had retired for the night. The moon was high by the time Amenmose and Nebet climbed the stairs under its silvery light.

Nebet took her copper mirror and an eyepaint container from her cosmetic chest and set them on its lid, the mirror propped against the bedroom wall. Like the handle of the sistrum, the mirror's handle bore the figure of Hathor, and the kohl tube was supported by the dumpy figure of Bes. The shaggy-headed dwarf deity, Hathor's companion, was traditionally invoked to repel evil spirits and to neutralize the effect of poisonous bites and stings. On a mat in front of this makeshift shrine she set a small loaf of bread and a cup of beer. Beside these simple offerings Amenmose placed a pottery saucer containing a few embers from the kitchen fire. He blew gently on the coals until they glowed, and then sprinkled over them a tiny pinch of precious incense. As both parents watched the thin spiral of bluish smoke rising towards the divine figures, they prayed that their invocation would be enough to bring the gods' protection on their son.

When the embalmers at last sent a message to say that Montmose's body would be ready for collection in three days' time, Nebet felt both relieved and apprehensive. No matter what effort she had put into the funeral preparations, no matter how much of Montmose's wealth had been spent on providing him with grave goods suitable to his station, she was sure someone would find fault. For the hundredth time she went over in her mind the list of things to be done.

Just as she was beginning to congratulate herself on thinking of everything, Khaemwase asked, 'Do you want me to ask Master Nedjemger about flowers?'

Flowers! How could she have forgotten? The ceremony was not to be an elaborate affair but still flowers were expected for garlands for the mummy and for the funeral guests, as well as floral arrangements for the tomb. It was the middle of winter. Where would she find enough flowers at this time of year?

'Oh Khay,' she said, 'I'd forgotten about flowers. What is there to be had in this season? What shall we do?'

'Don't worry, Muti, there are still a few wild flowers around the vegetable gardens and on the edge of the cultivation. There are bound to be some berries, too, and we might find a few early clover or vetch flowers, but if we don't there's plenty of greenery to be had.'

'But will that be enough?' she wondered.

'That's why I suggested asking Master Nedjemger. There are plants in the temple gardens that he has flowering long after their season, especially the water lilies, and he keeps dried flowers. I'm sure, if I asked him politely, he would let me have a few. Shall I ask him?'

'Yes, my son,' she said, 'please do. What would I have done without you?'

'You'd have thought of it a little later, that's all,' Khay said, smiling at her. 'Don't worry. I'll find enough for the funeral.'

Khay was true to his word, and more. On his own initiative he asked Satra whether she would like to come with him to discuss the flowers with his master. This made her feel important and took her away from the house, leaving Nebet alone for a few blessed moments of peace. Khay also sent Neferti and Iset to pick whatever wild flowers and fruit they could find. He asked Bak to pick bunches of herbs from the vegetable plots, and Gemni went with Menna to cut young papyrus heads and flowering reeds from the banks of the canal. When Satra and Khay returned from their visit to the temple gardens, they were followed by one of the under-gardeners, who carried a bulky basket stuffed full with plants of all sorts.

'By all the gods!' Nebet exclaimed when she saw it. 'How generous of your master, Khay. How will we ever repay him?'

Satra answered, 'Master Nedjemger has given these flowers and leaves to me as a gift. He requires no payment.'

Nebet felt sure she was missing something. Satra was looking extremely smug, just as she did when she thought she had the better of an argument, but without the malicious tinge to her voice that usually accompanied such smugness. She glanced at Khaemwase, who merely shrugged. However, there was no time to lose. There were garlands and bouquets to be made and while Satra was in a reasonable mood they might be able to get the job done with the minimum of fuss.

By the evening of the last day of the month they had made garlands of celery and coriander leaves threaded between water-lily petals for each member of the funeral party. As he had been taught by Nedjemger, Khay prepared the cores for several large bouquets by binding bundles of reeds with leaves stripped from date palm fronds. Neferti then helped her mother to tuck leaves and flowers into the bindings, forming layer upon layer of living colour over two-thirds of the length of the core. Satra, meanwhile, determined to play the central role in this final aspect of her father's funeral, busied herself in making a broad floral collar to place about the mummy's neck. On to a linen background she sewed olive leaves interspersed with dried safflowers, shiny nightshade berries, lotus petals and halved fruits of the mandrake.

When it was finished, Nebet had to admit that Satra had done a good job, and she told her so. Satra received the praise graciously.

As they placed the floral offerings in the cool of the cellar to await the arrival of Montmose's body the next morning, Nebet took a surreptitious look at her sister. Was it imagination, or had Satra mellowed since that horrible argument? If she had, what had brought about this welcome change? And would it last?

CHAPTER SEVEN

Third Month
of Winter

THE TJATY WAS STILL IN ATTENDANCE ON HIS MAJESTY AT PER-RAMESSE. There was a great deal of speculation in Waset as to the nature of the urgent summons that had taken Paser to the northern capital and kept him there for a month and more. Nebet had no time to think about such weighty matters. Her attention was fixed on the final arrangements for the funeral, and Amenmose, busier than ever helping Paser's deputy Meryra run the Tjaty's office at the Mansion Temple, had been confident that she would not let him down. He and Satra had agreed, for once, on the simplest and cheapest form of embalming for their father, which had taken a mere forty-five days, thirty-five of which had been taken up by the process of drying out the body. To keep the cost to a minimum the family had provided all the necessary linen for the bandages and the shroud, and Nebet was very proud of the way Neferti had worked day in and day out on her hand loom to produce the outermost strapping bandages.

The necessary amulets, purchased from a faience-worker known to Nebet through his work for the temple, were considerably cheaper than those offered by the embalmers as part of their 'all-in package'.

The same craftsman had offered to make a set of *shabti*s but at the back of Montmose's storeroom Nebet had found a small collection of nearly twenty of these servant figures which he had acquired over the years in anticipation of his funeral. The *shabtis* were all similar in size and style, each a mummiform figure holding agricultural tools and bearing the simplest version of the inscription that would bring the figure to life in the next world to carry out any work that Montmose might ask to be done. None had been inscribed with his name, but the collection was stored in a box shaped like a primitive reed shrine and painted with a scene of Montmose, together with his *ba*-spirit, in the form of a human-headed bird, receiving food and water from Hathor, Lady of the Sycomore. As far as they could tell, this was the only funerary equipment Montmose had purchased himself. Everything else had to be paid for out of his estate and Satra begrudged every *deben* that reduced her potential inheritance.

Hoping that she would be able to recoup the cost from the disposal of Montmose's house and furnishings, Nebet had also made a deal, involving the sale of one of Hedjet's kids, to acquire a painted funerary mask to place over the wrapped mummy's head and shoulders. She had not obtained as good a price for the animal as she had hoped, because it was still too young to have proved its worth. However, Tjeti had made the bargain and she knew he always haggled for top prices for the beasts in his care. She was glad to leave the business to him and she doubted that anyone else could have done better. The mask was made of scrap papyrus and linen, layered together with paste and moulded into the shape of a human face complete with ceremonial wig and floral collar. It was not a true likeness of Montmose, in fact to Nebet the features looked rather feminine, but it became a portrait of him as soon as his name was written into the blank space on the short inscription panel.

She was most pleased with the funerary stela she had been able to buy with the surplus left after paying for the coffin. It was of wood with a thick layer of plaster, which made it look like limestone. The surface was divided by horizontal lines into three registers. In the upper third, beneath the arched top, the stela had been prepared with a standard picture of the deceased and his wife kneeling before Osiris. The two lower registers were already laid out for personal details to be filled in. The craftsman who sold it to her had been a little put out that she did not want him to complete the decoration, but Nebet refused to pay for a job that could be done by any of the scribes in her family. Pakhred had been eager to carry out this commission as his contribution to the funeral. For the middle register he composed a stylish version of the funerary offering prayer, followed by a simple statement of Montmose's name and titles. In the lower part of the stela he drew the seated figure of Montmose receiving the homage of his children: Amenmose accompanied by Nebetiunet with Satra standing behind them. Even Satra had found no fault with his work.

Before sunrise on the morning of the funeral, the body was carried to the house from the embalmers' workshop to be received by Young Amenmose, standing in for his father, who had not been able to return to Waset the previous evening. The body, now enveloped in several layers of bandages, the innermost stiffened with oils and resins, lay on a litter for which the embalmers had provided six bearers. Satra placed her floral tribute round her father's neck with a tenderness that surprised Nebet. She was also surprised at how much more imposing the mummy was than Montmose had been in life, and at how much bigger it was than the body she had last seen lying peacefully on his own bed. By contrast, the Canopic chest, the modest box containing Montmose's preserved viscera, was light enough for two men to carry easily by means of poles passed through staples in its sides. Ramose had ensured that the coffin itself would be delivered from the workshops of the Place of Truth directly to the tomb.

Montmose's family and friends assembled at dawn to escort him on his last journey in this world. All were dressed in the unrelieved white of mourning. Amenmose, who was to lead the procession in his role as the 'Son Who Causes Their Names to Live', had made his way, with Ramose, across the river on the early-morning ferry. The two men were waiting at the jetty for the barge that would soon carry Montmose over to the West Bank. The procession consisted of the least number thought proper for Montmose's rank. Nebetiunet and Satra were the only female family members present, representing the goddesses Isis and Nephthys, sisters and mourners of Osiris. The pre-dawn chill had caused both women to wear shawls over their thin linen gowns.

It had been very difficult deciding who should be asked to be the principal mourners, known as the 'Nine Friends of the Deceased'. Amenmose's three sons and the husbands of his two elder daughters were included by right of the closeness of their relationship to the dead man, but that left at least four places to be filled. Satra had not wanted to employ professional funeral attendants, as their presence would advertise her father's lack of connections and thus diminish his status. Amenmose had asked around the taxation offices where Montmose had worked and had found two colleagues who were glad to be able to pay their respects in this way. Nebet had prevailed upon her friend Senetnay, who had persuaded her husband, Ahmose, to join the party.

Not wanting to be outdone, Satra had invited another guest, none other than Nedjemger, the Chief Gardener of Ipet Esut. Nebetiunet had marvelled at Satra's audacity in approaching a man who was hardly more than a casual acquaintance. Nevertheless, she welcomed Khay's boss and thanked him for his kind attention, wondering all the while if there was something more to be read into his appearance at the funeral of a man he had not known.

Neferti handed out white mourning bands and she and her mother helped the funeral guests to tie them about their foreheads. Nebet was pleased to see that Senmut's wound had healed again and the mourning headband hid it completely, making him look almost presentable. With the assembled bearers, including Montmose's former house servants and others 'borrowed' for the day from friends, and a small troupe of professional female mourners, a very respectable funeral party made its way through the twilit streets to the public quay just below the Southern Sanctuary. There Amenmose greeted his wife and sister and formally took over responsibility for his father's funeral.

The vessel was provided with a funerary bier protected by a simple canvas canopy in place of a cabin. The body was carried on first and the Canopic chest was placed below it, hidden by the heavy cloth draped over the bier. While the servants stowed the tomb furniture wherever there was space, Satra and Nebet arranged the floral offerings. They placed four of the formal bouquets at the corner posts of the canopy, and the remainder of Nedjemger's flowers and greenery were strewn around the bier to disguise the plainness of the mummy wrappings. Khay had insisted on taking charge of the basket in which the fragile collars had been packed. They would not be required until after the funeral rituals. The guests had been invited to return to the Place of Truth, where Mutemwiya and Mutnefert, together with some of Wiya's new friends in the Village, were preparing a feast in celebration of Montmose's achieving everlasting life.

Nebet worried that the boat was not big enough to take the whole party but the captain made his living from funerals and he knew exactly his vessel's capacity. While Amenmose dismissed the litter-bearers, who would return the borrowed litter to their masters, the Nine Friends took their seats on the plank benches to either side of Montmose's body, and Nebet and Satra took up their places at the head and foot of the bier. The servants huddled at the prow, keeping out of the way of the rowers. The wailing mourners were left on the east bank when the boat was cast off. Another group would be waiting to receive the coffin on the far side. The boat followed a diagonal course, rowed across the current and drifting with it, to reach the Western Town jetty.

The causeway linking the Maatkara-Hatshepsut mansion to the riverbank had become a major thoroughfare, as well as a processional route for the most important religious festivals of Waset. Almost every day funeral parties could be seen making their way along the well-kept path. Long since, the temple itself had been closed and was hardly more than a tourist attraction, but the holiness of the ground remained and the people of Waset had established many family tombs in what had been the sacred precinct of the temple.

Amenmose's mother had been buried in a tomb which had originally been excavated hundreds of years ago, probably during the time of Nebhetepra-Montuhotep, but which had been robbed at some time during the troubled period when Kemet was subject to the rule of foreigners. The tomb, like many others in the area, had stood derelict for years before the guardians of the cemetery had given permission for new owners to be found. Montmose had paid men to clear out the short entrance corridor leading to the single rectangular chamber, and to excavate a second, smaller chamber beyond, deeper into the cliff. The tomb had never been decorated, because the rock into which it was carved was of mediocre quality, tending to crack and crumble so that the stonemasons could not achieve a good, flat surface to the walls. The only sign of ownership was a temporary grave marker set up in the tiny courtyard area outside the entrance at the time of the funeral of Montmose's wife. Now that would be replaced by the finely painted stela set in a niche cut into the wall to one side of the tomb entrance.

As the boat neared the farther bank Nebet could see that another funeral barge was already tied up to the jetty. There were many people milling around as the first vessel discharged its mournful cargo. She strained her gaze to pick out Sendji, who, she had been told, would be waiting with the ka-priest, the funerary sled and the donkeys with their handlers. It all looked quite chaotic and she began to fear that the dignity of Montmose's funeral would be compromised.

She need not have worried. The funeral directors of Waset were acknowledged to be the best of their profession in all Kemet. By the time Montmose's mourners began disembarking, the funeral ahead of them was well on its way along the causeway. The servants unloaded the tomb furnishings and offerings and packed what they could into panniers on the backs of the donkeys. The larger pieces of furniture, including Montmose's favourite armchair, would have to be carried individually. A sled drawn by a pair of white oxen would bear the mummy, which was the last thing to be taken off the boat. Nebet and Satra gathered up all the flowers and rearranged them about Montmose's body before taking up their positions for the funeral procession.

At the front was a small group of female mourners, paid to weep and wail in a manner that was considered undignified for members of the family. A mortuary priest walked behind them, sprinkling the path with milk and water. Amenmose came next, wearing a borrowed cheetah-skin robe to indicate his role as officiating priest for the funeral. He burned grains of incense mixed with dried, sweet herbs in a censing spoon. The way was thus purified for the passage of the deceased, who was dragged along the smooth causeway by the sturdy oxen and escorted by the Nine Friends, who took hold of ropes to ensure that the sled did not deviate from its stately course. The donkeys and the servants bearing the tomb goods made up the remainder of the procession, which moved sedately through the cultivation and into the desert land beyond, their path rising steadily towards the foothills of the Peak, the mountain of Meretseger.

The sun was climbing the sky behind them and the world was coming alive. The causeway was a route favoured by farmers, herdsmen and traders, and by priests and administrators visiting the mansions that flanked the newer causeway branching off to the south. They were passed frequently by such parties going in both directions. The funeral cortège moved even more slowly than a shepherd with his small flock, who had to lead his animals down the embankment and through the narrow headland of a barley field in order to overtake them. Fieldworkers paused in their tasks and bowed their respect to the body as the procession passed by. Women, gathered at a cistern by the bank of a canal, sprinkled water from their jars over the path in front of the sled and added their voices to the ululation of the mourners.

Such reactions were commonplace. The only certainty in life was death. It came to everyone, rich or poor, man or woman, priest or peasant. In Waset, where kings had been buried for uncountable generations, the funeral had been developed to a more sophisticated level than anywhere else in Kemet. In Waset death was part of everyday life.

Nebet fell into a sort of dream-state, lulled by the slow rhythm of their progress. She found it difficult to keep her mind on death and the hereafter. Disconnected thoughts flitted across her mind. Memories of Montmose jostled with inconsequential domestic problems. She found herself thinking how lucky it was that Montmose had not died in high summer, because the heat would have made the funeral journey intolerable. Then she chastised herself for the uncharitable thought. Looking at the farmland to either side of the causeway, she noted everywhere the rapidly growing wheat and barley, still green, the colour of new life but proof, if proof were needed, of Osiris's powers of regeneration and resurrection. New stems were emerging from the bases of the clumps of reeds and sedges that colonized the banks of the irrigation channels. A field of clover grown for animal fodder was already hazed with pale mauvish flowers. The countryside had come to life again, reborn from the bounty of Hapi, the bringer of the inundation.

At the edge of the flood plain, where the rich, dark soil gave way abruptly to the buff, sandy desert, they passed on their right the mansion of the King's father, the divine Menmaatra-Sethy. To the south, beyond His Majesty's own temple, lay the mansions of earlier kings, their towering pylon gateways facing proudly towards the River. Their builders had been kings of great renown whose names were still spoken with reverence.

Nebet idly wondered how long Montmose's name would be remembered. He had done nothing out of the ordinary in his lifetime. Like countless others, he had worked hard, a competent and respected civil servant. He had brought up two children of whom he had been very proud, and they would remember him for the rest of their lives. But what then? His name was part of his personality, part of his very self, and as long as his name survived he would continue to exist. But what would happen when there was no one left to speak it, or remember it, when no one visited his tomb to read his name on the funerary stela? Would the name fade from memory? If so, would Montmose himself fade away, becoming as insubstantial as the smoke of incense, drifting on the air to merge with the millions of disembodied souls who had gone before? How long would that take? Would he survive for hundreds of years in the memories of his descendants or would he be forgotten within the next generation?

Nebet felt a pang of guilt when this train of thought reminded her of her own parents. She had no memory of her mother, who had died in childbirth when Nebet herself was only one year old. Her father had remarried, taking as his wife Nebet's wet-nurse, but the marriage was not a success and after only two years the woman had returned to her first husband. The relationship had lasted long enough, however, for the divorce settlement to be expensive, especially following so quickly on the funeral of his first wife.

Nebet had understood little of what was happening, and had pieced together the story in later years, relying heavily on the memory of her sister Nubnefert, six years her senior. Her sister was of the opinion that their father had been tricked into his second marriage by a wife who stayed with him just long enough to have a claim against him for maintenance. Whatever the circumstances of his marriage, he was a wrecked man after the divorce, with hardly the means to support his two daughters. He had struggled on, living largely on the charity of his brother, long enough to see Nubnefert married and settled. He had died, broken in spirit and heart, when Nebetiunet was nearly ten. His brother, Nebneteru, had immediately sent for Nebet to be brought up with his children on the family estate just south of Iunet. The move, the love of new parents and the companionship of brothers and sisters had served to blot out the pain and distress of the first ten years of her life. Her childhood memories now were exclusively of that period when she had become the darling of a loving family and had, in her turn, idolized her older siblings, especially Paser. They were her true family. She had experienced more grief at Nebneteru's death than she had felt for her real father, and in recent years she had been closer to Montmose, her husband's father. Despite his affectations and his exploitation of Satra, Montmose had been a good man and she hoped that his goodness would promote the survival of his name.

Nebet felt guiltier still when she had to search her deepest memory even to recall her mother's name. She had never visited her parents' tomb at Iunet, so she could not tell if their names were properly commemorated. She offered up a silent prayer to their memory, hoping that Montmose would understand if her attention was not wholly devoted to him.

A little way into the desert a lesser path diverged from the causeway in the direction of the Place of Truth. Here was a sentry post where cemetery guards checked the authority of those who sought to enter the sacred land. It was the guards' duty to ascertain that the funeral guests were not a band of tomb robbers in disguise and they had to be seen to be doing their duty. This should have been a mere formality, as it was quite obvious that the party had legitimate business in the area and the guards had been advised of the funeral in advance. Amenmose had chosen to dismiss the female mourners at this point. He had paid their fee when they had first arrived at the riverside that morning. The women, and the young girl apprenticed to their profession, were so eager to return home that Nebet suspected they had another death to attend that day. The guards were another matter. Amenmose was just beginning to wonder whether he would have to grease a few palms to allow the procession to go on when one of them recognized Ramose. The change in their attitude was dramatic. A quiet word from the Scribe of the Tomb had one of the sentries ducking into his mudbrick guard-post to fetch a jar of water and a cup so that all the guests and, after a little extra persuasion from Ramose, the servants, too, could take a drink. This short respite was very welcome, especially to throats dry from breathing in the dust of many feet, both human and animal. Ramose thanked the guards, who stood to attention on either side of the road as Amenmose signalled for the procession to move off again.

As she passed them, keeping her eyes to the front, Nebet could not help thinking that Montmose would have accepted this mark of respect as no more than his due. Yet it was Ramose's position, and the high esteem in which he was held by the local officials, that had earned this little courtesy.

Breasting the rise they came within sight of the Maatkara-Hatshepsut mansion. Though it could be seen from the River, Nebet had only occasionally seen the temple at close quarters and she was struck again by its elegance. Nestling in a deep bay in the cliffs, the temple was built as a series of broad terraces supported on colonnades, each level reached from the one below by a long ramp. The white limestone of the walls and columns had mellowed over the years to a soft honey colour, blending in with the cliff-face so that they seemed to have been carved from the very rock.

As they approached closer, however, the toll of years became evident.

The avenue leading up to the first ramp had once been planted with trees. They had long ago died and their pathetic stumps could still be seen between the granite sphinxes and standing statues of Maatkara-Hatshepsut. Nebetiunet had once told Khay about the trees and he had expressed disbelief that anything could have been made to grow in such an inhospitable environment. How she wanted to point them out to him now, to see and hear his wonder. She hoped he had remembered what she had described and that he could see them well enough to recognize what they were.

The funeral procession turned northwards, following the well-worn path along the foot of the bluff into which many tombs had been cut. They had reached the end of their journey and it was just after midday. The party halted below the shadowed rectangle that marked the entrance to Montmose's tomb. It was easily identified because waiting in the courtyard in front of the tomb entrance were two men standing on either side of the coffin. Amenmose and Ramose climbed the steep path to the tomb to speak to the coffin-makers and to inspect the seals on the tomb door. Happy that the tomb had not been violated, Amenmose took a small knife from his belt and cut the cords binding the door-bolts in place. The two wooden door flaps were pulled open as far as they would go and the four men entered the tomb.

While Amenmose was checking the available space inside his father's tomb, Nebet and Satra spread reed mats on the ground and began to set out a simple meal of bread, cheese and fruit for the guests. Satra broke the seal on one of the jars of beer that had been provided for Montmose's enjoyment in the Afterlife. As she said, the intention was as good as the deed and the empty jar, labelled with a proper description of its original contents, would be magically refilled by the words of the funerary offering prayer. The animal handlers had brought bundles of feed and skins of water for their oxen and donkeys, as well as lunch baskets, which they shared with the servants. Nebet had wanted to bring the servants' food from home but the funeral directors who hired out these services had their own customs. Food for the bearers, even if not as good and certainly not as cheap as she could have provided herself, was included in the funeral costs. The meal was quickly over and everyone's attention returned to Montmose and his journey to the Land of the West.

The tomb courtyard, hardly more than a ledge on the cliff-face, had been kept clear by use during the festivals of the dead held throughout the year, but it was not big enough to accommodate the whole funeral party. First Amenmose called on the servants to help reorganize the goods from his mother's burial to make space for his father's coffin. When that had been taken inside, the servants helped to transport the rest of the tomb furniture and food offerings up the steep slope and into the tomb, to be stored wherever room could be found for them. The mummy was the last thing to be carried, at shoulder height, up the treacherous path. Nebet found herself clenching her fists with anxiety, dreading that one of the servants would lose his footing and send Montmose tumbling ignominiously to the desert floor. But all was well. The body was set upright in front of the tomb entrance, wedged in place with heavy stones and supported by Ramose, who had donned the mask of the jackal-headed Anubis, guardian of the cemetery and god of embalming. That having been accomplished, the servants were dismissed to return to Waset with the sled and the donkeys.

The rituals were conducted with due decorum, despite the lack of space which meant that those of the Nine Friends who were not of the family had to watch from the path below the tomb. The body was censed, libated and anointed with the seven sacred unguents. The offering formula was recited in its fullest form to provide all Montmose's needs in the next world. Though the food that had been stored in the tomb might crumble to dust or evaporate into the air, the magical words of the offering prayer would constantly replenish all the jars and baskets.

Finally Amenmose performed the Opening of the Mouth ritual, touching the iron blade of the sacred adze to the eyes, ears, nose and mouth of the funerary mask to reactivate Montmose's senses. He was thus enabled to see the obstacles in his path, to hear the challenges of the gatekeepers, to breathe in the divine perfumes of the other world, and to speak his name and make his statement of justification before the King of the Dead. At last he was ready to go forth on his journey to the Realm of Osiris.

As she watched the funeral ceremonies Nebet became aware that Satra was weeping openly. This might have been expected of any daughter at a funeral, but not if that daughter was Satra. Nebet wondered whether she was being too hard on her sister. Perhaps it was a genuine outpouring of pent-up grief but all her tears had been self-pitying until now. Nebet doubted that she had had such a dramatic change of heart, especially when she saw Nedjemger almost shyly taking

Satra's hand between his own and whispering some comforting words. Satra's discreet sobs were then muffled as she leaned her head against Nedjemger's shoulder.

So that's the way of it, Nebet thought. I might have known.

Beside her the architect Ahmose muttered, 'Well, well, who'd have thought he had it in him?'

Nebet gave him a quick, disapproving look but then had to bow her head to hide the rueful smile that threatened to spoil the dignity of the occasion. She could see through the part that Satra was playing. Satra was a calculating, scheming, selfish bitch and Nedjemger had not stood a chance from the moment she had set her sights on him.

The rites having been completed, the professional ka-priest collected up the sacred implements and saw to it that the body was reverently placed in the coffin. The remainder of the ritual oils was poured over the mummy before the lid was secured with cords and clay seals. Amenmose, the last to leave the tomb, bowed one more time to his parents, then closed the tomb doors. Once again the bolts were slid across and bound in place with strong cords. Into the heavy mass of fine-grained clay that was smothered over the knots the priest pressed an oval wooden seal, the mark of the burial ground. To this impression Amenmose added his own from a faience signet ring. Lastly, the funerary stela was set in its niche in the wall, so that all who passed should have an opportunity to read the inscription and perpetuate Montmose's memory and thus his very existence.

Later in the year, at the Beautiful Feast of the Valley, the family would return to pay their respects. Then the tomb would be opened for the last time. The stela would be taken inside and the doors would be resealed and finally bricked up to provide Montmose with extra security. In the meantime the ka-priest, whose duty it was to care for the kau, the spirits of the departed, had been paid to perform a much-abbreviated offering ritual twice a month.

The officiants returned to the path. Amenmose divested himself of the cheetah-skin robe and handed it back into the safekeeping of the priest, who then took his leave of the funeral party. The sun, now just about to dip behind the western cliffs, was casting long shadows on the desert floor. The mansion of Maatkara-Hatshepsut was already so deeply in shade that it was difficult to distinguish the main part of the building from the natural rock. Only the fiery glow picking out the avenue of statues indicated that here was a work of human endeavour.

With the shadows came a cool breeze and Nedjemger offered to replace Satra's shawl about her shoulders. Had it been anyone else Satra would have voiced her impatience in strident tones, but she submitted to Nedjemger's fumbling ministrations with a sweet, coy smile. Nebet hardly knew whether to laugh or cry. She told herself that Nedjemger was old enough to know what he was doing but she felt sorry for him nonetheless. She wondered what Wiya and Mymy would make of this development when the party returned to the Place of Truth for the funerary meal.

Tamiu had caught a bird, an injudicious and unlucky sparrow found pecking around the quern in the kitchen court. This was not unusual; after all it is in the nature of cats to catch birds. What Nebet found surprising was that her fat, elderly pet had bestirred herself enough to catch *anything*. She could only imagine that Tamiu, from her favourite perch on the staircase, had not been able to resist the temptation and had

simply jumped down, killing the bird by weight and surprise. The most astonishing thing about the whole incident was Satra's reaction. Nebet had never thought of Amenmose's sister as a sentimental person, and yet Satra had cried over the pathetic little feathered body. What was more, her tears seemed more genuine than those she had shed at her father's funeral. When she had been persuaded to relinquish the tiny corpse she had run away to continue her grieving in private.

Nebet said in bewilderment, 'What was all that about?'

Not thinking that Tia would have heard her, she was taken aback when Tia said succinctly, 'Guilt'.

'What are you talking about?' Nebet asked. She was unprepared for the flood of response this question unleashed from the usually taciturn Tia.

'That one's feeling guilty about her poor father. She knows she didn't show proper respect at his death. She was too busy making eyes at that gardener. And what now? Her father's dead and gone to Osiris, leaving her nothing but dreams. She thought those dreams were going to come true and what happens? Her admirer hasn't sent her so much as a flower from his garden, let alone a message. She thinks her father has spoiled things for her again, that he's been watching everything she does.' She pointed emphatically at the dead sparrow.

It was a few moments before Nebet realized what Tia was suggesting. It was said that the *ba*-spirits of the dead could return to visit the people and places they had loved in their earthly lives. Some believed that the *bau* kept protective watch over their loved ones, while others said that they were still looking after their own interests. If the spirits witnessed wrongdoing or saw their relatives acting against their express wishes, they would report these matters to the deceased and the transgressors could be called to account in the next world. The *ba* was thought to appear as a bird. On Montmose's *shabti* box his *ba* had been conventionally portrayed as a bird with a human head. The body of Montmose's *ba*-bird, now Nebet brought it to mind, had strongly resembled that of a sparrow.

Tia saw by Nebet's expression that she understood Satra's fear, and nodded sagely. 'I don't say that this little pest was the old Master's soul, you understand, but that's what young Satra thinks at the moment. It's shaken her up well and truly and once she's over the shock she'll be looking for someone to take it out on.'

Nebetiunet was of the same opinion. 'Dispose of the body. You'd better bury it, somewhere where Tamiu won't find it. If Satra thinks we've treated it with honour she might not–'

'Huh!' was all Tia could say.

Amenmose had managed to take the two rest days off and was looking forward to relaxing in familiar surroundings and enjoying the company of his family. From the moment he entered the house it was clear that his expectations were to be dashed.

Senmut had come home from school with another bad report from his tutor. He would have tried to lose it somewhere, had it not been for the fact that his teacher, knowing Senmut only too well, had already sent a verbal message. The report was written on precious papyrus, wrapped and sealed so that Senmut had not been able to read it himself. There was no alternative but to hand it over to his mother when he returned home for the rest days. Nebet suspected something of its content and insisted that her wayward son should present it to his father the moment he came home, and then wait to hear his doom.

As Amenmose read the report the rest of the family maintained a tense silence. He looked up from the papyrus and stared hard into his son's eyes. Senmut, at first unabashed, could not bear his father's disapproval and lowered his gaze to stare uncomfortably at the floor.

'You may well look ashamed,' Amenmose said. 'This says you've been playing truant again. You even failed to attend the class when you knew the Head of the House of Life was paying a visit. You are nearing the end of basic training and you should be thinking about your future. Very few boys are given this sort of opportunity. A graduate from the House of Life can achieve great things, can earn great rewards and the respect of his fellows. But that's not good enough for you, oh no! You choose to antagonize your teachers and to insult the very people who can do so much for your career. What in the name of all the gods were you thinking of?'

Senmut muttered something.

'Speak up, boy. Mumbling won't help you,' Amenmose snapped.

'I said, I don't want to be a scribe,' Senmut said loudly and vehemently.

In a scribely family this statement was tantamount to heresy. Satra broke the stunned silence. 'You're an ungrateful boy,' she said. 'My father would have beaten you for your insolence.'

'Stay out of this, Satra,' Amenmose said.

'Yes, stay out of this Satra,' Senmut yelled, his voice breaking with emotion. 'I've had enough of your constant criticism.'

'How dare you speak to me like that. I–' but Satra was shouted down by a now unstoppable Senmut.

'I dare because no one else dares,' he said. 'We all go out of our way to be nice to you and all we get is spite in return. Don't think I don't know about the way you treat Neferti. She talks to me, I'm her brother. And if you go on being cruel to Iset you might get more than you bargained for. As for Khay, it's not his fault that Nedjemger hasn't contacted you since the funeral, so don't take it out on him.'

'Senmut,' Nebet said in her most dangerously quiet voice, 'you will apologize to your father's sister. Now.'

For the first time in his life Senmut disobeyed his mother. He turned and ran from the room, ducking under his father's arm when Amenmose tried to stop him.

Satra stood watching him go with a self-satisfied smirk on her face. 'Well,' she said, 'that just proves I was right about him all along.'

Nebet moved swiftly across the room and delivered a stinging slap to her sister's face.

'No,' she said. 'It proves only that I was wrong,' and she hurried out of the room in search of her son.

Senmut had raced through to the back of the house and up the stairs to his room. Nebet found him there packing his few belongings into a shoulder sack. He glanced at her as she entered the room but did not stop what he was doing.

'It's no good, Muti, I can't stay in the same house as that woman a moment longer.' His controlled voice told her that he meant what he said.

'So are you running back to school?' she asked, trying to sound calm. 'I'm not sure that you'll find a welcome there just now.'

'No,' he said firmly, 'I'm not going back to school. I'll go to Mymy for now. She's always made me welcome.'

'But you will go back, eventually?'

'I don't know. At the moment I feel as if I never want to see the place again.' He pulled the bag's drawstring closed with an angry tug before looking directly into her eyes. 'Why should I continue to go to school if it makes me so unhappy?'

'Because it makes your father happy.'

Senmut started at this blunt reminder of his duty. His eyes filled with tears, which he brushed away roughly with the back of his hand. His voice quavered as he said, 'But he let Khay give up school. Why am I different? Why am I punished? What have I done wrong?'

Nebet's motherly instinct made her want to take her son in her arms and hug him until the pain went away, but she knew that would be the wrong gesture. Senmut had demonstrated, loudly and forcibly, that he had become an adult.

'You're right, my son,' she said, though it hurt her to say it. 'You're old enough to make your own decisions. Go to Mymy, so that at least I'll know where you are and won't have to worry about finding you dead in a ditch somewhere.'

Senmut smiled in spite of his distress. 'I'm sorry, Muti. I don't want to hurt you or Father. I've been thinking about this for some time and when Satra started . . .'

'Oh dear, Satra. I hit her, but you didn't see,' Nebet said.

'Really?' Senmut said in wonder.

'Yes, I really did, I hit her.'

After a brief moment contemplating his mother's bewildered expression, Senmut began to chuckle. He tried to stop but his emotions were so much on edge that his laughter only became more hysterical, and infectious. Soon he and Nebet were clinging to each other and shaking with sobbing laughter, expressing both the humour and the anguish of their situation.

Nebetiunet refused to apologize to Satra, on the basis that, as Mistress of the House she had authority over all the female members of the household and could mete out whatever punishment she deemed fit. In fact, by not apologizing and keeping herself apart from her sister as much as was humanly possible in the circumstances, she registered both her displeasure and her superiority. Amenmose knew enough not to press the matter. He was as exasperated by Satra's behaviour as everyone else, and he could only guess what the rest of the family had been suffering at her hands and tongue in his absence. However, for the sake of a little peace, he did send a message to Nedjemger. Khaemwase was only too pleased to deliver it, since it held the prospect of resolving the family tensions. Amenmose's little scheme bore fruit almost at once, but unfortunately not before he had had to return across the River.

'There's a visitor to see Lady Satra,' Meryt announced. Satra looked as if she were about to say something but bit her lip. She had learned a little discretion from the outburst a few days before.

'Who is it?' Nebet asked.

'Master Nedjemger,' Meryt said, pleased that her news flustered Satra into a blush. 'I asked him to wait in the garden.'

'Do you wish to speak with this man, sister?' Nebet asked Satra.

'Yes, I do, sister,' Satra replied with great modesty.

'Well, then, go and speak to him.'

Amazed that Nebet had not suggested chaperoning at this meeting, Satra needed no second bidding.

Nebet caught the broad grin on Meryt's face. 'Let's not jump to any conclusions,' she said.

'No, Mistress,' Meryt replied, seriously but with a twinkle in her eye.

By the time Amenmose was able to take another day off work Nedjemger was visiting regularly. Satra had also spent considerable time being shown around his garden domain and had agreed to be his companion at a dinner party. Nebet had lent her sister her festival wig, which Meryt had helped to dress. Nedjemger came to call for her and, before leaving, Satra turned unexpectedly to kiss Nebet on the cheek, whispering, 'Thank you,' as she did so.

A little later Amenmose and his wife were enjoying the luxury of a quiet game of *senet*, something they had not done for a long time. They sat on opposite long sides of the playing box with its three rows of ten squares. Amenmose had drawn the spool-shaped dancers and Nebet was playing with the conical pieces. Ameny tossed the throw-sticks and put his hand to his chin as he contemplated the best move to make with his throw. Nebet had been telling him about Satra's uncharacteristic behaviour. 'I was stunned,' she said. 'She's a changed woman. We still have the occasional spat, especially with Iset, but I suppose you can't expect miracles.'

'Do you think there's true affection there?' Amenmose asked as he passed her the throw-sticks.

Nebet made her throw but found all her pieces blocked by spools. With good humour she handed the throw-sticks across the board for Amenmose's next turn, saying, 'Yes, I think so. I wasn't sure at first. I suspected her of base motives but Nedjemger's too wily a bird to be snared by one such as Satra unless he wanted to be caught. She's still trying to convince herself that this is all part of her plan to get her hands on Montmose's legacy, and Nedjemger is a very eligible man. But you only have to hear the tone of her voice when she speaks to him to know her heart has softened. She probably wouldn't go so far as to admit to love, but I have high hopes.'

Amenmose moved one of his dancers on to the house of Beauty. 'There, that's another piece done.'

'Not so fast,' Nebet smiled. 'You have to get over the house of the Waters before you can take that piece off the board. Don't assume too much.'

'Again you're right,' Amenmose chuckled, 'and perhaps we should take that as a warning. Our problems with Satra aren't over yet. There are many obstacles still to overcome, some we may not even have thought of, so let's just be grateful for the little changes and hope that their sum is worth waiting for.'

'Would it be wrong to pray for a happy outcome?' she asked.

'I suspect Satra has been praying hard enough for two already, but a little more wouldn't hurt. And I think we should pray for Nedjemger too. He's going to need all the help he can get if he's going to take on my sister.'

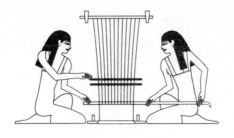

CHAPTER EIGHT

Fourth Month
of Winter

SATRA'S GOOD HUMOUR DID NOT LAST. NEDJEMGER CALLED LESS AND less frequently and she visited the temple gardens less often. No one dared to ask why, at least not of Satra herself. Nebet pointed out, to anyone who did ask, that there were many reasons why the two might not be able to see each other as often as they liked.

For example, the busiest time of the year for gardeners was just beginning. Trees and vines needed pruning, the annual flowers needed coaxing to extend their blooming period and the constant battle against weeds in the vegetable plots grew fiercer, and Nedjemger had never been one to sit back in the shade while watching his underlings doing all the hard work. Since he was out of practice in the courtship game he probably did not realize that the reduction in the time he could devote to his lady-love, necessary though it undoubtedly was, might be interpreted as evidence of cooling ardour.

Equally, with so much going on in the temple gardens, Satra found visiting there hardly worth the effort. She had said so, loudly, in the hearing of most of the household and the family next door, which only made her listeners think she was making too much of the matter. If she understood and accepted the circumstances that had taken Nedjemger from her side, there was no call to make such public excuses for their separation. In temper, having improved markedly during the height of

Nedjemger's attention, she was rapidly returning to the volatile, unpredictable nature that all knew and feared. Nebet found herself wondering how much longer she could keep silent, knowing that speaking to Satra was likely to stir up all the old resentments.

Meanwhile Khaemwase was learning so much from Nedjemger that Nebet allowed him to practise one of his new skills by pruning the vine in her garden. While watching him tending the plant his mother asked him, 'You probably think I don't have a right to know, but have you brought any messages for Satra recently?'

Khay was so good-natured that he had readily agreed to be the intermediary between Satra and his boss. He knew how much it meant to the rest of the family to keep Satra happy, but he had soon discovered what an unenviable task he had taken on. If the message he bore to Nedjemger received no reply at once, he was accused of forgetting to deliver it, of losing it or of deliberately withholding it out of spite. On the occasions when he had brought a message for Satra, she somehow managed to blame him if the letter was too short, or if its content was not to her liking. Nebet was proud of the way that, despite the aggravation and in the face of all Satra's accusations, Khay remained cheerful and smiling. He was smiling now, and humming gently to himself, totally absorbed in his work. She decided that he had not heard her question and felt bad about asking it again. She would have been surprised to know that her son had heard her perfectly well but had chosen not to answer.

Khaemwase had only that morning delivered a letter for Satra and it was the longest she had received in many days. Khay also knew something of the letter's contents, because it concerned him. The King's Mansion on the West Bank was so far advanced as to be ready for gardens to be laid out there. When Nedjemger had taken over responsibility for the gardens of Ipet Esut they had already been well established. Much as he loved his plants, Nedjemger also loved the creative challenge of starting a garden from nothing, and now Lord Tjia, Superintendent of the Mansion, had offered him the greatest challenge of his life, the job of setting out the gardens at the new temple.

It was a great honour to be chosen but it would mean moving across the River to take up residence in new quarters at the Mansion. He had been told that he could nominate some of his staff from Ipet Esut to accompany him to form the core of the new complement of gardeners and he had already asked Khay informally if he would like to be one of them. As the matter had not been made public, Khay had not yet had to approach his parents for permission, though he was fairly sure that his father, who was still spending a great deal of time with Lord Tjia and the Tjaty's deputy, Meryra, would already know of the plans.

Nedjemger, believing that Satra would not want to leave her family so soon after her father's death, had written to explain that he was moving away from Waset and that their friendship, much as he had valued it, would necessarily cease. Never having been skilled in the art of diplomacy as it applied to love letters, Nedjemger had expressed himself in very formal, unemotional terms. Even as Khay and Nebet were engrossed in the vine, Satra was reading what she interpreted as a cruel and casual dismissal, which dashed all her hopes. She was, understandably, furious.

The first person to suffer for Nedjemger's thoughtlessness was Iset. The girl had never taken to Satra, who had complained about her careless work on visits, long before she had moved into the house herself. Iset was clumsy and lazy. She had become clever at finding ways to avoid hard work or to skimp the tasks she had been set. Her attitude towards her employers had not changed. In fact, she had become increasingly resentful as she saw Neferti taking on a more adult role in the management of the household. Nebet had tried to teach her some of the simpler skills of being a lady's maid and, in a moment of perversity, had decided that Iset and Satra deserved each other. She had offered Iset to Satra as her personal attendant. This relationship had been fiery from the start.

Satra had taken her letter to the top of the stairs, hoping to find some privacy in which to read it. She did not know that Iset was on the roof, shaking mats and spreading them out to air. The servant girl surprised her mistress by swinging down the ladder from the roof almost on top of her. Satra knew perfectly well that Iset could not read, and yet she accused the girl of spying on her and slyly peering over the parapet of the roof to read her letter over her shoulder. Satra's pent-up frustration, anger and sadness were let loose on the unfortunate Iset. Nebet and Khay came running through from the garden at the sound of Iset's piercing screams. They were in time to see Satra with one hand entangled in Iset's unsuitably long hair to hold the girl still, while with the other hand she delivered blow after blow to her head, face, neck and arms. Clearly Satra was almost as hysterical as Iset.

'Satra!' Nebet called urgently. 'What are you thinking of? Let her go.'

Satra looked down at her sister, her face contorted with violent emotions and glistening with tears. She looked back at Iset, still squirming in her fierce grip, and as if she had woken from a dream she released her hold on Iset's hair. The girl teetered for a moment on the edge of the top step of the staircase, trying desperately to regain her balance, but in vain. She tumbled backwards in an ungraceful somersault, her head thumping once on the brick steps, and only Khay's quick thinking saved her from more serious injury. Even as his mother was speaking he had leaped to the foot of the stairs, and he was halfway up the flight when Iset fell. Her body knocked him against the outer wall, but he braced himself and was able to catch her round the waist. Together they subsided in an untidy heap on Tamiu's favourite step. Satra stood as if turned to stone, her eyes unseeing, tears now falling freely.

There was no one else in the house. Tia, unusually, had gone with Neferti and Meryt to the marketplace and Gemni had accompanied them to help carry back their purchases. Nebet assessed the situation in an instant. Iset was the more in need of help at that moment.

'Is she all right, Khay?' she asked. 'Can you bring her down?'

'I'll try,' he said. He eased himself from under Iset's limp body. The girl was stunned but not unconscious. Remarkably, there was no blood and no bones seemed to be broken. She had a large bump on the back of her head and her right eye was already half closed by the swelling of her cheek. Within a short while she would have an impressive black eye, and other bruises, both from her fall and from Satra's attack, would come out over the next few days. She began to come to her senses as Nebet bathed her face and told her to hold a cool, damp cloth to her eye. Her shoulders began to heave with sobs of pain and shock. Nebet could do nothing other than hold her close as she would have held her own daughter.

Looking at Khay over the top of Iset's head, she saw he was rubbing his arm where he had collided with the wall. 'You aren't hurt badly?' she asked.

'A few bruises,' he said. 'I've had worse.'

Satra was still immobile at the top of the stairs. 'You'll have to take charge of Satra. Take her into our room,' Nebet whispered. 'See if you can get her to lie down on the bed.'

Khaemwase nodded and slowly, so as not to frighten Satra into a similar tumble, he climbed the stairs, took her gently by the arm and led her into his parents' room.

Iset's sobbing subsided and she relaxed in Nebet's arms. Nebetiunet put a hand under her chin and lifted the girl's tear-stained face to hers.

'There, child, it's all over. Be sure I will never let anything like that happen to you again. Let's find you some good strong beer to take away the pain. Would you like that?'

'Yes,' Iset whispered, 'and a honeycake.'

Nebet had to smile. Iset had impressive powers of recovery. When Neferti returned she would be eager to show off her war wounds and give an exaggerated account of how she had come by them. As long as the story remained within the family, all would be well. However, Nebet had a suspicion that Satra's unwarranted cruelty would have far-reaching repercussions once it came to the ears of Iset's mother, as it most surely would. And if Nedjemger were to hear of it, Satra could say goodbye to all hope of marriage, either with him or with any other.

Neferti, Meryt and Tia were later returning from the market than Nebet had expected. She had instructed them to purchase pigeons for grilling and to find some new storage baskets. A recent inspection of the boys' clothes basket had revealed rodent damage, with two corners eaten away and tell-tale droppings staining some of the clothes inside. The large household linen container, with a lid almost as deep as the basket itself, was also showing signs of age. The weight of the sheets and coverlets had distended the base, causing some of the stitching to split. Both needed replacing but, ever thrifty, Nebet planned to give the lid of the linen basket to Mymy as a crib for the baby.

She had given Neferti two large baskets full of sharp-tasting cheeses, round and white, some covered in dried herbs for added flavour. Hedjet was still producing more milk than they could drink and the days were becoming warmer. The best way to prevent the milk from going to waste was to turn it into cheese. Tia had a light touch with the curd and her cheeses had proved to be very popular. This was the main reason behind her going to the market that morning. She liked to bask in the praise offered by her customers. The cheeses should have sold quickly, though it was unlikely that they would be exchanged directly for baskets of the sort Nebet required. However, it was well past midday when the marketeers returned, their mission accomplished. Neferti was eager to show her mother the fine linen press she had acquired and to explain the complicated series of exchanges that had brought about its purchase.

'Not now, Neferti,' Nebet said with an unusual tetchiness in her voice which made the girl fall silent in mid-sentence. Nubnefert, who had rarely known her mother to display bad temper without good reason, realized something was amiss. Nebet saw the look of concern in her face and said, 'I'm sorry to be so sharp with you but something happened while you were out and I've been worrying about it while waiting for you to return. Iset has taken a fall down the stairs. She appears to be unhurt, that is, not seriously hurt, but she'll have a fine crop of bruises by tomorrow. I've settled her in the women's room for now but I don't want to leave her alone, so would you, Meryt, go and sit with her?'

'Of course, Mistress,' Meryt said. 'Should I take her something to eat or drink?'

'She's had some beer but that has made her a bit drowsy and she didn't touch the honeycake I found for her because she suddenly felt nauseous. She did get a nasty bump on her head. I think it would be best for her to stay awake, so try to keep her talking.'

'Yes, Mistress, of course.'

Tia said, 'I'll come with you. The best thing for Iset is to get her walking as well as talking. We'll take her on a turn or two of the garden, splash her face and suchlike.'

'Yes, that's an excellent idea,' said Nebet. 'Thank you, Tia.'

Neferti tried to go with the two servants, but her mother caught hold of her hand and held her back. 'Come with me,' she said urgently.

Nebet led her daughter up the stairs and into her bedroom, where Neferti was astonished to see Satra apparently asleep on the bed, with Khay sitting on a little folding stool by her side. Nubnefert was bemused. She could not imagine what Iset's injuries had to do with Satra and yet there was clearly a link.

Nebet asked Khay, 'Did you find out what it was all about?'

'Not from Satra but I think I know,' he said, holding up Nedjemger's letter which he had found dropped at the top of the stairs.

'Have you read it?' Nebet asked.

'No, Muti,' Khay said severely. 'It's a private letter and I have no right to read it unless Satra gives me permission and she's . . .' He completed the statement by indicating the curled-up body on the bed.

Nebet swallowed her annoyance. Khay's righteous and somewhat pompous words had effectively prevented her from reading the letter herself, so she would have to wait to discover its contents. Then she had a thought. 'If you haven't read it, how can you be so sure that it's the cause of all this trouble?'

Khay was about to speak when Neferti asked in desperation, 'Will someone tell me what's been happening here? Is Satra ill? Did she fall, too? What's going on?'

Quickly and concisely Nebet outlined the morning's events as she understood them. Khay completed the picture by telling his mother and sister what he knew of Nedjemger's letter.

'So that's what Iset meant,' Nebet said, half to herself. 'She was muttering about Satra's "stupid letter" and how she wouldn't have wanted to read it even if she could. It makes sense now.'

'It makes no sense at all to me,' Neferti said. 'What happened? What possible connection could there be between Iset's fall and Satra's letter?'

'I think your father's sister has lost her temper once too often. For once, I suspect, Iset was completely innocent of any mischief. She just happened upon Satra at a sensitive moment and suffered the full blast of her anger. I don't know how I'm going to explain away her bruises. There are finger marks already showing on her face where Satra slapped her again and again. They can't be put down to the fall. And we can hardly keep her indoors until the bruises have all faded.'

Satra stirred. She uncurled and lifted herself up from the bed on one elbow. Her eyes still blurred from weeping, she was nevertheless quick to see her letter in Khay's hand. 'Give that to me. How dare you read my letter?'

Khaemwase had had just about as much of Satra as he could stand for one day. He resisted the temptation to argue his innocence. Instead he rose from his stool, tossed the letter on to the bed and left the room.

'I suppose he couldn't have read it anyway, with his bad eyes,' Satra sniffed.

Nebet's patience snapped. Any sympathy that Satra might have expected from her sister evaporated in an instant. The stream of recrimination and condemnation that Nebet unleashed on Satra soon had Neferti creeping from the room in embarrassment.

Amenmose had not been expecting to come home for a few days but the message he received, brief and cryptic as it was, caused him immediately to seek permission to return across the River. It was a most inconvenient summons, since the annual tax returns were coming in to the Tjaty's office and there was much work to be done in checking and filing the surveyors' reports and issuing the tax demands which were to be fulfilled after the harvest was in. He knew Nebet would not have called for him at such a crucial time if the matter had not been really urgent.

Nebet had hoped that they would be able to resolve the problem of Iset and Satra without Amenmose having to know anything of it. Being all too familiar with the stubbornness and resentful nature of both, she should have known better. Though she had rehearsed over and over what she was going to say to him, Nebet's relief at seeing her husband drove all that from her mind. She flew to his arms and wept with the release of the tension of the last few days.

'Oh, Ameny, thank the Lady you're back. Satra has been driving us all to distraction and now Iset has run away and who knows what tales she'll be telling about her treatment here.'

Calmly Amenmose led her into the garden, shutting the door firmly behind them, to the irritation of his children. Khay and Pakhred had been waiting with Neferti and Mymy to hear their father's reaction to the latest family crisis caused by his sister.

'That's it then,' Pakhred said. 'Father will soon sort things out.'

'Where's Satra?' asked Mymy, who had been sent for to mediate between her mother and her father's sister. Nebetiunet had not trusted herself to keep her temper, having once lost it so spectacularly.

'Hiding,' Neferti and Khay said in unison.

'Does anyone understand why she was so beastly to Iset?'

'Disappointment,' they said, again together.

'You two are no use at all. Trying to get anything out of you is like trying to get fur from a snake.'

Her siblings smiled sweetly. It was like old times, the days before Satra had appeared like a cat in the dovecote.

When their parents came indoors again the children were relieved to see that their mother had regained her usual calm. Amenmose, on the other hand, was frowning. He abruptly dismissed his daughters to go with their mother to the kitchen and sent the boys upstairs. The time had come for him to deal with Satra, who he knew was hiding herself away in the women's room. He had been patient long enough. He and Nebet had given her a home and treated her more than fairly, and she had repaid them with nothing but heartache. The time had come for her to acknowledge the debt she owed her brother's family and to make good some of the damage she had done.

The interview was not an experience Amenmose would wish to repeat. Satra tried all the old tricks he remembered from their childhood, the same tricks that had kept their father in the palm of her hand. She wept, she fluttered her eyelashes, she knelt at his feet and looked up at him with the doe-eyes of a doting baby sister. He was impervious to all her wiles and remained stony-faced throughout. When she at last realized that nothing would work on him, she fell silent and bowed her head as he explained exactly what he was going to do.

Montmose's house had yet to be sold. Although several people had expressed serious interest in it, the final price would not be decided until one or other of them came up with the goods and commodities, or firm promises of those goods, to pay for it. Now Amenmose had every intention of pushing the deal along, even if it meant taking a lower price than Satra thought the house was worth. The family was already suffering from a lack of negotiable assets because of the expenditure incurred by the funeral. Once the house was sold, Amenmose would take from the proceeds what he was owed and then, and only then, would he draw up a statement of what Satra might expect as a dowry.

She knew the implacable look on his face well enough not to argue, even though it was to her advantage to sell the house for the best possible price. But she could not hide her disappointment and, seeing this in her face, Amenmose held back his condemnation of her treatment of Iset. Satra was not young and she was far from wealthy. Her brother knew that Nedjemger had been her last realistic hope for a husband. Now her prospects of marriage seemed highly unlikely. He also knew that he could not suffer her presence in his family home for much longer. The only way to solve both his problem and hers was to revive Nedjemger's interest.

Khaemwase was not in the least surprised when his father gave him a letter to take to the Chief Gardener. 'Do you think this will work, Father?' he asked.

Amenmose looked at his youngest son with a quizzical expression. Physically Khay was still only a boy but his character had matured beyond all recognition since finding his vocation in the gardens of Ipet Esut. Amenmose realized that Khay had borne the brunt of Satra's intemperate behaviour with dignity and decorum. He had not run away like Senmut.

'I hope so, my son,' he responded with a sigh, 'I really hope so. You know Nedjemger better than any of us. Why do you think he's avoiding Satra?'

'I don't think it is a matter of his avoiding her,' Khay said with a wisdom beyond his years. 'Have you heard about his promotion?'

'You mean to the job at the Mansion?'

'Yes. I'm sure the letter Satra received was about that. I believe he was telling her he won't be able to continue seeing her once he has moved across the River.'

'Why ever not?' Amenmose asked in amazement.

'Exactly,' Khay said with an ironic smile. 'My master is not the most worldly of men, and he sees the River as an impassable barrier between them.'

'But people go back and forth all day long, every day.' Amenmose was still bewildered.

'You and I know that,' Khay said. 'Satra knows that. But my master has never lived anywhere but here in Waset. He sees the West Bank almost as a foreign land. When he came to your father's funeral, I believe it was the first time he had crossed the River since his first wife's death and that's so long ago that no one can remember when it was.'

'I knew he was attached to his garden but I had no idea he was so, shall we say, unadventurous.'

'Which makes it all the more remarkable that he agreed to go to the funeral. And as for starting to court Satra in the first place, the under-gardeners are still gossiping about that. Though she undoubtedly made the first move, I believe he truly cares for her. He's as upset by this separation as she is, but he honestly thinks that he can't ask her to move away from her home and family.'

'What, all the way across the River?' Amenmose laughed out loud. 'This situation is becoming more ridiculous by the moment. We must get those two back together and give them a good talking-to. They need to know a few facts of life.'

'So do you still want me to take this letter?' Khay asked.

'No, I'll go and see him myself.'

Nebet had complete faith in her husband's ability to solve the problem of Satra. She was not so sure as to what to do in the matter of Iset. The girl had vanished overnight. There were always gruesome tales circulating about young children, especially girls, wandering out into the dark, never to be seen again. Crocodiles were rare now in the River at Waset, having been driven away by the constant noise and turbulence of boat traffic, but that did not prevent the scare-mongers' lurid descriptions of bodies being dragged out of the water, lacerated and mangled by the teeth of the sinister reptiles, and totally unidentifiable. Nebet tried not to think about that. She hoped that Iset had returned to her mother's house, but if that were so she would have expected to have had an indignant Henut knocking at her door long before now. She wondered about paying Iset's mother a visit, but she knew that would be seen as such an unusual occurrence as to arouse Henut's suspicions immediately. She had had Bak and Menna scouring the locality without success. Hotepu and Didet had been pressed into revealing those little hiding places to which Iset used to escape from unpleasant or hard work, but a search of these had also proved fruitless. It was as if the wretched girl had disappeared into thin air.

Meanwhile Nebet had other things to think about. The Temple was preparing for the festivals associated with the harvest. The most immediate needs were for streamers to decorate the papyrus bowers of Renenutet, Lady of the Threshing Floor. In this incarnation the Goddess was represented as a snake, a great cobra who waited in the papyrus clumps of the irrigation channels bordering the fields to deter or destroy pests that endangered the success of the harvest. Renenutet's festival was not a grand affair like Opet. Bowers in her honour, decorated with fresh green papyrus stems, would be set up in villages all along the length of Kemet, from Suan in the south to where the River emptied into the Great Green. Nebet had never seen the huge expanse of salt-water which, so she had been told, lapped the northern shores of Kemet and stretched away beyond the comprehension of ordinary citizens. The reapers, threshers and winnowers would sing songs in her

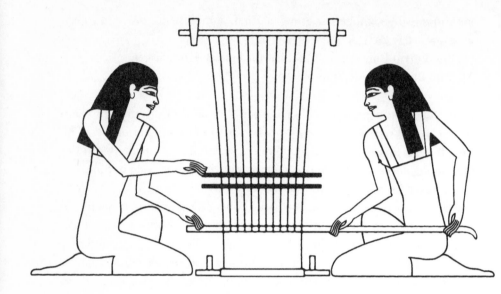

praise as they went about their work. This aspect of the Goddess was highly regarded by all concerned with the production of grain crops and, since the livelihood of everyone in the Two Lands depended on the harvest one way or another, Renenutet was a popular deity.

But she was also honoured as the nurturer of the King, the Lady who provided sustenance for His Majesty, and thus for all Kemet. She was recognized as the guardian of the King's clothing, imbuing the very cloth with her magical power and protection. As a weaver and seamstress who had made both kilts and gowns for the Royal Person Nebet felt very close to this manifestation of the Goddess. She liked to think that her needle had been guided by the Lady and that, in some small way, Renenutet's magic had been fixed in the garments by means of Nebet's stitches.

Nebet was surprised to find how few lengths of ribbon-width linen there were in the stores. The festivals of Amen-Ra and Mut had taken up more than she had allowed for, mainly because of the extra decoration for the new court at the Southern Sanctuary. Dyes were a problem, too. Renenutet's colours were green and yellow; while safflower would provide the colour of ripe corn, achieving a fresh, papyrus green was more difficult. Nebet experimented with several combinations of blue and yellow dyes but none of them pleased her. They tended to make a dreary olive colour, which would look grey when the ribbons were fluttering against the sky.

'I don't know why you put yourself to all this trouble every year,' Djehuti said as she frowned over the latest test batch of linen. 'You know what the solution is: the same as you did last year and the year before.'

Nebet bowed to the inevitable. She would make up batches of pale yellow and blue and twist them together.

Each of the Renenutet bowers would also require an amulet woven from new straw in the shape of the crescent moon. These would hang from the canopies, just as similar protective charms would hang over the threshing floors and grain stores throughout the Two Lands. Although it was in honour of the Lady, Nebet had never liked working with straw. It was harsh to the fingers and a seamstress could not work properly with rough hands. In the weaving sheds, where reeds and rushes were woven into mats, the men who worked the great looms were identifiable by the scars on their arms and hands. Scratches and splinters were natural hazards of their occupation just as much as the stiffness in their joints and a permanently bent spine. But no man had the delicacy of touch required to twist the amulets, which had to be newly made each year.

In previous years Mymy, though she had not inherited her mother's skill with either the spindle or the needle, had shown that she had a talent for making these little charms. Nebet had provided her with the raw materials and had said that, once the needs of the Temple were satisfied, Mymy could do what she liked with the leftovers. Mutnefert had made a basketful of amulets, far more than the Temple required, and, before she took them to sell in the market place, she had brought a selection of them so that her mother might choose one to hang over the grain bins in her own storeroom.

The problem with rodents had become more acute since Tamiu had become almost useless as a mouser. The boys' clothes basket was not the only victim of vermin. Nebet had set traps to catch them, Tia had put down foul-smelling mixtures to deter them, Khay and Gemni had searched out every mousehole and blocked them with mud and stones, and still the little beasts found their way back into the store. The corn in the bins was quite safe – even a rat could not chew through the thick pottery containers – but most of the dried goods were kept in sacks or baskets, which proved no barrier to mice.

Tia swore that the magic in the amulet from last year had worn thin.

Certainly it was looking a little the worse for wear, so Nebet was glad to choose a fine new charm from Mymy's collection. The amulet gleamed with the golden shine of the new straw. In comparison the old one was faded and colourless, its surface dull with a year's-worth of dust, and when she took it down a shower of tiny insect bodies fell from it.

Tia had taken charge of the replacement charm, which she held in one hand while in the other she held a wand made of hippopotamus ivory inscribed with many magical symbols, including the snake-headed figure of Renenutet. This wand had been handed down through Tia's family along with the knowledge of the appropriate words to recite for different occasions. She moved throughout the whole house, touching the door-jambs and sills with the wand, waving it over storage boxes and baskets, and holding it high above the beds as she intoned an almost meaningless chant she had learned from her mother. At last she reached the basement storeroom, where together the chant and the wand activated the magic in the straw amulet, providing protection for the food stores and prosperity for the coming year.

Mymy, discreetly holding a hand to her swollen belly, smiled a contented smile. The Renenutet ritual was as much a fertility rite as it was protective magic. The amulets that she was about to take to the market would be sought by women who wanted to conceive, as well as by housekeepers wishing to protect their pantries. The fact that the seller was obviously well advanced in pregnancy would be seen as a good omen and her amulets would find eager buyers. Nebet, seeing her daughter's unconscious gesture, wondered, not for the first time, if there might be a divine hand at work here. 'Mymy' was the nickname her elder sister had given her as an infant, because her childish lips could not pronounce the baby's given name. To Wiya, the syllables had been just an easily repeated sound which everyone in the family came to use as a name. But 'Mymy' meant 'seed corn', a word potent with the idea of life and procreation. Nebet had given up persisting in the use of Mymy's real name. Now that she had sailed through the most dangerous months of her pregnancy with ease, her nickname seemed fitting. This line of thought reminded Nebet of Wiya. She had picked out the very best of Mymy's amulets and would make sure that Tia's magic was worked over it to concentrate its powers. She would not consider herself a caring mother if she missed a single opportunity to help her daughter achieve her greatest desire.

The little household ritual complete, they hung up the amulet with new ribbons, hoping the mice would be suitably impressed. Tia took the old one into the kitchen court and they all watched as the evil it had absorbed over the past twelve months was destroyed, along with the ragged straw object, in the kitchen fire.

Nebet was not expecting to see Mymy again quite so soon, though she was glad to see her at any time. Mymy had come to report on the success of her market visit, but also to bring some news.

'I've seen Iset,' she said.

'Where?' Nebet had almost given up hope that the wretched girl was still alive. Her only consolation was that, since they had heard nothing from Henut, the fact of Iset's disappearance was not yet known to her own mother.

'In the marketplace,' Mymy explained. 'She was helping one of the stall-holders.'

'Oh, thank the Goddess, she's not dead,' Nebet said fervently. 'But where has she been all this time? What has she been doing?'

'That's the surprising part,' Mymy said, 'she was with Takhat.'

'The wig-maker?'

'Yes' – Mymy was warming to her subject – 'and I didn't recognize her at first. It was only when she tried on a wig for a customer that I realized who it was.'

'Do you mean . . . ?'

'Yes, she's cut off her hair!' Mymy almost squeaked with disbelief.

Iset's hair, the subject of many arguments and the object of Neferti's envy, had been long, straight and dark. Iset had been extremely proud of it, despite the fact that girls of her age usually wore their hair short. Henut had encouraged her daughter to grow her hair, and Iset had seen it as her only means of defying authority. Nebet, though she was the girl's employer, could not go against the mother's wishes and had been unable to persuade Henut of the inappropriateness of her daughter's hairstyle. Mymy's news suddenly made everything clear.

'That's what Henut wanted all along,' she said, 'to have Iset's hair grow long enough to sell.'

'That's what I thought, but I don't think Henut knows yet that Iset has sold it,' Mymy said.

Nebet began to laugh. 'Oh dear! Poor Henut! She had such high hopes and Iset has gone and ruined them.'

'I don't know what she will have got for the hair,' Mymy said, 'but it was enough for Takhat to give her lodging, and it seems as if Iset has been taken on as a wig-maker's apprentice. She looked quite happy and Takhat seems pleased with the arrangement.'

'I'm not surprised. If she can keep Iset interested in the work and can make her stay long enough, the girl's hair will grow again and she'll have another crop.'

'Rather like combing a goat.' Mymy too was laughing.

'Oh, this is wonderful,' Nebet said, 'but what will Henut do when she hears of it?'

It was not long before they found out. The next morning Henut called, only to find that Nebet was at work in the weaving shed at the Temple. Tia, who had answered the door, reported that Henut had been in a belligerent mood. She had refused to believe Nebet was not at home and had accused Tia of lying.

'She was in a right foul mood,' Tia reported. 'She wouldn't tell me what it was all about but it's clear she's found out about her precious little daughter. It seems she's ready to blame everything on us and she was determined to have it out with us then and there.'

Nebet was amused by Tia's use of the inclusive 'us'. Though Tia had complained just as much about Iset as anyone else, they were both servants and Henut might have expected Tia to take her daughter's part. Clearly, though she could have let Nebet, as Lady of the House, take full responsibility for recent events, Tia still saw herself as one of the family and so sided with them.

'Did she make any specific complaints?' Nebet asked.

'No, not her,' Tia said dismissively, 'though I dare say she's a deal put out to discover that Iset has taken her life into her own hands. That Henut was always a lazy madam and she'd hoped to be living off Iset for the rest of her life. For once the girl has got the better of her mother, and good luck to her, I say.'

It was so extraordinary to hear Tia saying anything in the least bit complimentary about Iset that Nebet could hardly believe her ears.

'Will Henut call again?' she asked.

'Of course she will,' Tia sniffed. 'She's worked herself up to say her piece and she'll not be denied that pleasure.'

Tia had assessed Henut's mood very well. Early the following morning Iset's mother was knocking at the door again, determined to catch Nebet before she left for the Temple. Nebet was annoyed that Henut knocked at the garden gate, rather than walking down the alley to the side door, but she had Meryt show the woman into the reception room where she was waiting, sitting on Amenmose's chair on the raised platform. This gave her an immediate superiority over her visitor, who, when offered a low stool which would have put her at an even greater disadvantage of height, preferred to remain standing.

In her sweetest, most reasonable voice, Nebet asked, 'What can we do for you, Mistress Henut?'

'You know very well,' the woman blustered. 'You've driven out my little girl with your cruelty. She's been out in the city, all alone and afraid for days, and no one thought to tell me, me who's her mother and worried sick about the dear girl.'

Nebet thought Henut was exaggerating her motherly feelings just a little but she accepted that the accusation of cruelty had some basis, even though Iset had not suffered injury at her own hands.

Maintaining her calm expression she said, 'I'm very sorry Iset chose to leave this house but I have been assured that she is perfectly safe and, in fact, that she has found other employment which is much more to her liking than being in service here.'

'That's as may be,' Henut persisted, 'but when I put her here I thought at least she'd be well treated, not knocked black and blue and kicked out into the street.'

'Now that is just not true,' Nebet said in a very reasonable voice. 'Iset went of her own accord. There is no question of her being dismissed. If she wants to come back, we will welcome her.' She felt proud of the way she had avoided the matter of Iset's bruises but hoped Henut would not encourage her daughter to reclaim her old position.

'What about wages?' Henut asked. 'Surely she's worth more than her keep now. She's been with you for nearly two years.'

This is the heart of the matter, Nebet thought; this is why Henut is so agitated. In a placatory tone she said, 'Much as it pains me to say it, you must know that Iset is not suitable as a lady's maid. I've tried to instruct her but you know your daughter's character well enough to understand my difficulty. If she wants to come back as a kitchen maid I know Tia would be happy to take her on, but I could not offer the sort of wage you are thinking of. Iset is just not worth it. And besides, I hear she has found her own vocation as a wig-maker. If she's happy doing that, I cannot see why we should interfere. Surely, as a mother, you only want your child to be happy?'

Henut grunted, 'What about compensation?'

Astonished at the woman's audacity, Nebetiunet drew herself up in the chair and looked sternly down on Henut. 'Compensation for what, may I ask? Iset cannot expect anything for herself, because she was the one who left us. As for you, she was not supporting you in any way while she was here, so you have no call upon us. I suggest you have a serious talk with Iset. What she may choose to give you is entirely a matter between mother and daughter.'

Henut looked startled and then deflated, like a sail when the wind drops suddenly. She had always considered Nebetiunet somewhat soft and had expected to be able to wring some sort of guilt payment out of the family. Now she realized she had met her match. She fell to her knees and started blubbering pathetically.

Nebet could distinguish a few words like 'starving' and 'lonely' but she hardened her heart against the miserable woman at her feet. 'I am sorry for you, Henut,' she said, 'but there is nothing I can do. Perhaps if you had shown more interest in your daughter's welfare while she was in my service, she would feel some sort of obligation to you now. I cannot say that I have any great affection for the child but she deserved more from her own mother. As long as Takhat treats her fairly and as long as Iset is happy where she is, I see no reason why she should not make a good life for herself there. I think that is all I have to say to you. I bid you good day.'

Henut had the grace to know when she was beaten. She scrambled to her feet and, to Nebet's intense satisfaction, bowed before leaving. Meryt, who had been waiting in the inner room, ushered her out through the kitchen gate.

Satra burst from the women's room and flung her arms about Nebet's neck. 'Thank you, sister,' she said, gushing with emotion. 'I thought she was going to accuse me. Thank you for protecting me.'

Nebet disentangled herself from Satra's unwelcome embrace. 'I did not do it for you,' she said. 'If Henut had asked how Iset came by her injuries, I would have told her. Iset is not the only one who has to learn a lesson from this. I only wish, Satra, that you were as easy a problem to solve as Iset.'

Until she had come to live in Amenmose's house, Satra had never been spoken to like this. She had been the darling of her mother and the constant companion and support of her father. Those years of pampering and indulgence had created a very selfish, spiteful and bitter woman. Only in the last few months had she come to recognize this. Nebetiunet was the perfect example of a happy, fulfilled and contented woman. Satra thought that she could do no better than to model herself on her brother's wife. She hoped it was not too late.

CHAPTER NINE

First Month of Summer

GEMNI CAME RUSHING IN THROUGH THE SIDE GATE INTO THE KITCHEN court, where Nebet was supervising the preparation of the evening meal. He had been down at the riverside with Ibi and the other washermen, and his face was red from the exertion of running as fast as he could to be first with the news.

'There's a royal boat coming in from the north,' he panted, 'a big one. I think the King's coming.'

'More likely it's the Tjaty returning,' Nebet said, though she doubted that. If Paser had been on his way back to Waset, Amenmose would have been the first to hear of it. It was even more unlikely to be His Majesty, because the King's visits to Waset were always heralded well in advance. Also, from conversations with her friends on the Household Staff, Nebet knew the current state of the royal apartments at Ipet Esut, and they were in no way ready to receive visitors.

'It's a big boat,' Gemni repeated, as if restating this observation would add weight to his argument.

'I've no doubt it is,' Nebet said patiently, 'but you weren't sent to watch for boats. Where's the laundry?'

'Oh!' Gemni's expression said more than words. In his excitement he had come away from the River empty-handed. He would have to go back to fetch the bundles of linen.

'Before you go,' Nebet said, 'did you ask Ibi about pleating the festival gowns?'

'Oh yes, Mistress,' Gemni said, relieved to be able to demonstrate that he was reliable after all.

'Well?' Nebet folded her arms and began to tap her foot, a sure sign that her patience was wearing thin.

'Ibi said' – Gemni screwed up his face in his effort to remember Ibi's exact words – 'if you want the garments for the Harvest Festival you'll have to get them to him soon because you're not the only family as wants to look their best for the occasion, and everyone knows that Ibi's pleating is the best in Waset so customers'll be lining up to get their dresses done.'

'Very well. Since you're here you can take the gowns to Ibi when you go back for the laundry. First, go to the Lady Satra and ask her to find them for you. I want Ibi to pleat her gown and mine and the Master's over-tunic. Can you remember all that?'

'Yes, Mistress.' Gemni hesitated.

'What are you waiting for?'

'Do I have to ask Lady Satra?'

'Yes,' Nebet said firmly, 'there's nothing to fear from her. She won't bite.'

'I wouldn't be so sure of that,' Tia muttered darkly.

Nebet turned to frown at the cook, whose hearing appeared to be very selective at times. Tia quickly busied herself with stoking the fire beneath the stew pot in which the first of the new season's beans were cooking with onions, garlic and herbs. Hotepu and Didet, who were making meal cakes, put their floury hands to their mouths to stifle their giggles, only to giggle all the more when each saw the other's whitened face.

As a means of registering her displeasure Nebet admonished them with a hurt look before leaving them to their silliness. She was disappointed in the servants' reaction to even the merest mention of Satra. Amenmose's sister had become much easier to live with over the last few days and, though she had said nothing about Nedjemger, Nebet had the distinct impression that the romance had been resumed. Her husband had paid the Chief Gardener a visit in order to deliver an invitation to accompany him on a trip across the River so that Amenmose might show him around the site of the proposed new gardens at the Mansion. During the river crossing and the tour of inspection

Amenmose had had a prolonged heart-to-heart talk with Nedjemger. He had confirmed everything Khaemwase suspected, and it was all Amenmose could do to stop himself laughing at Nedjemger's ridiculous predicament.

The gardener was a grown man in a responsible position. He was obviously good at his job or the promotion would not have been offered him. He was well off because he had lived a simple, some would say frugal, life while earning a very respectable income. The contents of his private storerooms and the credit he had accumulated at the royal commissaries must be considerable. Despite Satra's fears, he was not worried about finding a woman with a large dowry. The fact that he had not been looking for a woman at all when first he met Satra convinced Amenmose that Nedjemger's affection for his sister was genuine. The promotion had come as a complete surprise and had left the Chief Gardener in total confusion. Having had so little experience of life outside the confines of his gardens, Nedjemger was in no position to appreciate that the news, which was so startling to him, would be of great satisfaction to Satra. Amenmose reported much of this conversation to Nebetiunet, though some things would remain confidences between the two men.

'I had no idea that a grown man could be so ignorant of life,' Amenmose said. 'He really thought Satra wouldn't want him if it meant she'd have to move across the River. I reminded him that our daughter moved even further away to the Place of Truth only a few months ago and that we still see her regularly. It's not as if Nedjemger is moving to Suan or Per-Ramesse. I pointed out that we can actually see the Mansion from our roof-top so the distance is hardly worth mentioning.'

'Are you sure his excuses weren't just a way of getting out of any obligation to Satra?' Nebet asked, voicing her gravest fear. She could not help but wonder if Nedjemger had finally seen Satra as her family saw her and had tried to extricate himself from her clutches before it was too late. She would not have blamed him if that were the case, but she had come so close to ridding her house of Satra's disruptive presence that she would say almost anything, was prepared even to lie, to persuade him of her sister's suitability as a wife.

'Oh, I'm sure he's completely besotted by her, hard as it is for a brother to believe that his beastly little sister could be loved by anyone of intelligence,' Amenmose laughed.

'What will happen now?' Nebet asked in trepidation. Since the relationship would have to be repaired, and the courting couple would have to sort out the complications relating to Nedjemger's promotion, she could not see an early resolution to the problem of Satra.

'I think it's going to work, given a little time,' Amenmose said. 'She really can't hope for better so she'll see sense soon enough. Nedjemger's not going away, after all, only moving across the River. If he can cope with that, so can she if she wants to. I've given him my blessing, and as she's old enough to know what she's doing I don't see why we have to bother about watching out for her every step of the way.'

'And the dowry?' Nebet asked.

Montmose's house had at last been sold but the purchaser had paid only a part of the cost and had drawn up a document of agreement to pay the rest in instalments over two years. Amenmose was quite happy with the arrangement as it would provide him with a steady income for that period, and if the purchaser failed to make a single payment the house would be forfeit. If that happened, Amenmose would keep what income he had already received and would be able to offer the house for sale again. Despite the apparent good character of the scribe, who had bought the house as a marriage gift for his son, and despite the common nature of such agreements, Nebet was unhappy that there was not much to show for the sale of Montmose's house. She had hoped by now to have a substantial collection of goods set aside in their storehouse for Satra's dowry. The longer it took to accumulate the necessary supplies, linen, furniture and household equipment, the longer she would have to suffer Satra's company.

'Don't worry about the dowry,' Amenmose said. 'That's all taken care of. Nedjemger's unworldliness can be used to our advantage.'

'Don't think Satra won't have something to say about that,' Nebet said.

'I'm sure she will, but remember, Nedjemger has no family to give him advice so he makes up his own mind about such things. He knows I won't give him short measure, and as long as he's satisfied with our arrangement Satra will have no cause to complain.'

Nebet suddenly realized the significance of their conversation. 'Are you telling me you got as far as discussing marriage terms with Nedjemger?'

'Yes.' Amenmose grinned broadly.

'The Lady must have heard my prayer,' Nebet sighed with heart-felt relief.

'She must have done,' Amenmose said. 'Let's hope that my sister realizes how lucky she is.'

'Rather hope that Nedjemger doesn't have a change of heart at the last moment.'

'Oh, he won't. As I said, he's besotted. I think he'd take her without a dowry.'

'Hah! You'd never get Satra to agree to that.'

They laughed together and Amenmose reached for his wife's hand. Soon he would return across the River to resume his work for Paser but he treasured such precious times when they could be together. He had missed Nebet's company in the last few months and he regretted that his absence had put such a heavy emotional load on her.

He studied her face, noticing for the first time the lines forming at the corners of her eyes and by her mouth, the creases at her neck and the grey hairs shining among the black. Her hands were still soft because she kept them so by using many different ointments and lotions, but he knew she was already suffering some discomfort of joint-stiffness. She would not admit it but he knew she had largely given up spinning, at which she had been truly proficient, and restricted her sewing to the most important royal commissions. Most of her work for Djehutiemheb was now supervisory, training young weavers like Neferti and overseeing the manufacture and maintenance of the Temple linens. She was thirty-one years old and the proud mother of three boys and three girls. Her own mother had not lived as long, and Amenmose's mother had died at thirty-two. Both had borne only two living children. Amenmose was acutely aware of how much harder and more dangerous life was for a woman than for a man. He could not visualize life without Nebetiunet by his side but all the men in his family and hers had spent their last years alone. He wanted to come home, to make the most of what little time was left to them. His duty to the Tjaty had to take priority but another half a day would not matter. He led Nebet through the house and up the stairs to their bedroom, where he firmly bolted the door behind them.

The boat Gemni had seen turned out to be carrying a group of senior army officers who went immediately to report to Lord Tjia at the

Mansion. The most important of them, especially in his own estimation, was Ameneminet who, like Paser, had been a boyhood companion of His Majesty. Whereas Paser had followed his father's profession, becoming a scribe and administrator and ultimately the King's Chief Minister, Ameneminet had chosen the army life.

Under the rule of Menmaatra-Sethy, Ameneminet had accompanied His Majesty, who was then the King's Eldest Son, on several campaigns, acting as personal attendant and, when he was old enough, as charioteer. When the King's Father had gone to join Osiris, His Majesty had appointed his old friend Commander of the Royal Chariot Division, which was stationed at Waset. Since the campaign season was short, his army duties occupied him for only a small part of each year, so he had also been awarded the honorary title of Overseer of the King's Building Works at Waset. This set him in authority over Senetnay's husband, Ahmose, who was the King's Chief Architect in the City and the man who did all the work for which Ameneminet gained all the credit and all the praise from their royal master.

The swaggering charioteer would expect a welcome suitable to his high position in the King's favour. He would make a cursory inspection of the buildings under construction for which he was nominally responsible without really seeing them. He would receive reports from Ahmose and other senior officials of the Works Department, which he would never read. He would ask what he thought were the right questions but, knowing he would not understand the answers, he would simply not listen to them. Ahmose's frustration and animosity towards his supposed superior was well known and Nebet knew those feelings would be refuelled by Ameneminet's return to Waset. She knew also that her friend Senetnay would need someone to talk to.

The Festival of the Coming Forth of Min to celebrate the harvest was a highlight of the year at Waset, bringing in people from the countryside all around to watch the colourful procession. The success of the harvest was vital to Kemet. If Min withheld his blessing, many of the poorest people would starve, along with their animals. If the seed corn kept from this season's crop was bad and failed to germinate next year, famine would spread and even the richest landowners would suffer. The god of fertility and procreation was a god for all. The health of the Two Lands depended on Min's goodwill at this end of the agricultural cycle just as it did on the blessing of Osiris at the time of planting. At the height of the festival Min would emerge from the Temple to receive the first gifts of the harvest and the adulation of the pilgrims gathered in Waset.

Min's statue was carried on a float draped with heavy red hangings decorated with gilded rosettes and edged with fringes. Each year since the drapes had been replaced for the first Harvest Festival celebration of the King's reign, more renovation had been necessary. Not surprisingly the fringes tended to fray and come away from the bottom of the hangings when trodden on by the priests carrying the float on their shoulders. The weighty bronze rosettes were easily snagged and pulled off the drapes, sometimes tearing the thick linen.

In order to clean the cloth Nebet had to decide whether she could simply shake it out and brush off the dust or whether it had to be washed. If it was to be properly cleaned with natron the rosettes and fringes would have to be removed first, and their replacement would take several needlewomen several days to complete. When she looked at the hangings spread out on the floor of the weaving-shed, she sighed with resignation. The dirt of four years, caused by countless people crowding around the god, their feet stirring up the dust and their sweaty hands reaching out to touch the divine float for luck, had discoloured the blood-red linen to a murky brown.

'That will never do,' Djehutiemheb said. There was genuine regret in his voice, for he knew how much work was required to make the hangings respectable.

'If only I'd looked at them sooner.' Nebet sighed again. 'There's no time now to make new hangings so these will have to be cleaned. I'll need extra hands if this is to be done in time for the Coming Forth. Can I bring in some friends to help me? They're all good workers and trustworthy.'

'Of course, my dear,' Djehuti said. 'I'm sure anyone you choose will be perfectly acceptable. But what do you think about the colour?'

Nebet had been worrying about that. The deep red had been achieved by successive dyeing with a combination of vegetable and mineral dyes. When washed with natron, to remove the greasy hand marks and the stains of dripped unguents, the colour was likely to fade and she could not be sure the drapes would still look red, no matter how much care she took of them.

'They'll have to be washed but I'll suggest to the launderers that they try just hot water at first. I'll decide whether to use natron once the worst of the dirt is removed.'

'That's my sensible girl.' Djehuti patted her arm.

The work had to begin at once to remove the trimmings before the drapes could be sent for washing. Nebetiunet immediately called in her team of helpers. She had already warned Meryt and Neferti she would be needing them, and even Satra had volunteered her services. Amenmose's sister could not sew a straight seam but she could thread a needle and was capable of simple repair work, which was really all that the task required. Wiya had recently arrived to stay for the duration of the festival, and she was almost as good a needlewoman as her mother. Together with some of the Temple weavers, she would have a jolly little party to work on this sacred task. It seemed a highly opportune time to ask Senetnay to join them.

The first task was to remove the rosettes. Nebet provided her helpers with sharp blades to snip the threads holding the gilded bronze in place. Where the cloth had been torn it had to be darned to prevent further fraying before the hangings were washed. The women sat in a circle with the dusty, heavy material spread over the floor in front of them like a red pond, its folds lapping their knees. Sometimes one of the younger girls was sent to crawl under the drapes to loosen knotted threads, or to tiptoe carefully across the fabric to reach the sections furthest from the edges.

Despite the urgency of the work, there was a friendly atmosphere in the room and everyone, even Satra, joined in the gossip and banter that always attended such gatherings.

Nebet was surprised to see that Satra was willing and eager to share gossip with people she would have considered her social inferiors only a short while ago. Once she would have hesitated to introduce Satra into such company for fear her sister would make herself disagreeable. Now she felt quite happy at leaving her among the unmarried weavers. Their language and conversation could be scandalous at times but Satra seemed perfectly at ease in their company and laughed along with them, though Nebet suspected she did not always understand what she was laughing at.

Wiya had settled herself between Meryt and Neferti so that she could give them the benefit of her experience. She caught her mother's eye every now and then when a hoot of laughter from the opposite side of the floor silenced all other conversation, especially once when Satra seemed to be the originator of the joke. Wiya was clearly as amazed as Nebet at the change in Satra.

Nebet had made sure Senetnay was sitting beside her, and was waiting for an appropriate moment to broach the subject of Ameneminet. Her friend had a somewhat distracted air. Though her hands went through the motions, it was as if her mind was elsewhere, but when she pricked her finger with a bronze needle she seemed to awaken from her dreaminess and instinctively put her finger to her mouth.

'Are you all right?' Nebet asked.

'Yes,' Senetnay said. 'It's only a tiny scratch, only a drop of blood, but I don't want to get it on the cloth.'

'Don't worry about that,' Nebet said, adding wickedly, 'blood won't show on this colour. And anyway it's going to be washed as soon as we're finished here.'

'It's my own fault,' Senetnay said. 'I should be using a thimble to push the needle through this stiff cloth but I never could get used to using one of those things.'

Nebet knew exactly what she meant. It had taken her months to get used to the cumbersome grooved stone, which fitted over the middle finger of her needle hand and was held in place by the first and third fingers. She was grateful that, for the fine work at which she excelled, a leather band round the fingertip was all that was needed to push the thinner needles through delicate fabrics.

'Your thoughts aren't entirely on the task, are they?' Nebet asked kindly.

'No.' Senetnay paused, considering the wisdom of telling her friend her true thoughts. Her mind was made up by the sympathetic smile on Nebet's face. Nebetiunet was a good friend, who could be trusted to keep a confidence, and Senetnay had a great need to confide in someone. She bent her head over her work and with a sideways glance indicated that if Nebet were to do the same they could whisper to each other without being overheard.

Still, when it came to speaking, Senetnay did not know where to begin so Nebet prompted her by saying, 'I hear the Overseer of Works is back in town.'

Senetnay's sharp intake of breath told Nebet that she had hit the mark. In a low undertone, fortunately smothered by the general noise in the room, Senetnay began to pour out her feelings.

'It's so unfair! Ahmose has been working for days at a time, from sunrise to sunset, trying to complete the Mansion on time. He's well ahead of schedule and everyone here in Waset has praised him for it. But now that man has arrived, and he treats Ahmose as if he was a nobody. He'll take all the honour for himself and my husband's part in this grand enterprise will go unrecognized.'

'Surely Lord Tjia and the Tjaty know Ahmose's worth?'

'Oh yes, of course they do, and I've tried to tell Ahmose that, over and over again. But Ahmose is ambitious. It is the King's recognition he craves and he won't get that if all His Majesty is told is what Ameneminet chooses to tell. In the official records it will be shown that Ameneminet was Overseer of Works and Ahmose was only his subordinate, following his master's instructions. I tell you, Nebetiunet, Ahmose is angrier and more bitter than I ever thought he could be. The work has kept him away from home for days on end and then, when he does manage to get back across the River for a time, his temper is so short that the boys fear to enter a room if they know he's there. I thank the gods that at least Amenhotep has started school, so he's not at home eight days out of ten but Simut adores his father and to see his little face crumple when Ahmose shouts at him for no reason, it breaks my heart.'

Senetnay muffled a little sob.

Nebet reached out to touch her hand, saying, 'I know exactly how you feel. Amenmose has been living at the Mansion since the Tjaty left for Per-Ramesse. I miss him dreadfully, more than I've ever admitted to him. But at least my children are grown up enough to understand what's going on. Your first concern must be for the little ones. It's only natural to be protective of your children, and it hurts all the more when you have to protect them from the very people they look up to.'

'Please, Nebetiunet,' Senetnay said urgently, 'don't think that Ahmose would ever hurt them. He loves them and he'd do anything for them. In fact, it's because of them that he has this ambition. He wants to safeguard their future. Whether or not he's justified in his belief, he sees Ameneminet as a monster preventing him from doing what a good father should do.'

'He may be right, but perhaps he should consider the possibility that Ameneminet is also looking to his own future. Who can blame him for taking advantage of his friendship with the King? I suspect he has no idea of how his actions or his attitude may be interpreted by others.'

Senetnay looked up sharply and hissed, 'Nebetiunet, that man knows perfectly well. If he was a typical empty-headed, muscle-bound soldier, Ahmose could laugh off his interference as plain ignorance. But he's an intelligent man, born of a noble family and with a good education. He knows *exactly* what he's doing and, more to the point, Ahmose thinks His Majesty knows, too. Ahmose is sure he's being used to further Ameneminet's career.'

Nebet regretted her instinctive attempt to see both sides of the argument, but she was shocked to hear that Ahmose was harbouring treasonous thoughts. She hastened to apologize for her unthinking comment and Senetnay graciously accepted her apology.

They knew each other too well to fall out over this matter but at the same time both knew that it was best not to continue this conversation. They worked on in silence for a short while before, to Nebet's surprise, her friend said, 'I must say sorry, too. My emotions are very fragile at present. I am with child again.'

Nebet had to restrain herself from hugging Senetnay in congratulation. Instead she whispered, 'How long have you known?'

'It's four months since my last moonflow. I'll begin to show soon.'

'Ahmose knows?'

'Of course.' Senetnay seemed surprised at Nebet's implication. 'He was the first person I told, but I haven't told the boys yet. Baby has been very niggly of late. I think she has more teeth coming through. She hasn't been feeding properly, crying day and night, keeping the whole household awake, and Simut said only the other day that he hates his sister and doesn't want any more babies in the family.'

'You know he doesn't mean that. He's hardly more than a baby himself. He doesn't know what he's saying.'

'I know but I'd rather keep quiet about my pregnancy until Baby's settled. Once she's all sweetness again her brothers may take more kindly to the idea of another child.'

At last the red hangings had been stripped of all adornment. When the patched and darned fabric had been spread out in a single layer over the floor, the fading of the colour became startlingly obvious. Where the rosettes had protected the cloth from the bright sunshine there were circles of deeper colour, almost as bright as the original dye.

'At least we'll be able to see where the rosettes have to be sewn back,' Satra said.

'Thank you for all your work, ladies,' Nebet announced. 'I'll arrange for the cloth to be cleaned and then I'll have to call on you again. The first day of the Coming Forth festival is fast approaching and it's only with your dedication that I'll be able to complete the task on time.'

Nebet could hardly bear to watch the launderers at work but felt she had to be there to take responsibility for what happened to the god's drapes. Wiya stayed with her mother to give her moral support and, as they watched the wet cloth being slapped with wooden paddles, she held Nebet's hand. In an attempt to take her mind off the red-tinted water running away along the gutters beside the laundry's stone floor, Wiya asked Nebet what she had planned for the festival celebrations.

'Your father's determined to spend several days of the festival at home, so I want to do something special. I've told Tjeti that the yearling goat is to be slaughtered, and Amenmose has agreed to broach some of the wine we had from Montmose's cellar. We'll have a fine feast.'

'Won't that be rather extravagant?' Wiya asked. She was surprised that her mother, usually such a prudent housekeeper, was talking about making a considerable dent in the family's supplies.

'There are times, Wiya, when we need cheering up. We've had so much upheaval in the last few months, so much bad feeling, that I think the time has come to put all that behind us and look to the future. A really good party will make us all feel better.'

'I suppose we might have a family event to celebrate too,' Wiya said.

Nebet turned to look at her daughter, her face a picture of astonishment and pleasure. 'Are you telling me that you're going to have a baby?'

A fleeting look of pain crossed Wiya's face before she shrugged and said casually, 'No, I only meant that Satra might announce her intention to marry. That, surely, would be the greatest possible cause for celebration.'

Nebet's heart felt heavy with the emotional turmoil of hopes so quickly raised and just as suddenly frustrated. That Mutemwiya had so calmly brushed aside the suggestion that she might, at long last, be pregnant was almost as heartbreaking as the news that she was not.

When the hangings for the god's float were at last dry, Nebet was relieved to see that the leaching out of the dyes by washing had been balanced by the removal of a few layers of dirt and dust. The fabric was definitely paler than it had been before but its useful life had been extended for another year or more. However, the Chief Launderer of Ipet Esut had insisted that the hangings be spread out to dry indoors to prevent further fading in the sun, so the drying had taken longer than she had expected. When her group of needlewomen gathered to restore the hangings to their full glory, they all knew time was against them. Talk was muted and generally more serious as the women concentrated on their task.

Once again Nebet sat with Senetnay but this time she was determined to keep to neutral or uncontroversial topics of conversation. She asked, 'And how is the little one? Has she got over her teething troubles?'

'I think it may be something more than just her teeth,' Senetnay admitted. 'She is still very fractious and won't be comforted, even by her nurse. To tell you the truth, I'm getting a little concerned about her.'

'I always found a sip of honeyed water a soothing remedy.'

'I've tried that,' Senetnay said, with a tinge of desperation in her voice, 'but it's not enough. I may have to resort to a potion of lettuce sap.'

The white sap from lettuces was said to be at its strongest at this time of year, because the plant was sacred to the fertility god Min whose festival they were about to celebrate. Troughs planted with lettuces, whose tall, pointed shape was seen as symbolic of the god's erect member, were being prepared for offering at the Harvest Festival. At the propitious moment they would be cut and the sap, symbolizing the god's semen, would be allowed to drip on to the ground to renew the fertility of the soil. Lettuce sap was sought after by men wishing to enhance their sexual performance, but for children it was also a strong sedative.

'That's quite a drastic remedy for one so young,' Nebet advised. Then, not wanting to appear critical of her friend, she added, 'but you know best. Perhaps the fact that the child's trouble started at such a time should be seen as a guide to her treatment.'

'That's rather what I thought,' Senetnay said, relieved that her friend agreed with her. Having been reminded of the Harvest celebrations, she asked, 'Have you made any special plans for the festival?'

'Only a family gathering,' Nebet said, 'though I hope we'll be eating well. What about you?'

'Nothing in particular.' Senetnay smiled wryly. 'I don't know how long Ahmose will be able to take off work but I'm determined the boys will enjoy themselves, even if only for the first day of the holiday.'

'It's much the same with me,' Nebet said. 'Amenmose had hoped that the Tjaty would be back from the north long since but there's no news as to when he will return, unless Amenmose is keeping it a secret. So it looks as if we'll only have the opening day together for certain.'

'Why don't we combine our families in one big party?' Senetnay's face brightened with the idea. 'The more people around the jollier it will be for all of us, and if they're to have only one day at home we should give Ahmose and Amenmose a day to remember.'

Nebet was tempted by the idea but she knew she could not offer to host such a party at her house. By opening the reception room door on to the garden she could create a space that was just about big enough for the family to celebrate in comfort, but a larger group would require more seating space than she could provide. On the occasion of Montmose's funeral Wiya had arranged the meal for the mourners in the spacious court outside the north gate of the Place of Truth, according to the custom of the Village. Nebet had no such luxury in Waset.

'It's a lovely idea,' she said, 'but I just haven't the room.'

'Oh, I'm sorry,' Senetnay said. 'I never meant to invite myself to *your* party. No, I meant that *you* should come to *us*.'

The front court of Ahmose's house was more than twice as big as Nebet's little garden. Senetnay was very proud of her ornamental pond with its blue and white water lilies and its sycomore trees at each corner. The two reception rooms opened on to the garden through a shady porch built across the full width of the house. It was a very stylish setting for a festival party and Nebet was sorely tempted to accept.

'It's very kind of you but . . .' She hesitated. Was Senetnay offering to provide all the food and drink for both families or was she just providing the venue and expecting Nebetiunet to make all the other arrangements? Either way, that would put one friend under a heavy obligation to the other.

Senetnay understood Nebet's reticence in an instant and quickly reassured her, saying, 'Of course, you'll have started planning your food just as I have. What fun it would be to put it all together in one big feast. It'll be like a bigger version of our picnic at Opet. Please say you'll come. There's plenty of room for everyone. I believe I could even tolerate Satra and her gardener friend.'

How could she refuse? Nebet accepted gladly and for the remainder of the sewing session they discussed food, drink and garden furniture, and the practicalities of transporting the necessary goods from one house to the other.

The last of the gilded rosettes was sewn in place just a day and a half before the dawning of the Harvest Festival holiday. All that remained now was for the drapes to be hung round the god's float ready for the procession. Nebet had arranged special admittance into the Temple for Wiya so that she might help her mother with this last task. Nebet also had another reason for having her daughter there.

Min was portrayed as a man wearing the tall double-plumed crown of Amen and a shroud-like garment from which only his face, hands and erect penis emerged. The divine image of the god, about half the size of a living man, was made of wood with the crown and shroud covered in gold. The god's skin was coated with a shiny black bituminous paint in imitation of the rich black soil of Kemet, whose fertility was the gift of Min. The god was also the most powerful symbol of procreation and arousal. Many festival-goers would be hoping to touch the float to have some of Min's power rub off on them, but Nebet hoped to be able to ensure Wiya's chances of obtaining the god's favour by more direct means.

On the afternoon before the start of the Coming Forth of Min the float was brought from the Temple store and set down on the stone block in front of the god's shrine. The block was just tall enough for the priests to be able to walk with only a slight stoop under the carrying poles in order to take the float on their shoulders. When they lifted the float the priests would be all but hidden behind the red hangings, only their feet and the tops of their heads being visible to the crowds. However, before the drapes were replaced, making access to the float platform awkward, the statue was reverently removed from the shrine and set on the float ready to be carried in procession round the Temple walls the next morning. Nebet and Wiya were left alone to finish attaching the hangings to the poles while the guardians of the shrine sat outside the door, getting what rest they could in preparation for the long opening day of the festival.

There was something about the image of Min that was at once disturbing and reassuringly familiar. Of all the gods he was the only one who allowed his image to be revealed to the people. While other deities travelled outside their temples hidden away in the safety of their shrines, Min went out unveiled, beneath an uncurtained canopy, proudly displaying his massively engorged organ. The god was the patron of travellers and miners, of traders and quarrymen, as well as overseer of the harvest. But it was his blatant sexuality that set him apart from other deities. While the Goddess, Hathor, Mistress of Love, was revered by women and men alike, Min was powerfully and unequivocally male.

Though she had not given up hope that the Lady would eventually hear her prayers, Nebetiunet was casting around for other sources of help for her daughter. She could not entertain the thought that Mutemwiya might be barren but it had occurred to her that something might be wrong with the way in which Wiya and Ramose were trying to conceive a child. Wiya would never find fault with her husband and would take all the blame for her childless state on herself. Nebet thought that Min might be their last chance. His attributes, especially the most obvious, were created from the raw magic of the earth and the powers of the soil as harnessed by man. If only a little of that magic could be given to Wiya. If only a hint of Min's masculinity, so evident in his image, could be given to Ramose.

The moment arose so naturally that Nebet later saw it as divine intervention. Wiya was holding the cloth in place while her mother fastened it to one of the rings threaded over the pole. They had reached a point just in front of the divine statue and, as Wiya glanced up, the sunlight through one of the window grilles high in the wall cast the shadow of the god's phallus across her forehead. She blushed deeply, her cheeks turning almost the same red as the hangings, and fumbled the cloth in her embarrassment. Nebet looked up to see what had distracted her daughter and gasped. The sun was going down and the window was narrow. The shadow was already moving across Wiya's face.

Nebet said softly, 'It's a sign. Reach up and touch the god.'

Still blushing furiously, Wiya said, 'I can't, I dare not.'

'It's a sign,' Nebet repeated. 'You must follow your heart and the god's will. How much more clearly can he express his intention?'

Wiya slowly stretched her hand up towards the statue. She hesitated but Nebet urged her on and as the shadow fell across her mouth Wiya curled her fingers about the god's erection. She gulped at her temerity but as she was not struck down by the god's anger she grew bolder. She began to stroke the statue, caressing the god's penis with such tenderness that her mother had to look away. Then, suddenly overcome by the sacredness of what the god had permitted her to do, Wiya released her hold on the statue and fell to her knees, sobbing.

Nebet took her in her arms and murmured words of comfort and encouragement. She felt honoured to have witnessed this holy moment but she understood that no one else must ever know of it. It was a confidence accepted by mother and daughter as something not meant to be shared. Nevertheless, Nebet told herself, the god must have his reasons for revealing himself in that way. Now, surely, there would be a child.

The celebrations were declared to be satisfactory if not spectacular. Since the King had not travelled south for the Coming Forth of Min, the ritual had been led by his deputy, the First Servant of Amen, Nebwenenef. The High Priest had cut a sheaf of barley to mark the start of the harvest, although this was only a symbolic gesture since the harvest had been well under way since the previous month. Great piles of offerings had been presented before the god's image to secure his blessing, and the news of his acceptance of the first fruits was ceremonially dispatched to the four corners of Kemet by the release of doves. The rites over, the procession began and all the people of Waset, their numbers swollen by peasant farmers coming into the City from all around, began to jostle for position along the route of the god's progress. It was a noisy but good-natured crowd that sang and shouted the god along his way. It was a happy crowd that eventually dispersed back to individual homes, where the celebrations would continue long into the night and, in many cases, over several days.

Tia and the housemaids had spent most of the last two days helping Senetnay's servants prepare a real banquet, the centrepiece of which was the roasted goat supplied by Nebetiunet. The food was set out in the porch and the reception rooms, the wine jars in their racks were wrapped in damp cloths and draped with leaves to keep them cool, and servants stood by to pour drinks or offer trays of fruit and sweetmeats. The atmosphere was relaxed and pleasant and Senetnay, as her guests arrived, greeted them warmly, handing out garlands made of the flowers of the fields – poppies, cornflowers and daisies.

Nebet's family arrived in threes, each party welcomed as cheerfully as the next. Khay had come with Satra and Nedjemger, Pakhred with Mutemwiya and Ramose, and Mymy had had little trouble persuading Senmut to come with her and Abau when he heard that Ahmose was the host: the Chief Architect had a reputation for keeping an excellent cellar. Neferti, arriving with her parents, completed the family reunion.

As the sun set, torches were lit around the garden and the guests settled down to some serious eating and drinking. One of Tia's contributions to the feast provoked ribald laughter. She had moulded spicebread dough into cakes shaped like the god's phallus, and the married men made a great fuss of offering the breads to their wives to see which of the ladies could take the biggest bite. Nebet's was not the only red face that evening and she was grateful for the darkness that hid most of her blushes. Perfumed oil had been added to some of the lamps to scent the air and to help deter insects. A trio of musicians, a flautist, a lutanist and a harpist, played softly beside the pond. The party was a great success.

Nebet had not been able to keep track of how much Senmut was drinking. She was far more concerned about Amenmose, who appeared to be matching Ahmose cup for cup. Senetnay, too, was worried that her husband was setting a bad example to the two boys, who had been allowed to stay up for this occasion, so she did not notice that Senmut had appropriated a jar of Ahmose's date liquor. He was not a selfish lad and he was happy to share his prize with Abau. When the musicians stopped to take their own refreshment, a tuneless humming could be heard from under one of the trees.

Realizing that they were now the centre of attention, Abau and Senmut began to sing louder, adding words to their tune. It was, inevitably, an army marching song, praising the attributes of some of the well-known officers in the Division of Amen, starting with a squad leader and working up through the ranks to the Commander of the Host. The tune was barely recognizable, distorted as it was by drunken tongues, but the words of the song were familiar and so, at first, the audience laughed along with the ever more outrageous tales of the clumsy troop officer, the skinny platoon leader and the cross-eyed standard bearer.

Then Senmut launched into a verse which might have been his own composition but which was certainly new to his listeners. It was in praise of the gallant charioteer and it was quickly apparent to Nebet that her son was singing about Ameneminet. The name was not mentioned but she could tell from Ahmose's stony expression, and the anguished look on Senetnay's face, that they knew who was meant long before Senmut launched into the chorus.

'Oh, Ameneminet! Great Ameneminet!
Bold Ameneminet! Most Favoured Ameneminet!'

There was a loud crash of breaking pottery as Ahmose threw a beer jar at the garden wall. In the silence that followed he growled, 'I'll not have that name mentioned in my house.'

Senmut, not knowing of his host's feelings about the King's Charioteer, and being well beyond simple intoxication, staggered to his hero's defence. 'He's a great man, great man. Knows all 'bout horses, knows all 'bout ev'rything. Here's to the great Ameneminet!' He raised his cup to his lips but most of its contents dribbled down his chin.

Amenmose quickly took his son by the arm and tried to lead him out of the garden but Senmut, with the belligerence of the truly drunk, shrugged him off and started to shout, *'Oh, Ameneminet! Great Ameneminet!'* until Ahmose strode up to him and with one punch knocked him to the ground.

Later Nebet could not remember what she had said to Senetnay by way of apology. All she could think of was removing Senmut and Abau, who had fallen asleep against the tree trunk, as quickly as possible. Mymy was crying tears of mortification at her husband's part in the disturbance and Nebet knew that such strong emotions were not good for the baby.

Amenmose had spoken a few words to Ahmose and whatever he had said had cooled the architect's anger. Nebet's husband was wise enough not to blame Ahmose for his attack on Senmut. The boy's behaviour had been unforgivable and Amenmose accepted a father's responsibility for his son's actions. Nebet worried that Senmut had been hurt but she knew, in her heart, that he had deserved the blow. When his head was cleared of drink and he had recovered his senses he would receive further punishment, a tongue-lashing at the very least, from his father. A joyous occasion had turned sour and Nebet was not sure that her friendship with Senetnay would survive this calamity.

CHAPTER TEN

Second Month
of Summer

ONCE THE HARVEST WAS OVER, MANY OF THE YOUNG MEN RELEASED FROM
their work on the land were called up for military service. The arrival of
the army officers with Ameneminet had signalled the start of the muster
in preparation for the King's second campaign into Retjenu. The
previous summer, in Year Four, His Majesty had triumphantly exerted his
authority over the coastal ports of Retjenu, from which the great timber
ships sailed for Kemet laden with cedar and pine. Further inland the
army's progress had been halted just short of the famous fortified city of
Kadesh.

The capture of this place had been the King's first personal military
victory, in the reign of his father, the god Menmaatra-Sethy. That Kadesh
had soon after reverted to the control of the kingdom of Hatti, and that
Menmaatra-Sethy had accepted the loss of the strategic fortress, had
always rankled with the young Crown Prince, who had sworn to regain
Kadesh for Kemet as soon as he was able. This year the King was intent
on crushing, once and for all, the power of the one whom he saw as
Kemet's most dangerous foe and his personal adversary, the King of Hatti.

Ameneminet had already left for the north with his chariot division
and the troops levied from Waset. Abau, although not a soldier, was
attached to the support staff of the Division of Amen and had also gone
north with the Waset contingent. Mymy was putting on a brave face over

her husband's absence at this critical time in her pregnancy. It was not certain whether Abau would have to go with the army into Retjenu or whether he would remain in Per-Ramesse or Mennefer, once the troops departed. Either way, he was likely to be away from Waset when his child was born. Before Abau left the City Nebet had assured him that Mymy would be staying in her parents' house until he returned, but his wife had proved more stubborn than Nebet had thought possible.

'I'll be quite all right in my own home,' Mymy said. 'There are still many other army wives living in and around the barracks. I won't be alone.'

Her tone was so like Satra's at that moment that Nebet hardly dared argue. She said, 'Well, of course you won't be alone. I'll visit every day and–'

'There's no need for that, Muti,' Mymy said quickly, 'there's no need to fuss so.'

Nebet thought she saw a guilty look flash across her daughter's face but she could not imagine what Mymy had to feel guilty about. She had always been the most independent and strong-willed of Nebet's daughters. Perhaps, Nebet thought, having been so self-sufficient all her life, she does not want to admit that she is scared.

'My dear girl, I'm not fussing,' she said patiently. 'I'm only concerned that you should be with your family at such a time, and I did promise Abau.'

'There's at least a month to go before the baby's due,' Mymy said, 'and I'm feeling fine, so I don't see why I should move when I'm perfectly comfortable where I am.'

Nebet gave up the fight. When the birth was imminent Mymy might change her tune. If she did, her mother would be there for her.

Amenmose had received a long letter from Paser explaining what had kept him away from Waset and why his absence was to be prolonged still further, probably until the end of the year. The King had asked Paser to accompany the army into Retjenu. He was to be His Majesty's personal adviser, travelling in the royal party and sharing the royal quarters.

'It's unheard of,' Nebet said when Amenmose told her of the letter. 'The Tjaty does *not* go to war. Paser is *not* a soldier; he never was. I don't know what military advice His Majesty thinks he'll be able to give.'

'Oh, I don't suppose for a moment he's been taken along as a tactician,' Amenmose said. 'He's been formally attached to the royal household as guardian of the King's Sons. He'll be baby-sitting.'

Nebet was horrified at the notion of young boys, whether royal or commoner, going to war. 'Surely the King isn't taking his sons with him? What caring father would put his children in such danger?'

'Be careful, Nebetiunet,' Amenmose warned. 'You have no right to criticize the living God.'

She bowed her head at his admonition. He was right, of course. The King was the Guardian of Maat, upholder of justice, truth and order. To suggest that he was unwise or uncaring was, at the very least, a gross impertinence and, at the most, treason. However, she still had in her mind the picture of the Royal Sons as they had looked at Opet, proudly riding their chariots in the parade. By her reckoning the King's Eldest Son, Amenhirkhopshef, firstborn of the Great Royal Wife, Nefertari, was just ten years old, but then His Majesty had been only half that age when he had accompanied his own father, Menmaatra-Sethy, on a campaign into Nubia. The Royal Family's lifestyle might be opulent and their customs different from those of ordinary people, but their obligations and duties were harsh.

Such terrible tales were told about the conditions of army life, especially for soldiers campaigning in foreign lands, that Nebet wondered what had been the reaction of the King's Wife to the announcement that her sons were to go to war. Despite their privileged status there was a very real possibility that she would never see them again. It was probably a great comfort to Nefertari to know Paser was there to look after the boys, though he would not relish the responsibility.

Nebetiunet was anxious about Senetnay. She had not tried to see her since the party, knowing that an uninvited visit would not be welcomed by Ahmose. She had sent a message of apology, including the wish that they might remain friends, but Senetnay had not replied. Now Nebet had heard from Meryt, who had met Senetnay's maid in the market place, that her friend had other things to worry about. Baby was very sick. The little girl, whose real name Nebet could not remember hearing, had recovered from her teething troubles but now she had fallen victim to one of the many curses of infancy.

'Kiya said the little one has a fever. She doesn't eat, she hardly drinks, she suffers from loose bowels, and she screams day and night.' Meryt reported.

Nebet knew how serious that was. Her sister Nubnefert had lost two babies to summer fevers. In the hot months a small child suffering such ailments was unlikely to survive for more than a few days, and it was unusually hot for the time of year. Nebet also worried about the unborn baby. It was probable that Senetnay was not sleeping and was eating barely enough to keep herself going, let alone provide for the child growing in her belly. What a tragedy it would be if she lost two children at once.

The next afternoon there was a frantic knocking at the garden gate and a tearful Kiya was admitted. She had spent her day off with her own family only to find, when she returned to her duties, that her mistress had shut herself away in her bedroom and the other servants were unable to coax her out. The house was eerily quiet and Kiya had realized at once the significance of that silence. Baby was not crying. Without waiting to find out exactly what had happened, but fearing the worst, all Kiya could think to do was to fetch Nebetiunet.

'Please come, Lady,' Kiya pleaded. 'My mistress won't listen to any of us and the master's still away. I fear for Baby. I fear she's already dead.'

To Nebet's surprise Satra offered to accompany her. 'I can deal with the servants while you talk to your friend. If the baby's dead she'll need comfort, and the last thing she'll want to think about is household management.'

Nebet agreed. She had never expected to be grateful for Satra's company, but on this sad occasion she was glad to be able to rely on her sister's strength and authority.

The baby was dead and had been for some time. They found Senetnay sitting on the floor, rocking back and forth, cradling the pathetic, emaciated body in her arms. Her tears had given way to a terrible silence. The servants were huddled in the kitchen. Not one of them had been brave enough to approach their grieving mistress, even when it was apparent that the baby had died during the night. As Nebet fell to her knees beside Senetnay, Satra took control.

She addressed herself to Kiya, the only person in the house to have shown the least bit of sense. 'We'll need something to wrap the child in, a cloth, a sheet or an old garment of some sort. Can you find something like that?'

'Yes, Lady,' Kiya said, relieved to have someone giving orders.

'And someone will have to take a message to your master. He should be here. His wife needs him.'

'I'll send one of the men,' Kiya said, knowing that several of the servants would volunteer for this sad task, if only to get out of the house.

Ahmose had returned to his work at the Mansion the day after the party and had been back only once or twice since. The sun was already descending. It would set before Ahmose received the news of his daughter's death. He would probably wait until first light before crossing the River. Baby would have to be buried before then.

Kiya first thought to take a coverlet from the baby's crib but she found the sheets soiled with vomit and excrement. They would be burned. Instead she found a shawl which had been used by the baby's nurse as a sling in which to carry her charge. The nurse herself had fled the house. Her purpose in being there had ceased as soon as the little girl died.

Nebet murmured wordless comfort as she gently released Senetnay's hold on the tiny body. Without taking her eyes from her friend's face she handed the baby to Satra, who wrapped it quickly in the shawl and carried it out of the room. Nebet pulled Senetnay into her arms.

Satra bullied a kitchen maid into fetching a bowl of water and rags so that she could wash the body. When they saw what she was preparing to do, other servants began to offer their help. The doorman took the kitchen boy into the garden to dig a grave beneath one of the sycomore trees. The cook found a reed basket which she lined with more rags. The smooth bone that the baby had used as a teether was placed in the basket by one of the housemaids. Kiya added the little amulet, in the shape of the bandy-legged dwarf god Bes, that had hung about the child's neck, and said, 'May Bes grant that she won't have nightmares now.'

When the body had been cleaned, Kiya anointed it with a little of her mistress's lotus-flower perfume, then wrapped it in the linen shawl again and placed it in the basket. Before drawing the linen folds over the baby's face Satra carried the basket to Senetnay, who was sitting with Nebetiunet against the wall under the garden porch.

Little Simut, who had been hiding all this time in the garden, had crept up and squeezed his way in between the two women. Frightened and not understanding what had happened, he needed to be close to his mother, but she was hardly aware of his presence. Nebet felt her hand clutched tightly as Senetnay leaned over to kiss her child for the last time. Then she nodded her resignation, giving Satra silent permission to bury the babe.

The cook placed the lid on the basket and, escorted by the full complement of servants, Satra took the makeshift coffin into the garden. There was no ceremony, no ritual. Compared with Montmose's funeral, this burial was nothing. But it would have been cruel to separate the little soul from her parents, so the child was laid to rest in the only place she had ever known. When Senetnay died, the baby's body would be exhumed to be reburied alongside her mother.

The setting sun threw long shadows across the garden as the servants resumed their routine tasks. It was comforting for all to have something to do. At Nebet's signal Kiya took Simut by the hand and led him away to find food and drink. The little boy had already missed one meal that day, probably two. His belly was growling with emptiness. He could not be expected to understand why his mother was ignoring him. His most immediate concern was his hunger. His mother was unhappy, he knew that, but, as she had told him so often before, everything would be all right tomorrow.

Ahmose arrived shortly after dawn the next day. Nebet had stayed the night with Senetnay while Satra had taken little Simut home with her, promising that Neferti would find him some honeycomb. It was well into the darkest part of the night before Senetnay had finally cried herself to sleep. Nebet told Ahmose what had happened as succinctly as possible and then withdrew discreetly to the garden. A little later he came to find her and sat down beside her on the bench in the porch.

'I must thank you, Nebetiunet, for being a true friend to my wife, and to me,' he said, 'even though I hardly deserve such a friend after the way I treated your son.' Ahmose's cheeks were still damp from his tearful reunion with Senetnay. Nebet had never seen him so low in spirit. She felt she had to reassure him.

'If you hadn't punished Senmut for his thoughtless, discourteous behaviour, his father would have done so later. But that's all forgotten now. I missed Senetnay's company over the last few days. I was glad to be able to help when she really needed a friend and I'm only sorry, so sorry, that it should be such a great sadness that has brought us together again.'

Ahmose shuddered with suppressed emotion and then pointed towards the garden. 'Is that where she's buried?'

'Yes, beneath the tree there. Satra saw to it that the body was clean, and the little one looked very peaceful. The Lady will care for her now.'

'You will give my thanks also to Lady Satra?'

'Of course.'

There was a long silence during which Ahmose gazed across the garden towards his daughter's grave, his eyes brimming with more tears. Then suddenly he stood up, his hands clenching and unclenching in helpless rage. He turned to Nebet and said, 'I should have been here, and then my daughter would still be alive.'

'No, Ahmose,' she said. 'There was really nothing you could have done. I've seen this before. The summer fever is cruel but quick. Your being here wouldn't have stopped it.'

'But I'd have been here if it hadn't been for that bastard Ameneminet. How long will my family have to suffer because of him?'

Nebet was bemused. Senetnay had told her about Ahmose's dislike of the King's Charioteer but she had never realized that he harboured such a deep and irrational hatred for Ameneminet. What possible link could there be between Ameneminet and the death of an infant?

Ahmose was pacing up and down the porch, punching his right fist again and again into the palm of his left hand. He was muttering. His words were largely a string of incoherent complaints, laced with invective, but Nebet heard enough of what he was saying to understand something of his thoughts. He had been working so hard that he was carrying an enormous burden of guilt about neglecting his family.

Unable to carry the burden alone, he had, in his own mind, laid a large part of his guilt on Ameneminet. The Charioteer, oblivious to this antipathy, had only reinforced Ahmose's opinion of him when he had arrived in Waset, full of his own importance and basking in the King's favour. He had gone almost as quickly as he had arrived, totally unaware of how his brief presence in the City had fuelled Ahmose's hatred.

What was worse, Ameneminet had taken with him a large band of recruits for the army, including several of Ahmose's most promising apprentices from the Works Department at the Mansion. This had left Ahmose short-staffed and even more overworked, and his visits home had become fewer. Senetnay had never complained. She had never blamed either her husband or Ameneminet. She had simply accepted that this was the way things were. Ahmose had not his wife's placid temperament. He needed someone to blame and Ameneminet was convenient.

Before she could think of words to comfort him they were startled by a piercing cry from the room above. Ahmose ran into the house and bounded up the narrow stairway, with Nebet following as quickly as her narrow-hemmed dress allowed. They found Senetnay doubled over with pain and it was all that Kiya could do to support her. Ahmose began to weep helplessly as he fell to his knees to take his wife in his arms. Nebet saw the blood on the skirt of her friend's robe and knew at once that the tragedy was not yet over. But, though the unborn child was bound to be lost, Senetnay might still be saved.

Nebet took charge of the situation. 'Get her on to the bed, Ahmose. Do it now. She must lie down. Stay with them, Kiya. I'll send one of the servants for a physician and then I'll be back.'

'Don't go, Nebet,' Senetnay moaned. 'I'm so frightened.'

'I know, dear one, but Ahmose is here, and Kiya.' Nebet turned to the maid, who seemed a little more aware than Ahmose. 'Try to keep her quiet. She must keep as calm and as still as possible, or her life will go along with the baby's.'

Senetnay was lucky. The goddess watching over her must have thought she had already suffered more than enough. In a few days she was walking around and, though very pale, appeared to be recovering well. Nebet was relieved to see that her friend's health and strength had apparently survived the double blow.

However, Senetnay's misfortune had set Nebet's resolve as far as her own daughter was concerned. She could not bear to think of the girl living on her own at such a time. Crowded as the house would be, she knew it was her duty to bring Mymy back home, by force if necessary. She discussed the matter with Satra.

'The problem is, where do we put everyone? The women's room is already too small for you and Neferti. If Mymy does come back it means Senmut will have to come, too, because I'll not hear of him fending for himself in Mymy's house. That fills up the boys' room and I can hardly put her up on the roof.'

'She'd never climb the ladder,' Satra said with a twinkle in her eye.

Nebet had become familiar, over the years, with the way in which Satra's temper waxed and waned like the moon. One day she would be sharp and shrill, snapping the head off anyone who said as much as 'Good morning' to her. The next she would be as sweet as honey and as mild-mannered as a milch-goat. She had been argumentative, demanding and domineering all her life and yet, just occasionally, she could be reasonable, helpful and considerate. Nebet now looked on Amenmose's sister as someone she could rely on, as she had done when Senetnay was in need. And Satra seemed to have developed a sense of humour. What a wonderful thing love was!

They were no nearer to solving the problem of where to put Mymy until Satra said, 'Of course, Khay will be leaving home soon.'

Nebet had been trying not to think about letting go of her youngest child. Khaemwase had formally approached his father for permission to go with Nedjemger as his personal apprentice when the Chief Gardener moved into his new quarters at the Mansion. It was a great honour for such a young boy and an opportunity that he could not be denied. Amenmose had readily agreed and Nebet knew his decision was right, but that knowledge was not enough to comfort her. Though her baby had grown up, she could not help worrying about who would look after him, whether he would eat properly, whether the other gardeners would tease him because of his short-sightedness. To Khay it was all a great adventure. He had a life of his own to lead which he was eager to start.

Nebet found his eagerness hurtful. He did not need her any more. He could not wait to get away from her. She knew such thoughts were as ridiculous as Ahmose's unreasoning hatred of Ameneminet, but she was still Khay's mother, and mothers were expected to care.

'He's not gone yet,' she snapped.

'No,' Satra said reasonably, 'but until he does go, surely he wouldn't mind giving up his bed to his sister? It's warm enough now for him to sleep on the roof.'

'That's hardly a solution,' Nebet said. 'There's still Young Amenmose and, as I said, I'll have to find room for Senmut.'

'Pakhred is only home from school for a couple of nights at a time as it is. Could you not ask him to stay in the students' dormitory until after Mymy's child is born?'

'I suppose so,' Nebet said, unwilling to admit that Satra's suggestion was a sensible one, 'but what about Senmut?'

'The roof, of course,' Satra laughed. 'It's what he would expect anyway.'

Still unwilling to accept the inevitable, Nebet found one last objection. 'But what shall we do when the weather turns colder?'

'Oh really, Nebetiunet, you're just finding excuses.' Satra's words were severe but her tone was playful, teasing, without the cruel edge that Nebet was accustomed to. 'If you're really that worried about Mymy, you'll find a way. And remember, I shan't be living here for much longer, either.' With that enigmatic statement, Satra left the room.

Nebet was taken aback by this throw-away comment. What could Satra have meant? The only reason Nebet could imagine for Satra moving out was that at long last she and Nedjemger had resolved their difficulties and were planning marriage in the near future. Was it possible? Were her prayers about to be answered? Still, whatever Satra's plans might be, Mymy was her immediate concern. She made up her mind to visit her daughter that afternoon and not to return home without her.

Mymy was still blooming. No one could predict how pregnancy would affect a woman and Mymy was blissfully unaware of how lucky she was to have avoided all the many problems and dangers that often went with her condition. However, when she opened her door to her mother she flushed and seemed reluctant to let Nebet in.

Nebetiunet was not in the mood for argument. 'I've come to take you home. Call Senmut and he can help us pack your things. You're both coming back with me today.'

Mymy hesitated, still holding the door and barring her mother's entry.

Nebet could tell she was close to panic. 'What is it, child? Have the pains started already?'

'No, Muti, no,' Mymy whimpered.

'Then let me in, child. What's the matter with you?'

'Oh Muti, Senmut's gone.'

Nebet felt her face drain of colour. She had suspected something was wrong days ago when she suggested daily visits to check on Mymy's progress, but all her thoughts then had been for her daughter. She had not even considered her son.

'What do you mean, "gone"?' she asked.

'You'd better come in,' Mymy relented, 'and I'll tell you everything.'

Senmut, it seemed, had been more deeply affected by his humiliation at Ahmose's hands than anyone had realized. Having already been driven from his own home, he felt he was no longer welcome anywhere. These feelings of rejection lowered his self-esteem to such a depth that he had been ready to clutch at any offer of friendship from whatever quarter it might arise. The offer had come from an army recruiting officer. Senmut had enlisted with the Division of Amen and had sailed for the north with Ameneminet.

'I didn't know,' Mymy wailed. 'One moment he was here and the next he was gone. I didn't make the connection until Abau asked where Senmut was. When we realized what he must have done, Abau made inquiries but then he had to leave for Mennefer himself so we never found out exactly what had happened. Abau promised to send word as soon as he discovered where Senmut was. He said he'd find him and put him on a boat back to Waset. He's probably on his way home now.'

Nebet tried to believe that but she knew her son's character better than Mymy. Senmut was stubborn. A notion or whim fixed in his heart would be seen through to the bitter end. He would not give up, whatever the consequences. Nebet feared that her son was now well beyond her reach and beyond her help, but he would never be beyond her love or her thoughts. If only she could be sure he knew that.

'We'll just have to hope Abau was able to talk some sense into him,' she said. 'Meanwhile I'll take no argument from you, young lady. You're coming home with me, now.'

When Abau's letter arrived, it was short and to the point. He had found Senmut, who, typically, had refused to consider a return to Waset. He said he had joined the army of his own free will and he would not go back on that decision. Abau had used every tiny bit of influence he had to have the lad transferred from the infantry to the chariotry, and had promised to keep him as much as was possible out of harm's way. He could not persuade him to join the commissariat staff but had found him a post as groom to a very well respected chariot officer. Abau tried to reassure the boy's family that Senmut was unlikely to come close to real fighting.

The letter was dated the first of the month. Because Abau had had to rely on finding a southbound civilian vessel with an amenable captain to take the letter, it had taken fifteen days to reach Waset. The cargo boat had been overtaken by a royal courier ship bearing a letter to Amenmose from Paser. The Tjaty's letter had been written on the eve of the army's departure from Mennefer and was dated the eighth day. By the time Abau's news reached Nebet and Amenmose, their son had crossed the border with the army and was on his way to Kadesh.

When Mymy heard the news she became mildly hysterical. She had been hiding the truth from her parents for so long that it was a great relief to let loose her fears and feelings. Her greatest worry was naturally for Abau. At the time of their marriage she had accepted the fact that he was under army orders but also she had convinced herself that, since he was not a soldier as such, Abau would never have to go to war. The fact that he had not been called upon to go with the army on any of the King's previous campaigns had lulled her into believing he would never have to go.

Abau had delayed telling his wife of his call-up until the last possible moment, by which time they had already discovered Senmut's absence. The news that her husband would be away from home and even beyond the borders of Kemet at the time of his child's birth would have sent most women hysterical. Mymy was made of sterner stuff. She knew it was his duty to go with the Division of Amen. She helped him pack. She urged him to be careful and the last thing she said to him on the quayside before he boarded the transport vessel was, 'Give my brother a good slap from me.'

Now her brave façade had crumbled. Now she had someone else with whom to share the worry, she could afford a show of emotion. When the crying fit had passed she felt much better. Being back in her childhood home with all her loved ones around her, she fell easily into the old family routine. Eating Tia's cooking, giggling and gossiping with Neferti and Meryt and, most of all, sharing quiet times with her mother, Mymy became reconciled to her situation.

There had, of course, been changes to the household since Mymy's marriage. The most obvious difference was Satra's presence, and Mymy was pleasantly surprised at how well her father's sister received her back into the home. She had expected to find the same embittered, vinegar-tongued woman she had both pitied and despised before. To see Satra and her mother talking together like friends, if not sisters, was a revelation.

Though the population of Waset had been terribly depleted by the departure of the army, life had to go on as normally as possible. The full moon of the month heralded the second most important of the festivals of Amen-Ra, the Beautiful Feast of the Valley. Since the King himself would not be present, the festival would be a rather subdued affair, without the elaborate pageantry that was expected of a royal occasion. However, the Feast of the Valley was unique to Waset, and the people of the City, especially the villagers of the Place of Truth, would not be deprived of their chance to celebrate. The High Priest, Nebwenenef, had announced a reduced programme of events to be conducted over several days. The people would not let the reduction in the official celebrations spoil their fun, and many plans were being laid for family reunions, lavish entertainment and vast quantities of food.

Nebet, too, was determined not to let her worries about Senmut and Abau dampen the family's enthusiasm for the festival. Wiya was involved in the planning of the very special party held at the Place of Truth, and she and Ramose had invited the whole family to join them and their new friends after the usual gatherings at the family tombs. Having paid their respects to the dead and shared food with them, they would return to the Village to share an even grander meal with the living. Amen's Valley Feast was a time for family.

At the weaving workshops the first of the new season's flax was being processed. The stench of the retting ponds hung over everything. The youngest stems produced the finest, whitest fibres, which would make the softest, sheerest linen, but it was unlikely that any cloth could be made from the latest harvest in time for the festival. As the King's official gift to Amen-Ra, Mut and the other gods of Waset, Djehutiemheb had been instructed to have new gauzy curtains made for the shrines that were to be carried in the procession.

The giving of gifts was an important part of the Beautiful Festival of the Valley and Nebet regretted that, with so many other matters occupying her thoughts, she had had no time to think about, far less choose, gifts for her family. As she helped Djehuti find the curtain fabric from the temple stores, she found herself imagining what wonderful clothes she could make from the different types of linen that were all around her, stacked on the shelves and packed in boxes and baskets. Her eye lighted on a bale of soft, closely woven cloth which would be ideal for a new tunic for Amenmose to wear under his festival gown in the cooler weather and for simple day dresses for Neferti and Mymy. Beneath it was a length of unbleached fabric which would make smart but serviceable kilts for Pakhred and Khay. The same linen that she selected for the shrine curtains would make beautiful draped over-gowns for Wiya and Satra.

'Dreaming, Nebetiunet?' Djehuti asked.

'I'm sorry,' she said. 'Did you say something?'

'I asked if you were dreaming,' he said kindly. 'Your thoughts were obviously very far away. Perhaps you were thinking about your son in the army.'

'No, surprisingly, I wasn't,' she said, with a small pang of guilt when she realized the truth of this statement. She had not even considered what garment she might make for her absent son. 'I was thinking about making festival gifts but it was only dreaming. There's no time to make anything before the full moon.'

'But you could give the cloth as a gift with the promise of making it up when you have more time,' Djehuti suggested.

'I could,' Nebet laughed wryly, 'if I could afford it.'

'I think I might be able to help you there.' Djehuti smiled in a way Nebet had come to recognize as conspiratorial and waved his hands around, indicating the huge stock of linen in the divine storeroom.

'You're not suggesting that I steal from the gods?' she said, horrified at the very thought.

'No, no,' Djehuti said hurriedly. 'I only meant that you're entitled to choose your own festival gift from the god and, if you were to choose to take your gift in linen, you could then do what you liked with it.'

Nebet considered his offer. In past years she had accepted mere token gifts in recognition of her service to Amen-Ra and his consort Mut, sometimes in the form of food or wine from the divine offering tables.

Gifts of linen were traditionally handed out to public and Temple servants as a mark of their status, but Nebet had rarely taken all she was entitled to. She had been employed at the Temple all her married life, first on a full-time basis and then part-time as her family's needs took priority. She had risen from a lowly winder of thread to an accomplished spinner and weaver, and eventually a talented seamstress. The young female apprentices looked up to her and respected her skills. They admired her as a teacher and a role model. She was never one to criticize unfairly and was ready to give praise when praise was due. Djehutiemheb would be the first to admit, though not necessarily in Nebet's hearing, that he could not do without her. Perhaps it was time to take a more appropriate reward for all her work.

'What *are* you suggesting, then?' she asked.

'Tell me first what it was you were dreaming of and we'll see if we can't make a few dreams come true.' Djehuti was almost giggling with his own cleverness.

She had nothing to lose. Djehuti could only say 'No' and she would be no worse off than before. As she listed the garments she had envisaged the Master Weaver nodded thoughtfully.

'And can you see any fabric that might suit your needs?' he asked.

'Here?' she asked, surprised at his casual acceptance of what was quite an expensive wish list.

'Of course,' he said. 'I have no authority over any other store.'

Emboldened by his businesslike attitude, she indicated the folds of cloth that had caught her eye.

'You can always tell the best stuff at a glance, that's one of your many talents,' Djehuti said, patting her arm in his over-familiar way. 'Hmm, let me see.'

He studied the wooden dockets attached to the bales of cloth. Each label gave the date of manufacture of the linen, a statement of its quality, and the length and width of the piece in cubits.

'I see no problem in your having the close-weaves,' he said in a more professional tone, 'but there's only just enough of the sheer to make the curtains. What about this?'

He pointed out another length of cloth, not quite as finely woven as the first, but still of high quality and thin enough to drape attractively. Nebet could hardly believe that she was being offered such riches from the god's own storehouse.

'Oh, really, I couldn't,' she stuttered.

'Why not?' Djehuti said sternly. 'It's no more than is due to you after all this time. I insist, and I shall see to it that you have enough linen to make a gown for yourself as well.'

Overcome with his generosity she took his hand and kissed it. 'You're a good man, Djehutiemheb.'

The Master Weaver accepted her compliment as a matter of fact. Always seeing the best in people himself, he believed that everyone saw nothing but the good in him. With only a little false modesty he said, 'The gift is the god's, Nebetiunet. He put it into my mind to reward you this way. Take the linen and welcome. Amen is pleased with you.'

Nebet and her family, including Nedjemger, went across the River on the day before the start of the festival. Amenmose had arranged to meet them with Sendji and two donkeys, one to carry the party goods and the other for Mymy to ride. To Nebet the Place of Truth did not seem so far this time as she walked arm in arm with her husband amid the happy chattering and laughter of young people.

Mutemwiya and Ramose were waiting at the north gate to welcome them.

'I'm so glad you could all come,' Wiya said as she kissed each of her family in turn. 'Kanefert has kindly offered to find room for Satra and Master Nedjemger. I thought the boys could go up on the roof . . .'

Khay groaned and Pakhred pouted, both with good humour. They felt they were expected to make a small protest about their accommodation. However, they were used to sleeping in the open air, especially at this time of year, and the rooftops of the Place of Truth were much more interesting than the roof at home.

The houses were built in two blocks with only a narrow street between them. The rooftops were effectively a series of interconnecting courtyards, each divided from its neighbour by a low brick wall or woven reed fence. On the roofs the Villagers had their storage shelters and work huts, drying racks and even the occasional loom. Some children and servants slept under matting canopies on the roof all the year round. There was a constant movement of people at roof level, where the linked courts had become the main thoroughfare of the Village.

Nebet found this aspect of Wiya's new life difficult to accept. She had always valued privacy and had acknowledged her children's rights to be alone whenever and wherever possible, even though, in a large family, this was not always achievable. In the Place of Truth everyone knew everyone else's business. They lived, literally in some cases, right on top of each other. There was no escape from neighbours, and the roof was the last rather than the first place where solitude might be found. But it was festival time and everyone was prepared to forgo comfort for the conviviality of the gathering.

'Oh, you two haven't changed,' Wiya said, wagging a finger at her brothers. 'As I was saying, Father and Muti will stay with us, of course. That only leaves Neferti and Mymy–'

'Mymy must stay with us,' Nebet interrupted.

'Don't fuss, Muti,' Mymy said. On the journey she had complained that the donkey's uneven gait caused her some discomfort and she had walked the last part along the desert path. She was somewhat red in the face and stood pressing both hands into the small of her back to stretch out the aching stiffness. 'I'll be fine as soon as I can find a comfortable place to sit in the shade. I don't mind where I sleep.'

Wiya gave her sister an odd look, part concern and part envy, and said, 'I have two suggestions. Kaha's wife, Tuy, has offered two beds, or rather one folding bed and a pallet, if you think that will do.'

'Of course it will,' Mymy said.

'And I'll be right next to you if you need anything,' Neferti said, quickly forestalling her mother's objections. Wiya was grateful that her second suggestion had not been needed, because finding room for her sisters in her own home would have been uncomfortable for everyone, even for two or three days.

Nebet reluctantly agreed to the arrangements. 'I suppose Tuy is a close neighbour so Mymy won't be far away.'

Amenmose and Ramose began to laugh and Wiya, smiling broadly, said, 'Oh, Muti, you are funny. Everyone in the Place of Truth is my close neighbour.'

There was nothing else to settle. After the evening meal, which was a modest affair as all were saving their appetites for the feast the following evening, the family said their good nights and dispersed to their various beds.

On the opening day of the Valley Festival, the gods of Waset embarked on their sacred barges to be towed across the River. On the West Bank the divine procession led the gods on a tour of inspection of the mansion temples of the deceased kings and their tombs. The latter part of the procession took the gods beyond the public gaze into the Great Place, the hidden valley where for many generations the Kings of the Two Lands had chosen to excavate their final resting places.

Paser had told Nebetiunet something about the Great Place, recounting his experience of attending the last rites of the King's father, the god Menmaatra-Sethy. Now Paser's appointee, Ramose, was supervising the excavation of the King's own tomb and others for members of the Royal Family. All current enterprises would be subject to the scrutiny of Amen-Ra, Mut and their adopted children, the moon-god Khonsu and Montju, god of war. If the gods were satisfied with what they saw, the efforts of the Workmen of the Place of Truth would be reported back to the Tjaty, who would in turn report to the King. Of course, with both Paser and His Majesty out of the country, the reports would not be delivered for some while. But since no one could remember an occasion when the gods had been dissatisfied, it was assumed that the works in hand would pass inspection and everyone was planning to celebrate anyway.

Ramose was up and out of the house before dawn. He and the Foremen of the Gangs, the two senior workmen in the Place of Truth, had to attend the gods' inspection of the Great Place. This was the first time Ramose had officiated at the Valley Festival as Scribe of the Tomb, and as the Tjaty's chosen representative he felt his responsibility keenly.

The family had decided that the best place to see the procession was at the end of the causeway to the Mansion of Maatkara-Hatshepsut. After paying a courtesy visit to the temple there the gods would leave the ceremonial way to be carried up and over the cliffs and down into the sacred valley beyond. This place was too far from Waset to become overcrowded with sightseers, and it was convenient for the tombs where the family would be paying their respects and sharing a midday meal. As the procession came into view, the sunlight glittering off the gilded shrines, Nebet was pleased to see how well the linen curtains looked. The morning breeze made them flutter delicately, almost as if moved by the breath of the gods. When the priests and temple acolytes started to climb the steep cliff path, she and almost every other spectator offered up a silent prayer for the safe journey and return of the gods.

After the solemnity of Montmose's funeral the family gathering at his tomb for the Valley celebrations was a much happier affair. They were soon joined by other families, from both sides of the River as well as from the Place of Truth, and along the whole length of the cliffs picnics were shared. In the hottest part of the day some of the more adventurous children went exploring the semi-derelict mansion temple. The innermost chambers of the temple which had housed the shrines of the deified Maatkara-Hatshepsut and her fellow-gods were still sealed securely with bronze-clad doors but many of the small side rooms were already choked with sand and wind-blown debris. The open colonnades on either side of the ramps leading from terrace to terrace were easily accessible and offered a little welcome shade. They were also vividly decorated and Pakhred in particular wanted to study the scenes his teachers had described to him in such glowing terms. When a glint of gold from the cliff-top announced the return of the sacred procession, and parents started to gather in their children, Pakhred was among the last to leave the colonnades.

That evening, in the orange light of flaring torches and under the silvery luminescence of the full moon, the Villagers and their guests celebrated with a huge communal feast set out in the court before the north gate. Professional singers and dancers with their accompanying musicians had been sent from Waset, their fees paid by the Tjaty's office as part of the King's official festival gift to the Workmen. With a little persuasion Kanefert's husband, the senior scribe, Huya, told stories of magic and mystery for the entertainment of young and old alike. Pakhred had made friends with some of the young craftsmen among the Villagers, some of whom had studied under Master Hori, and they were sharing experiences.

When one young painter began to scratch a portrait of Huya on a scrap of limestone, he started a competition. Pens and ink were fetched, small children were sent to find suitable flakes of stone and people crowded around, suggesting subjects and themes for the little sketches. Pakhred, whose training had concentrated on formal designs of the sort used in the decoration of temples, was fascinated by the easy way his new friends had with ordinary subjects. One drew a caricature of a stonemason with his mallet and chisel. Howls of laughter from the audience showed that they recognized the bulbous nose, stubbly chin and heavily pierced ear. Another draughtsman produced a picture of a herdsman with his flock, except that the herdsman was a jackal and his charges were geese.

Pakhred was encouraged to draw something but could not think of anything that would bear comparison with this spontaneous display of the artists' skill until Ramose leaned over his shoulder and said, 'Draw something you saw today.'

Immediately Pakhred knew what to do. He outlined a single figure, the most memorable from the temple colonnade where he had sheltered from the midday sun. In a few sure strokes he portrayed an enormously fat woman, with rolls of flesh hanging from her arms and legs. It was the wife of the King of Punt, the incense land far to the south. No royal wife of Kemet would have been happy to have herself shown thus, no matter how fat she was. Only because this lady was a foreigner could the artist afford such licence.

Ramose took the finished sketch and held it close under the light of the nearest torch. 'You have remembered well, Young Amenmose. This is a good likeness. May I have it?'

Honoured that his sister's husband should want to keep a casual doodle, Pakhred said, 'Of course, if you think it worth keeping. Call it my festival gift.'

'Thank you,' Ramose said. 'And thinking of gifts I think it's time to hand out the presents.'

The party went on until well after moonset. This was only the start of the holidays. No one needed to rise early tomorrow.

CHAPTER ELEVEN

Third Month
of Summer

NEDJEMGER TOOK UP HIS NEW POSITION OFFICIALLY ON THE FIRST OF THE
month. A house had been allocated to him in the small but select
residential area that had been established just to the south of the Mansion
on the edge of the cultivation. His new neighbours were the first priests
and administrators to be appointed to the King's mortuary foundation.

Even before the building complex was complete, certain parts of the
establishment were already functioning. Some, like the Tjaty's office, had
been operational for nearly a year. The many professional people who
worked there would be expected to employ housekeepers, personal
servants and menials as a demonstration of their status, so the houses
provided for them were neat, one-storey buildings, each with its own
kitchen courtyard and, in place of a garden, a separate block for servant
accommodation.

All the residents were employees either of the temple of Ipet Esut, the
senior religious authority in the region, or of the King himself.
Nedjemger's was a royal appointment and the house represented part of
his salary. The remainder of his pay would be drawn according to
carefully audited accounts from one or other of the storehouses of the
mansion temples. The same system applied to Amenmose, Ramose and
even the Tjaty himself.

Nebet was familiar with the petty bureaucratic minds of the

commissary clerks, having had several disagreements with them in her time. Once, shortly after Khay's birth, when she was still feeling rather fragile, one official had been extremely rude, accusing her of asking for more than her due ration. He had treated her with such condescension that, rather than argue the matter in front of other civil service wives, she went home empty-handed and in tears. That evening she had described the confrontation to Amenmose, blushing bright pink with embarrassment at the memory. Amenmose was furious and, had it not been long after the clerk had gone home for the night, he would have gone straight to the warehouse and beaten the man for his insolence.

By the next morning he had calmed down enough to see that there was a better way to deal with the problem. He went to the stores himself, choosing a time of day when the largest crowd of people was likely to be there. He wore his smartest wig and his second-best gown and took great care with the application of his eye paint so as to make himself look as impressive as possible. He took Sendji with him as his personal attendant, to add to his air of authority. When they came home they were hardly able to stand upright for laughing, and it was a long time before Nebet was able to piece together the story. Some of the details she discovered only much later from friends who had witnessed Amenmose's performance.

Pushing his way to the front of the queue was quite easy, though he later felt the need to apologize to the wives of a couple of his colleagues for his apparent boorishness. They both said it had been worth the temporary annoyance to see the uppish clerk reduced to sobs of mortification. Amenmose announced himself as the Tjaty's personal secretary, which was perfectly true, and immediately the stores clerk was wringing his hands with humility. The clerk invited his noble visitor to step inside where they could discuss their business in private. Amenmose had insisted on speaking to the man, very loudly, in the open under the very public scrutiny of an amused and ever growing crowd.

Amenmose demanded to know why the woman Nebetiunet had been refused her rightful food ration. The commissary clerk frowned as he tried to recall the name and the circumstances, but made the mistake of not checking his written record of the previous day's transactions. Amenmose knew at once, from the man's expression, that the clerk had not made the connection between himself and the Amenmose who was listed in the stores' records as Nebetiunet's husband. There were some advantages in having a common name. The official tried to bluster his way out of trouble by claiming, rather too vehemently, that he was well aware of the sort of tricks that women of *her* sort would try on. He was only doing his job and protecting the interests of the King. Amenmose, knowing Paser would back him up if necessary, had shamelessly implied that it was the Tjaty who wished to know the answer. The clerk blustered some more before he became aware of the hush that had fallen over the gathered crowd. At least he had the sense to recognize when things were not going his way.

In the silence Amenmose had delivered his final verbal blow, rendering the clerk temporarily speechless: 'The Lord Paser, the Tjaty, will be most interested to hear that his sister Nebetiunet has been misusing her position.'

When Amenmose turned to go, the clerk seemed to shake himself awake as if from a nightmare and flung himself on to the ground at Amenmose's feet. Only a few phrases could be made out from his largely meaningless blubbering, 'sorry' and 'I didn't know' being the most audible.

Nebetiunet had never again had any trouble from a clerk of the stores and these days she had no need to present herself personally at the commissary. Though that particular civil servant had never been seen there since, Nebet's name alone guaranteed that her supplies would be released into the hands of her representatives, be they family or servants. She had never used her relationship with Paser to her own advantage, but she was very glad on behalf of her children that she could claim an association with such an important and well-respected man.

Though Nebet would not dream of asking what salary the Chief Gardener could command, she was certain that Nedjemger and Satra would be very comfortably off. Satra had not yet announced when she would be moving in with Nedjemger, but it now seemed only a matter of time before the two were wed. Nebet was fairly certain that Amenmose had already finished the negotiations over Montmose's legacy. So, once Nedjemger was settled in his new house, there was nothing to prevent Satra marrying almost immediately. Meanwhile Nedjemger was taking the first step towards that end.

Khaemwase looked around his room for the last time. The image of every corner of this house was fixed in his heart. It had been his home for more than nine years and, though his vision of it was blurred, it was that imperfect picture that he would always remember, because it was all he had ever known. If there was a hint of a tear in his eye, it was nothing compared with what Nebet was feeling.

She was trying very hard not to cry. She kept pressing the back of her hand to her nose and surreptitiously wiping away the tears that threatened to betray her. She had told Amenmose she would be strong. She was glad that Khay had been given the chance to make something of his life, especially after its unpromising start and the disappointment of his schooling. But he was the youngest and that made him, in his mother's eyes, the most vulnerable of all her children. He was and always would be her baby. Now she had to tell herself that it was all for the best, while wanting to enfold her child in her arms and beg him not to go.

Khaemwase came down the stairs and picked up his sack of belongings. Tia handed him a small lunch basket just like the one she had prepared for him every day since he started school. She too was emotional, though for different reasons.

Khay was the youngest child of Amenmose, and Amenmose was the child Tia had nursed in his infancy, the man she now thought of as her son. To see the young boy, still under-grown in her opinion, about to leave home to take up his apprenticeship brought the full weight of her years down heavily on her back. She would not weep, not in front of him, but she might shed a few tears later and some of those tears would be for herself.

'Has Master Nedjemger arrived?' Khay asked his mother.

Nebet sniffed and said, 'Yes. He's gone into the garden with Satra. Give them a few moments.'

'Of course,' Khay said. Then, after an uncomfortable pause he went on, 'Isn't it funny how my master still thinks about the West Bank as being almost in another country? I told him I've travelled across the River on my own many times, but he insisted on coming back to escort me to my new quarters.'

'He cares,' Nebet said. 'Do you think I could let you go with anyone who didn't?'

'Oh, Muti . . .' He ran to her and suddenly they were crying and hugging each other tightly.

Nebet had one glorious moment of thinking, 'He'll stay,' but she knew that was wrong. All little birds had to fly the nest at some time. Khay's time was now. She gently detached herself from his fierce embrace and held him at arm's length.

'You're such a good boy and we'll miss you, but your future is on the other side of the River. Just remember what we've been telling Nedjemger all this time: the Mansion is not at the end of the world. We'll see each other often.'

Khaemwase wiped a hand across his eyes and said, 'And I'll be living with Father for the while, at least until the Tjaty returns.'

'Yes, so you see, it's not as if you're really leaving home, just moving house.'

Khay nodded. He bent to pick up his things and saw with dismay a puddle of beer spreading from the lunch basket. The jar had cracked when he had dropped it in his rush to embrace his mother. Tia, who had clearly been watching the emotional scene from the kitchen door, brought him a fresh basket without a word about his clumsiness. He kissed her cheek and said, 'Thank you, Tia. I'll miss you too.'

'Get away with you. It'll be midday before you've even left the house at this rate.' Tia's gruff voice could not disguise her feelings and Nebet knew they were all close to another bout of weeping.

Then Satra entered from the garden and said, 'Are you ready, Khay? Master Nedjemger is waiting.'

'Yes, sorry, I'll be off then, Muti,' and he kissed his mother. 'Tia.' He kissed the cook again. With his head held high he shouldered his pack and went out to start his new life.

Satra looked with amusement at the desolate faces before her. Tia was the first to pull herself together, and she returned to her tasks in the kitchen. She could soon be heard giving Hotepu and Didet the rough edge of her tongue for no apparent reason. Nebet felt at a complete loss. She sank down on Amenmose's favourite chair and gazed at the door that had just closed behind her son.

Satra came to sit down on the footstool beside her. 'If it's any comfort,' she said, 'I can assure you Nedjemger will treat him well. He thinks a great deal of Khaemwase.'

'I know,' Nebet said absently.

'And besides,' Satra went on, 'after the wedding I shall be running Nedjemger's house and, if you want and if Khay likes the idea, he can come to live with us. I'll look after him. That's the very least I can do after all you've done for me.'

Nebet looked at her in amazement. In a few short months the woman's character had changed out of all recognition. She was beginning to think of others before herself, and that made her an altogether better person.

'That's a very kind offer and I'm sure Khay will accept. Does this mean you've set the date?'

Satra blushed. 'Yes. Nedjem has suggested the Feast of the Sacred Marriage.'

The festival commemorating the divine union of Hathor with Horus, the hawk-headed god of Behdet, was second only in Nebet's affections to the Lady's New Year festival at Iunet. As the Goddess epitomized love and femininity, the occasion of her wedding was also considered by women an auspicious time of year for marriages. Nebet had not thought Nedjemger was that sentimental, yet Satra's glowing cheeks told her that it was the husband-to-be who had chosen this romantic season for his wedding. She also noted Satra's use of the diminutive form of his name.

Then she realized. 'That's this month! The Lady will be arriving in Waset in a matter of days.'

'Yes,' Satra smiled sweetly, 'but I don't foresee any problems. I'm sure you're only too eager to have the house to yourself again.'

'But Mymy's baby is due soon. I'm sure it'll arrive during the Festival season. How can I plan a wedding.'

Satra chuckled. 'My dear sister, I'll make all the arrangements. I'm old enough to know what I'm doing. I wouldn't dream of distracting you from your daughter at such a time.'

'Oh Satra, I didn't mean to say—'

'I know what you meant,' Satra said, 'and I'm not in the least offended. But, if you have time, I would like to have that lovely linen you gave me for the Valley Festival made up as a wedding gown. No one I know can sew as well as you, Nebetiunet.'

The flattery was overwhelming, coming from such an unexpected source. Nebet bent to kiss the top of her sister's head, saying, 'I'll be pleased to do it. In fact, we'd better start on it now while there's still time, before Mymy decides to go into labour.'

'She has a choice?' Satra asked with a playful twitch of her eyebrow. They both laughed.

The Lady of Iunet, Hathor the Gold, wife-to-be of the sky-god Horus, paused at Waset, on her voyage south, to pay a courtesy visit to her sister Mut, wife of Amen-Ra and Lady of the Two Lands. Her gold-plated barge was sighted at dawn rounding the bend in the River to the north of the City. Crowds of well-wishers thronged the banks of the River, spilling on to the mudbanks which had been left high and dry by the rapidly falling waters. To north and south of the landing, booths had been set up from which temple servants dispensed free beer and bread baked in the shape of the Goddess's horns. Everywhere the Lady's lovely, placid face could be seen; on her head she wore the horned sun's disc crown or the enshrined serpent power, the Eye, the uraeus. It was on the prow and stern of the great barge, the gilded horns of the Lady's crown glinting in the sunshine. It was on the handles of mirrors waved by women so that the golden morning light reflected off the copper surfaces sending dancing patterns over the crowds of pilgrims. It was on the sistra carried by the Chantresses of Mut, who had come down to the waterside to provide an escort for the Goddess as she made her way along the processional route to the Asheru Temple. Nebetiunet, Mutemwiya and Satra took their places in the procession and sang with all their hearts the praises of the Goddess.

In the crowd, cheering and laughing with the joy of the moment, were Neferti, Mymy and, to Nebet's delight, Senetnay. She had so hoped that her friend would be able to shake off her depression in time to be able to participate in Hathor's welcome. She was convinced that Senetnay would be comforted by the Goddess's calming, loving presence. Nebet had not pushed Senetnay into making a decision and she knew better than to hope she would take up her customary position among the Chantresses. Instead she had mentioned her own fears for Mymy's safety in the jostling crowds.

Senetnay, always generous in spirit, had said, 'I'll stand with her. Don't worry, Nebetiunet. I'll make sure she doesn't get over-tired.'

These days Mymy was really suffering from the heat. By midday she was already flagging and had not the energy even to climb the stairs to her room. Nebet had decided that the sleeping arrangements had to be reorganized, so Neferti and Satra were asked to swap rooms with Mymy. They agreed at once. Neferti was excited at the idea of sharing the bigger upstairs room and, when Satra said that it would be only a short while before she could have the room to herself, she was even more eager to help with the packing and moving of furniture.

It was amazing how much work was involved in this simple exercise. Moving storage boxes revealed unpleasant amounts of dust and dirt that had accumulated behind them. More than that, a suspicious hole in the women's room, in the corner against the outside wall, looked worryingly like a snake burrow. When Hotepu discovered it she upset the whole household with her screaming. Satra had to slap her face to calm her down.

'You silly girl,' she said, 'what have you to be frightened of? Nubnefert and I have been sleeping in that room for months and there's no telling how long that hole has been there. No harm has come to us.'

Hotepu, not in the least comforted by that thought, refused to go back into the room until the hole had been checked for occupancy.

Nebet had mixed feelings about the possibility of having a snake in residence. A cobra was undoubtedly a potential danger to humans, especially to small children, but it was also a very effective deterrent against rats and mice, and the creature was only unpredictable when cornered. For the most part, if a snake was left alone it would not bother anyone. Nebet understood that most of the time a snake would be more frightened of humans than they were of the snake. The cobra was also the symbol of the Goddess whom Nebet's family had revered in her various forms for generations. She had brought up her daughters to respect the Lady by giving them names which put them under the protection of Hathor or Mut. She hoped even now that the Goddess was looking after her namesake Senmut.

She also wondered whether Tia's magic at the Renenutet Festival might not have attracted a snake to the house. Renenutet was not only goddess of the threshing floor and protectress of the grain store, but also patroness of nursing mothers. Perhaps the magic of the straw amulet and the ivory wand had drawn the snake to the room where a pregnant woman was about to take up residence. This was not something that Nebet had considered at the time, when all her thoughts had been for Wiya, but the Goddess did not necessarily answer prayers in the way expected.

Whatever the explanation for the snake's presence, it could not simply be treated as a pest. Hotepu's outburst showed only that she did not understand the Goddess's mysterious ways. As Satra had said, she had nothing to fear. She told Hotepu what she had observed in the Place of Truth, where the villagers, who lived in closer harmony with the powers of the animal world than the town-dwellers of Waset, recognized the Lady in her serpent form as Meretseger. The very name chosen for their goddess, 'She Who Loves Silence', hinted at the way in which they believed snakes should be treated. Nevertheless, Nebet decided that the snake-catcher had to be called in to inspect the place, for the sake of peace in the household as much as for Hotepu's peace of mind. She smiled at the play on words. Hotepu's name meant 'Peace'.

Djedef was the last in a long line of snake catchers. He had learned his craft from his father, who had been taught by his father and so on, far back beyond the memory of anyone now living. Djedef had no son and the sister's son he had hoped would take over the family's traditional profession had rebelled against his teaching and had become a potter. The snake-catcher had had to take on as his apprentice Seneb, a young boy from the town of Per-Montju, a little to the south of Waset on the West Bank. Nebet had heard that Seneb had come looking for Djedef, asking to learn about snakes because his own father had died from the bite of a horned viper. Djedef, now ancient, stooped and half blind, was glad Seneb had proved a quick pupil, and Seneb clearly adored his master as a son loves his father.

When they arrived in response to Nebet's summons, Seneb carried the tools of their trade while the old man walked leaning on his tall staff and with one hand resting lightly on the boy's shoulder.

Tia, who had greater respect for Djedef than for the goatherd Tjeti, insisted on observing certain niceties when dealing with such a professional and her courtesy extended to Seneb. She was ready with beer, fruit and sweetcakes for them. Like Tjeti, the old snake-catcher had hardly a tooth left in his head and took time to soften the bread in the beer before he could eat it. Seneb, meanwhile, gobbled down everything set in front of him and looked around expectantly for second helpings. His slightly distended belly and his ravenous appetite suggested to Nebet that he suffered from a worm infestation which was so far advanced as to be untreatable. She dared not mention this to Djedef, since the old man had such high expectations of the boy carrying on the snake-catching profession after his death. But there was something about Seneb that made her think he had little time left. His very appearance belied the meaning of his name, 'Healthy'. He might not outlive his master, because the worms were sucking his life away from the inside. There would come a time when his skin would become pale and dry, the whites of his eyes would turn yellow and his gums would become almost transparent as the blood was drained from his body. It was a cruel death, but commonplace among peasant farming communities in the more rural districts, where even a travelling physician rarely paid a visit. The farmers, who recognized and treated such afflictions in their animals, seemed oblivious of the same symptoms shown by their sons and daughters. They seemed to put a lot more trust in the powers of names and amulets to protect their children than in practical measures.

There were vermifuges, vile-tasting potions for the most part, which Nebet had used occasionally for her own children. They had to be forced to swallow the medication, which usually had a strong laxative effect, or it might make them vomit. Children were quick to associate even the smell of such a potion with unpleasant sensations and Nebet, more than once, had had to drag her children crying from their hiding places to doctor them, telling them it was for their own good.

Once Djedef had taken his fill of Tia's hospitality, he turned to professional matters and asked for the details of their problem. Such things could not be rushed and Nebet was happy to leave the talking to Tia. The cook had consulted Djedef on many occasions in the past and considered herself his professional equal with regard to household magic. She explained at great length the nature of the spells she had cast with the help of her mother's wand, and made him aware of how important the Goddess was to this particular family. This information would help him decide how to deal with the serpent, but first he had to ascertain what sort of snake he was dealing with or, indeed, if there was a snake at all.

Throughout this discussion Seneb had been listening attentively. He was his master's eyes and had to see with his master's heart. He had learned much in the few years he had served Djedef and he knew that every snake was different. It was necessary to understand the snake's place within its surroundings. Only when they knew why the snake was there and what sort of threat, if any, it posed could they decide what to do.

Having listened carefully to Seneb's description of the hole, Djedef asked, 'How deep does it go? Is the other end outside the house or does it go down into the basement?'

To answer the first of these questions Seneb probed the hole with a flexible reed, but he could tell little apart from the fact that the burrow took an abrupt turn about a hand's-breadth into the wall.

Gemni was sent into the alley to examine the outer wall of the women's room. He reported by shouting up to the narrow window grille at the level of the ceiling, 'I can't see no hole out here.'

Down in the basement storeroom they found the hole that Nebet had noticed on her return from Iunet last New Year. It was behind the largest of the grain bins and well out of the way of human traffic but ideally placed for a snake lying in wait for its rodent prey.

'And you say you've never seen the creature?' Djedef asked.

Tia assured him that she had not and Nebet agreed.

'Well, I think the hole upstairs is irrelevant' was Djedef's professional opinion. 'Unless there was a ready food supply there for her, she wouldn't linger in that part of the house. But there must be another entrance hole. She wasn't born here. She must have come in from outside. She isn't here now so she must have another way out. I suspect we'll find the burrow goes through the thickness of the wall to the front of the house. Did I see a garden there?'

'Yes,' Nebet said, 'a small one.'

'But quite big enough for our friend. Shady corners with plants for hiding in, warm stone for basking on, and you have created the perfect home for our Lady.'

Nebet felt strangely proud that she had done something unintentionally to please the Goddess, and was reluctant to risk offending her by evicting her creature from her chosen home. She asked Djedef, 'What do you advise?'

'Be wary, especially in the garden. You shouldn't poke around without thought for the Lady. If you're worried about the burrow entrance in the women's room you can block it up, but leave a small hole so that she can observe the mother-to-be. There's no other reason for her to seek out that room, so we must assume it's the scent of women that has drawn her there. Consider this. Her presence was revealed only when you decided to give the room to your daughter. I think the Goddess has given you a sign that she will protect your daughter and her child. Now all we must do is check the garden.'

Seneb conducted the search for the cobra. He quickly found the small hole in the front wall of the house underneath the pomegranate tree and signs that something had been nesting in the leaf litter. The fragment of dried scaly skin, the remains of a snake's moult, found clinging to a twig at the base of the tree's trunk, was the clinching proof.

Djedef held the white scrap close to his face and pronounced, with authority, 'She is a cobra.'

That was what Nebet had hoped he would say. She had become reconciled to the idea of sharing her house with a snake and she would have been disappointed if Djedef had identified the creature as anything other than a cobra and female.

Having ascertained the nature of Nebet's problem, Djedef prepared his spells. He placed a handful of salt in one saucer and asked Tia to fill another with milk. These two offerings were laid underneath the pomegranate tree to show the cobra where she was welcome. The magic was activated by Djedef's recitation of a binding spell which, rather than driving the cobra away and risking the Lady's displeasure, was intended to restrict the snake to the garden and the area around the grain bins. The sense of his chant became apparent only when it was taken up by Seneb, whose unbroken voice gave clarity to the words. Djedef invoked the blessing of the Goddess on the house and its occupants and begged her to restrain her creature from harming anyone under her protection.

'I have come, that I may worship your greatness,
I have come, so that your power may be recognized,
I have come to give offerings of welcome,
I have come to seek your protection.
O Great Goddess, Hathor the Gold, Serqet of the Hot Breath,
Sakhmet the Eye, Renenutet the Nurse of All,
The Lady under all her many names,
Look kindly on this house and upon the Lady of the House, Nebetiunet,
Keep her in your heart and grant your protection to all her people.'

Nebet thanked Djedef and asked what reward he would accept for his consultation.

After a little whispering with his apprentice, he said, 'Food for me and the boy for two days.'

'Is that all?' Nebet asked, surprised at the modest request.

'You don't know how much this boy can eat,' Djedef laughed.

Satra had confirmed that she and Nedjemger were to become man and wife on the day of the New Moon, the very day when Hathor was to arrive in Behdet for her marriage to Horus. Apart from the wedding feast there was not much to be organized. A wedding was a very casual affair, usually no more than a parade of family and gifts as the bride moved out of her father's home and into that of her new husband. Most of the important business would have been conducted and agreed, in private, between the heads of the two households well in advance.

As her father was dead, Amenmose acted as Satra's negotiator and Nedjemger, being of mature years, was his own spokesman. This had made the drawing up of the marriage terms simple and the resultant contract was straightforward. There had been a time when Satra would have argued her case down to the last grain of barley but the transformation in her character seemed permanent and she was all smiles and reason. She had even agreed to draw up her own will, in which she stated that, should her marriage prove childless, her brother's children were to be her heirs. Thus her inheritance from Montmose would remain in his family.

The traditional marriage parade was complicated by the need to transport the bride, her possessions and wedding gifts across the River. Nedjemger and Amenmose had arranged for two boats, one for goods and the other for the guests. Several of Nedjemger's former colleagues from Ipet Esut, together with their wives, and some of the women from the weaving-sheds with whom Satra had become friendly, joined the family for the boat trip. Mymy came down to the quayside with Tia to see them off but even that short walk tired her and going any further was out of the question.

Satra went to great lengths to assure Mymy that she would not be offended by her absence from the celebrations. As she kissed her goodbye before embarking on the boat that was to take her to her new husband, she said, 'Take care of that baby. I'm sorry I won't be here for the birth but let me know as soon as it arrives. I shall be thinking of you.'

Mymy smiled and returned the affectionate kiss, saying, 'If you find yourself thinking of me in the next few days, Nedjemger won't be doing his duty as a husband.'

Satra blushed, not for the first or the last time that day. She was dressed in her best sheath dress with the fine over-gown that Nebet had been working on by lamplight, morning and evening, over the past few days. Nebet appraised her handiwork and was happy that the style suited Satra, accentuating her slender figure. Comparing Satra's shape with her own, Nebet sighed at her thickened waist, plump hips and thighs, and incipient double chin. There was little more than two years' difference in their ages but Nebetiunet's life had put more strain on her body and heavier demands on her physical strength.

Marriage and motherhood were the greatest joys and the greatest dangers in any woman's life. Knowledge of the good and the bad came only with experience. If asked to weigh her own experiences in the balance of Maat, Nebet would have judged her life to have contained more happiness than sadness, more success than failure, and more love than hate. But no woman starting out on a marriage could really know what lay in front of her. Satra at least had lived a full life, a healthy life, a longer life than many women could hope for, before she took the plunge into marriage. Nebet no longer harboured bad feelings towards Amenmose's sister; she wished her only happiness in her new life; but she also hoped that Satra fully appreciated how fortunate she was.

When Mymy climbed the basement stairs too quickly she complained of dizziness and had to sit down abruptly on the top step. Nebet told her off for going down into the cellar in the first place: 'Suppose you'd fallen? You could have hurt the baby. You must be careful.' Mymy was too listless to argue against her mother's sharp reproof which she knew was born out of anxiety. Nebet softened her attitude at once and called Meryt to help put Mymy to bed, but she saw the dizzy spell as a sign that the birth was imminent and started to make preparations.

With Tia in the house there would be no need for a midwife and Mymy would have plenty of female support. Both her sisters were on hand, since Mutemwiya had returned with her mother after the wedding. Meryt, Hotepu and Didet could all be relied on to play their part. Next to Tia, Didet was the most experienced, having assisted four of her sisters at the births of their children. Nebet had lost count of how many times the girl had taken a day off for such family matters. Didet's personal knowledge of all that childbirth entailed, including the death of one sister, probably explained why she had shown no inclination for marriage so far.

It would be a small matter to chase the men out of the house. They would prefer to go fishing anyway. Nebet's main concern was to prepare the place where Mymy would give birth. At the Place of Truth she had been shown the little birthing closet built into the corner of Tuy's front room, but it had looked very small and cramped to her, like most things in the Village. She had in mind the romantic idea of creating a birthing bower in the garden.

Like most women Nebet had always dreamed of giving birth in pleasant and peaceful surroundings, and like most women she had had to make do with a corner of a room curtained off for a little privacy. Now, with fewer people in the house to get in the way, she might be able to create her dream for her daughter.

She had Bak fetch out the festival awnings they had used at Opet. She told him what she wanted to do and, despite his scepticism at the practicality of the scheme, he did exactly as she asked. The awnings were combined in the garden to make a small three-sided tent, open at the front but with a curtain that could be drawn across to separate an inner room from a porch. Reed mats were strewn beneath the shade of the awnings and trails of bindweed and vines were twisted round the tent poles.

The birthing bricks that had been used in the family for at least three generations were brought out in readiness for the fourth. Tia blessed them with her ivory wand, calling upon their protective spirit, the goddess Meskhenet, to grant the pregnant woman a safe delivery. She also placed her collection of amulets about the tent, hanging them from the poles and rails. Many were images of the Lady as Hathor of the Horns, as Taweret the hippopotamus or as the frog Heqet, midwife of the gods. Tia's favourite divine statuette was that of the fearsome Bes, wearing his lion-skin cape and waving two knives above his head. He would be particularly efficacious if the baby should be born at night. The threat of the noise of the god's yelling and the clashing together of his knives would drive away the spirits of darkness that sought to take advantage of the vulnerability of a new-born babe and its mother.

Tia kept her precious amulets in a small chest, each wrapped in a square of linen, with the wand made from a hippopotamus tooth lying on top. Most importantly the box held the *pesesh-kaf* knife, the flint blade, forked like a snake's tongue, that was used to cut the umbilical cord. Tia took out the knife and checked that the curved edges were still sharp. Another essential part of the midwifery equipment was the Bes amulet, crudely moulded from clay, which Nebet had brought back from Iunet many years before. As the dwarf figure was employed in the spell to speed up a protracted or painful labour, it was to be hoped that Tia would not need to call upon this particular magic.

Such votive objects were readily available in the City of the Sycomore at festival time. It was said that the craftsmen of the Hathor temple made the most efficacious of charms for women because the Lady, who oversaw all their work, understood intimately their true value. Last New Year at Iunet, Nebet had bought a *menyt* amulet for Neferti, similar to the one she herself had worn for many years before giving it to Wiya. Both charms now hung in the birth bower, lent by the sisters for Mymy's added protection. The last and newest additions to the magical collection were the amulets given to Nebet by the King's Mother, Mut-Tuya, and the King's Daughters. Nebet had brought both from her jewel box and had given the blue hippopotamus emblem into Tia's keeping. She had taken to wearing the little vulture figure about her own neck so that it would be ready to hand when Mymy's pains started.

On a more practical but complementary level, oil lamps and fire-lighting equipment were set close at hand. A folding bed with a good mattress was placed in the inner compartment, along with the crib which had been the lid of the old linen basket, and one of Mymy's own straw amulets was hung in the centre of the tent, directly above the birthing bricks. Bowls and cloths and a jar of clean water were stored in readiness for the birth which, Nebet was convinced, would happen at any moment. So strong was that feeling that Nebet moved into the women's room to be close to her daughter. All her own labours had started in the hours of darkness and she had vivid memories of the first time.

She and Amenmose had been living in a smaller house then, with only Tia and a living-out maid as servants. She had been woken in the middle of the night by, as she thought, the need to pass water, but when she sat up she felt a strange sensation that was not pain and yet not the urinary urgency she had become accustomed to over the last few months. It was almost as if something inside her had split, like a ripe melon. When she stood up she could do nothing to stop the warm water that flowed from her. It was her first pregnancy. She had not been present at any birth before this. She knew nothing of what to expect.

Her sobs of embarrassment woke Amenmose, who was as ignorant of such matters as she was herself. In panic he rushed out of the room to fetch Tia, and in the brief moments while she was alone she experienced her first contraction, a wave of pain which began just below her breasts and rippled down to her thighs. By the time Amenmose had roused Tia and made her understand what was going on, Nebet's labour was well and truly started and she was weeping with fear and pain in equal measure. The baby girl was born just after midday but not before

Amenmose's mother and Paser's wife had arrived to lend their support. Nebet was exhausted but extremely proud of her lustily yelling daughter, though she would have liked her first child to be a son for Ameny's sake.

There was no question in her mind as to how the little girl should be named. It was the time of the Opet Festival when Mut, the goddess of Waset, had celebrated her own marriage by going forth in her sacred barque, her wiya, so the baby girl was called Mutemwiya, 'Mut is in her sacred barque'.

Mymy's cry was hardly more than a whimper but her mother recognized the tone and was fully awake almost at once. She lit a rushlight from the pot of embers she had kept from the kitchen fire. Mymy was curled up as far as her swollen belly would allow, and was grimacing with pain.

Nebet stroked her daughter's brow and said softly, 'It won't be long now, dear. I'll leave the light for you while I go to wake the others, then I'll come back to help you into the garden.'

The 'others' were all the women in the house. First Nebet woke Neferti and Wiya and sent them downstairs to keep their sister company. In the basement Didet, who had been sleeping in Iset's old place for the past few days, was quickly awake. Nebet had more trouble rousing Tia. She had to be shaken firmly but the cook knew immediately what must be happening and started muttering her protective incantations as she made her way up to the birthing bower. Meryt was still staying with her own family and would not arrive until the morning. Apart from Gemni, who was blissfully asleep on the roof, there was not a man in the house.

By dawn, when Hotepu and Meryt arrived, Mymy's pains were coming rapidly, one contraction after another. Seeing they could be of no immediate help to the midwives, the two servants went to the kitchen and started to prepare the morning meal. Mymy's body, naked except for the turquoise-blue Taweret and the golden Mut amulets hanging at her neck, glistened with sweat and the perfumed oil that Wiya had brought as her contribution to the birth spells. Tia insisted that the time had arrived for Mymy to squat with one foot on each of the birthing bricks. Her sisters knelt on either side of her, holding her arms, while Nebet knelt to support her daughter from behind. Didet busied herself with cloths and water and was ready to hand Tia anything she called for.

The cook knelt in front of the labouring woman and held the ivory wand to Mymy's belly, saying, 'We have come to give protection to this child. See, it is Hathor who lays her hand on her with this amulet of health!'

Although Tia had barely touched Mymy with the wand it was as if the pressure of its magic had been transmitted to the baby. Mymy gasped and her eyes widened with apprehension.

'It's all right, girlie,' Tia said, slipping out of her spell-casting role for a moment, 'the babe is on its way now. You'll have to give it a help along the way, though, so you'd better start pushing.'

Didet asked, 'Does she need the honey draught?' She was referring to the infusion of honey and fenugreek that Tia had prepared as a means of speeding up the labour if necessary.

Mymy, who had taken a great deal of interest in all Tia's preparations and so was far better informed about what was happening to her than her own mother had been, said through clenched teeth, 'How much faster do you think it can get?'

Tia chuckled. 'That's a sure sign that we're nearing the end, when the mother gets snappy.'

She was right. Meryt and Hotepu were summoned from the kitchen just in time to witness the birth and, with an ease that Nebet envied, Mymy's child slithered into Tia's waiting hands.

'It's a girl,' Tia announced as the baby uttered her first cry. Tia snagged the cord with the curved flint knife and deftly separated the child from its mother. She held the bloodied knife in front of the little girl's face to show her that the separation was complete. 'Now, little one, your life is your own. Live!'

In turn Mutemwiya, Nubnefert and Nebetiunet repeated Tia's wish. The baby was passed to Didet, who tied the cord and washed the wrinkled little body clean of birth fluids. Tia proceeded to deliver the afterbirth, which was then wrapped in a clean cloth and placed to one side. Later it would be buried beneath the threshold of Mymy's house to bring good luck to the home and lasting health to the baby.

Once Mymy herself had been bathed and given something to drink, she was settled in a low chair and her tiny daughter was brought to her. Calling upon Isis and Hathor, the Mother and the Nourisher, Nebet gave her daughter a moon-shaped amulet which would promote the flow of milk, and Didet put the baby to Mymy's breast. The child sucked almost immediately, a very good sign.

The sun had risen above the wall and the first rays spilled across the garden, casting a dappled light over the delightful scene of mother and child. Mymy, looking tired but satisfied, said, 'I shall call her Wadjet.

Nebet had hoped that the baby would be named for the Lady, but Mymy's choice surprised her. Wadjet was one of the Two Ladies, the protectors of Kemet, and patron goddess of the North Land. Abau's mother's family came from a village in the north close to the city of Dep, which was also known as Per-Wadjet, the 'House of Wadjet'. But Abau's family ties to the north had been severed long ago, even before he was born. His father had been a military scribe who had spent the early part of his career travelling about the Two Lands administering the great reforms of the army instigated by the King Djeserkheperura-Horemheb, before finally settling in Waset. Abau had been born in Waset and, having grown up honouring the gods of Waset, he had not shown any particular fondness for the goddess of his mother's birthplace. If his mother had been called Wadjet, Nebet would have understood her daughter's choice of name but, apart from a tenuous connection with the Lady of Dep, Nebet did not understand why Mymy had chosen this name. However, she was happy that, no matter how unusual the name might be for a child of Waset, at least Mymy had chosen to dedicate her daughter to the Lady. As a serpent goddess, Wadjet was also a

manifestation of the Eye of Ra and so was simply another aspect of the Goddess.

Then Wiya touched her arm and pointed across the garden. Beneath the pomegranate tree, swaying slowly back and forth and shining in the morning sun, was the hooded head of a cobra. The Lady had been there all the time.

CHAPTER TWELVE

Fourth Month
of Summer

MYMY HAD REGAINED HER STRENGTH AND, TO NEBET'S ASTONISHMENT and Wiya's envy, her figure in a remarkably short time. Little Wadjet was feeding well and putting on weight nicely. So often a baby which seemed perfectly healthy and of a good size at birth would fail to thrive despite all the mother's care. This might be because the woman had been so drained by the physical effort of giving birth that she had little milk or because the baby simply could not be taught to suckle properly. Wealthier families could afford to employ a wet-nurse, as Tia had been for Amenmose, to supplement or replace the mother's milk. Mymy would have to provide for her child herself, so Tia made sure that the young mother ate all the right sorts of food to promote her lactation. Each day for the seven days of Mymy's seclusion she boiled up a porridge of wheat grains, using milk instead of water and flavouring it with cassia and honey to tempt the appetite. She also insisted on Mymy drinking as much milk and beer as she could, since it was well known that a nursing mother needed to drink more than usual, especially during the hot months. When Mymy had emerged from her temporary home in the birthing tent, she looked radiant and her contentment had clearly been transmitted to her baby. Since then mother and child had continued to bloom. Wadjet was proving a model child.

Mutemwiya had delayed returning to the Place of Truth. Though still envying her sister, she had rejoiced with her at the birth of a healthy child and she was in no hurry to leave. Nebet suspected that Wiya was anticipating the interrogation she would be subjected to by the women of the Village on her return. In the close confines of the Place of Truth no one could keep secrets for long and even the most personal aspects of life were freely discussed. Wiya knew that her continued childless state, a great sorrow to herself and Ramose, was a cause for great speculation and gossip. The news of the birth of a child to her younger sister would have Village tongues wagging even more rapidly. Nebet was reluctant to broach the subject but felt that something had to be said, if only to reassure Wiya, before she went home. The problem was to find the right moment. In the event it was not until Wiya had announced her intention to go back to the Village and started to pack her things that Nebet contrived to have a little time alone with her daughter.

'Ramose will be glad to have you home, I've no doubt,' Nebet said lightly.

'I hope so,' Wiya said with a laugh that was just a little too merry.

'Surely there's no question that he's been missing you. He said as much when he came to see you.' Nebet was referring to Ramose's surprise visit a few days before. Ostensibly he had come to pay his respects to the latest addition to the family but Nebet had seen, from the way he and Wiya had looked at each other and at Wadjet, that the baby's arrival had accentuated their pain at having no child of their own. It was Ramose's all too brief visit that had prompted Wiya's decision to return across the River.

'Oh yes, he said he missed me, but . . .'

'But what?' Nebet asked. 'Ramose means what he says. He's one of the most honest men I've ever met. You couldn't ask for a better husband. What doubts can you possibly have?'

Wiya said, 'If I don't give him a child, he could set me aside as his wife.' She looked at her mother with a face so full of anguish that Nebetiunet only then began to understand what pain her daughter was suffering.

'No, never think that,' she said. 'Ramose is honourable. He considers you to be his only true wife; he's said as much to me and to your father. He loves *you*, and he loves you for what you are. He doesn't ask for more.'

'But every man wants a son and I can't give him one. I've failed him.'

'Mutemwiya, my dear child,' Nebet said softly, 'you haven't failed.

You're still young and there's plenty of time for children. Enjoy each other while you have the time together. Once the children start arriving, that luxury will become a precious memory.'

Nebet tried to sound convincing but she could hear the falsity of her words. For months she had been making every effort to help Wiya conceive. She had even sent her fruit from the mandrake plant in the garden with instructions on how they might be used to promote Ramose's ardour. Wiya had so far avoided telling her mother how successful that strategy had been.

The young woman wanted to believe her mother but everything she had been taught, all her experience of family life, had emphasized the importance of children. As parents nurtured their offspring, teaching them right from wrong and instilling in them respect for their elders, they were preparing for the time when sons and daughters would repay their debt of care by supporting their parents. Children were their parents' future. The future was bleak for a childless couple who had no one to call upon for help in their lonely old age.

Wiya was not crying and somehow that made her sadness all the more dreadful. She had resigned herself to the situation. She said, 'I know I'll never have a child and it's selfish of me to deny Ramose the opportunity to have children. I've told him I'm willing to adopt and rear any child he might father.'

Nebet was dumbstruck. This revelation explained why Ramose had returned to the Place of Truth so abruptly, having stated, on his arrival, his intention to stay with Wiya in Waset for a few days. Nebet, if she knew anything about Ramose, was sure he would have been deeply hurt by Wiya's suggestion that he should take other bedmates simply for the purposes of procreation. If he loved his wife as much as Nebet thought, he would never be so heartless as to ask her to rear the child of another woman. But she also feared that, in his hurt, Ramose might just take Wiya at her word.

Having packed the last of her belongings, Mutemwiya deftly tied the drawstring of her sack and said, 'I know you disapprove, Muti, and I know you think I'm taking a great chance, but I love Ramose. I love him enough to allow him this freedom and, because I am sure of how much he loves me, I know he won't abuse my trust.'

'My dear girl,' Nebet sighed, 'are you really that sure? You know I've tried to help in every way possible, but I'd never have encouraged you to do this. You know Ramose will be feeling terribly hurt.'

'Yes,' Wiya said, 'and that's why I must go home now. We need to talk this through, though where we shall find the privacy for that I don't know. I shall stand by what I said. Ramose said I didn't mean it and he'd give me time to think again, but I did mean it and thinking about it has only made me more determined. It's the only way and he'll see that in time.'

Rumours about the battle were beginning to circulate. Nebet never ceased to be amazed at how quickly news spread in spite of the fact that the fastest boat took several days to travel upstream from Mennefer to Waset. The City was already humming with anticipation of the return of the Division of Amen. Mothers, wives and sweethearts could talk of nothing else and yet no official messenger had arrived to confirm or deny the rumours.

Amenmose was dismissive of such stories, saying, 'The Tjaty's office would be the first to know if the King had returned. It's all wishful thinking.'

But Nebet knew better. She, too, had a sense – call it instinct or premonition – that Senmut was on his way home. Having worried about him for so long while he was so far away, she suddenly felt an overwhelming calm and relief. She knew Senmut was still alive.

The first official confirmation came in the form of a letter from Paser to his officials at the Mansion. He reassured his servants as to his good health and announced his intention to travel home to Waset immediately after the King's victory parade in Mennefer. This told Amenmose at least two things: first, the Tjaty had survived the campaign, and second, the battle had been won. For more detailed information he would have to wait until Paser arrived to tell his own story.

Meanwhile the long-awaited news of the army's return had people down at the River's edge at all times of the day and night, everyone hoping to be the first to spot the military transports making their way to the docks. This was no hardship, as it was the hottest part of the year when the River itself was at its lowest. The daytime watchers were glad of an excuse to sit in the shade of the stands of reeds and do nothing, while those keeping vigil by torchlight relished the cooler night air, which was a pleasant change from the baking heat of the day. Children splashed about in the shallows, the braver among them swimming between the mudbanks and daring their fellows to try the deeper water.

Occasionally a mother screamed with fear for her child's safety, but every sensible parent would have made sure that each child was protected from drowning by wearing the traditional fish pendant amulet, either around the neck or tied into the plaited sidelock. Mothers could not watch their children every moment of the day and had to learn to let go.

The first craft to be seen were two small messenger boats sent on ahead to give warning of the impending homecoming of the Division of Amen. One boat docked on the West Bank and the royal messenger immediately leaped ashore and sped up the causeway to take his letters to Lord Tjia at the Mansion. The other boat tied up at the quay before Ipet Esut, where a dense crowd had gathered. The Medjay soldiers accompanying the second messenger brandished their sticks to force people back so that he could make his way to the Temple. Hundreds of relatives and friends of the returning soldiers could do nothing but wait. Soon their hopes and fears would be realized.

Paser's barge arrived first and as the Tjaty stepped off the gangplank he was embraced by his old friend the High Priest, Nebwenenef. Accompanied by the division's senior officers, they passed along the ceremonial way and into the Temple precinct, where a welcoming feast had been prepared at the High Priest's residence.

Shortly afterwards the military vessels began to dock. Some tied up at the town quay while others sailed on upstream to land at the Southern Sanctuary. Yet more, rather than wait in midstream for berths to become available, steered for the farther bank to disembark their passengers at the royal quays. This left many soldiers stranded on the opposite side of the River from their loved ones and some people, initially elated at the thought of the army's return, searched the faces of the homecoming troops in vain.

Nebet, waiting with Pakhred, Mymy and Neferti, could not help but notice how few soldiers there were compared with the full division that had left Waset two months ago. Soldiers, some limping, many still bandaged and others sporting horrendous scars, were enfolded in the arms of their families. Most wept tears of joy at the reunion, but some looked vacantly around them as if hardly daring to believe they were home at last. Some men bore a burden of duty to their dead comrades and, having reassured their own families, they sought out others to deliver the saddest of news. Already the air was rent with wailing as parents, wives and children heard of the deaths of their menfolk.

'I can't see Abau.' Mymy had to shout to make herself heard over the general hubbub.

Pakhred, ever sensible, said, 'He's probably on one of the boats with the horses. They haven't started to land yet.'

'He could be on the other side of the River, in which case your father and Khay will see him before we do,' Nebet said.

'No, I'm sure they'll land the horses over here, where the stables are,' Pakhred said, reasonably. 'It would make no sense to take them off the boats once only to put them back on again. And I expect they'll wait until most of the crowd has dispersed. You know how skittish horses are at the best of times. Having been cooped up on boats for a few days won't make them any easier to handle.'

Logical as Young Amenmose's reasoning was, it made the waiting no easier. It was soon apparent that the horse transports were some distance behind the main fleet and would not dock until much later in the day. However, the delay allowed Amenmose and Khay to make their way across the River, and they were with the rest of the family when, at last, Abau and Senmut came ashore.

The relief Nebet felt when she saw her son was so overwhelming that she almost fainted. She had to lean heavily on her husband's arm as they pushed through the last of the crowds to reach him. Senmut had grown and was taller now than both Pakhred and Amenmose, but he had lost weight alarmingly. His cheeks were hollow, his eyes sunken and his mouth clenched shut. He looked grey and the scar on his forehead showed lividly against his unhealthily pale skin.

Nebet's first thought was that he was ill, that he had picked up some dreadful foreign disease. Then she realized that his face revealed horror rather than illness. The dreadful things he had seen and heard could not be shaken off in the same way as the foreign dust had been shaken from his sandals once he returned to the soil of Kemet. He said not a word as his parents embraced him. He hardly seemed to recognize his brothers and sisters.

By contrast Abau looked just the same. He laughed and cried and swept Mymy into his arms demanding to know where his child was, 'For it's clear to see you've had it. Well, have I a son or a daughter?'

'A girl, a daughter, and she's adorable,' Mymy said.

'I'm sure she is, if she's anything like her mother.' Abau kissed his wife soundly and, linking arms with her and Neferti, asked cheerfully, 'Where's the celebration party for our homecoming? I hope you've been busy brewing 'cos I've the most dreadful thirst!'

Nebet had the uncharitable thought that Abau had not changed at all. He was still more interested in beer than anything else. As he started the walk homewards, with a jaunty step and a giggling woman on each arm, Nebet and Amenmose turned to their son. Senmut had not uttered a recognizable word so far. He just stood there, as if carved from stone, almost unblinking. His body at least appeared to be uninjured but it was clear that his spirit was deeply hurt. Nebet knew that only time could heal his wounds, time and the love of his family. She took one of his hands and Amenmose, to her surprise, took the other. Gently they coaxed Senmut into motion and turned for home. There would be celebrations throughout Waset that night, but there would be mourning too. Senmut was, for the moment, oblivious to either mood. He would need time to adjust to ordinary life again. It would be some while before he was ready to tell anyone of the horrors he had seen.

Abau could not understand why Senmut was so withdrawn. 'He's been chatty enough ever since we met again after the battle, and in Mennefer he joined in all right with the celebrations after the victory parade. But as we got closer to Waset, just as you'd expect him to become more cheerful at the prospect of coming home, he became quieter and quieter until he stopped talking altogether. He'll snap out of it soon enough. Send him over to our place and I'll jolly him up a bit.'

Nebet politely declined his offer on Senmut's behalf. There was no question, for the time being, of Senmut returning with Abau and Mymy to their home. Neferti reluctantly gave up the second bedroom and moved back into the women's room with Meryt, who was living in again now that Mymy and Satra had moved out. After a few nights of the whole house being disturbed by Senmut's bad dreams Pakhred, who had not always got on as well with his brother as Nebet might have wished, agreed to sleep at home each night to keep him company. This proved to be the best medicine for Senmut's troubled *ka*.

Nebet's instinct was not to talk about the war so as not to stir up her son's memories. Amenmose had learned the official version of events as he wrote the Tjaty's report from dictation. He had then filled out the details from private conversations with Paser. Some of what he heard he kept in his heart, not wanting to worry Nebetiunet, and he would not ask Senmut about his part in the battle for fear of his son retreating even further into the shell he had so effectively created about himself. This was not a construct of bravery but a flimsy wall Senmut had built to keep out the images and sounds that threatened to haunt him for the rest of his life. Like an eggshell it was also desperately fragile, held together only by Senmut's will. Both Nebet and Amenmose were frightened of what might happen if his control gave way, so neither dared to press him. Pakhred, however, persuaded, cajoled and in some ways bullied his brother into talking about the horrors he had witnessed. Once Senmut started to talk, it was as if a dyke had been broached and there was no stopping the flood of memory.

The charioteer who had offered Senmut the position of groom had been seconded to a special detachment of veteran troops. Having passed along the coast road east of the River's mouths, the army had turned northwards towards Retjenu. The veterans were sent as a guard for the wagonloads of weapons and food, which were to be delivered to the supply bases on the coast. The detachment included many civilians such as Abau who were to be left in charge of the military supply dumps. Abau had spent most of the campaign season living comfortably in the garrison town of Gubla, sampling the local brews and developing a taste for the strong beer of Qode.

Having set up the store bases, the veteran officers were then charged with the muster of the garrison troops from the coastal ports and from smaller military outposts inland. Senmut had spent most of his time travelling from one walled town or fortified village to another, as often as not sleeping beneath his master's chariot, but well away from any real danger. However, once their complement was filled, the King had directed them to come swiftly and secretly to join the rest of the army for the battle before the hill-top city of Kadesh.

The city stood at a place where a stream joined a river, and so was surrounded on two sides by water. The King, coming from the south, intended to set up his camp to the west of Kadesh, knowing that his adversary would choose the opposite side of the river. It was on the last part of their journey, coming at Kadesh from the north, through territory already in upheaval and seething with rumours of the huge army that the Hittite king, Muwatallis, had called together, that Senmut became painfully aware of the facts of war.

All along the route this scratch fifth division, which called itself the Boys from Naharin, had encountered occasional opposition from local bandits who were quickly and efficiently disposed of. The nearer they came to Kadesh, the more serious the problems they encountered. Ambushes became more frequent and their assailants more ferocious. Some of their attackers were Hittite scouts or skirmishers and, since the presence of the Boys of Naharin was to be kept secret, the spies could not be allowed to take news back to their Lord. The first deaths Senmut witnessed were those of Hittite allies, local tribesmen for the most part, who were run down and trampled under the hooves of the chariot horses or speared to death to prevent them revealing the division's existence.

When they finally emerged from the pass through the ridge to the north of Kadesh they expected a warm welcome from their fellows already encamped above the city. Instead a terrible scene unfolded before them. A Hittite chariot troop had smashed into the shield wall round the

King's camp, where the Division of Amen had only recently arrived. The Division of Ra had been badly mauled and its remnants scattered by the Hittites' initial charge, and the two remaining divisions were still too far away to be of immediate help. The Boys of Naharin could only watch in horror as the King himself at the head of his hastily mobilized chariots came under pressure from a second wave of Hittite chariots sent across the river to capitalize on the first attack.

The veteran officers of the fifth division, some of whom had served with Menmaatra-Sethy at the last battle for Kadesh, swung into action almost out of instinct. There was no time to stop and let off passengers. Senmut found himself cowering down at the front of his master's chariot cab, clinging on tightly to the straps of the bow case and quiver, and trying to keep out of the warrior's way, while the chariot driver cursed him for taking up valuable space. Hittite chariots could carry three men at a time but the chariots of Kemet were built for only two. Senmut was in real fear of being pitched out of the bouncing cab, either by the roughness of the ground or, had the man not had his hands full controlling the chariot team, by the driver.

When he did find himself tossed to the ground he experienced a moment of relief before he was hit by the horror of what had happened. His master's pride and joy, the great black stallion that Senmut had been tending ever since they left Kemet, had been speared in the belly and had rolled, squealing in agony, turning over the vehicle and breaking the chariot pole. The second horse, the bay, was dragged sideways against the splintered end of the pole and suffered horrendous wounds to his flank as well as a broken leg. Both horses died, like so many others that day, thrashing and screaming amid the wreckage of their chariots and the human casualties. The only mercy was that most of the fallen charioteers were Hittites.

Senmut could not say how he had found the strength to crawl from the battlefield, nor how he had ended up sheltering in an olive grove outside the city walls. The Boys from Naharin had turned the battle in the King's favour. The Hittites were on the run. He watched as the Hittite troops started a desperate retreat across the river that claimed many more lives. The waters ran red with the blood of men and beasts.

Under the cover of darkness he had made his way back to the King's camp, guided by the flaring lights of cooking fires and torches. He was recognized by one of his friends from the stables at Waset and given food, drink and a blanket. After that everything became a blur. The army expected to resume the battle the next morning and there was an air of dejection over the camp. Everyone knew Muwatallis had thousands of foot soldiers waiting to be thrown into the fray. The army of Kemet would still be severely outnumbered even if the other divisions could be brought up in time. The Tjaty had been sent to summon the divisions of Ptah and Sutekh but no news of them had yet been received.

Then Senmut came to the most horrifying part of his story. By dawn the next day many of the soldiers of the Division of Ra who had taken flight at the first sign of trouble had come skulking back to the camp. Disgusted by their cowardice and their disloyalty, the King ordered a full parade of troops and proceeded to order summary executions to make known the depth of his displeasure. Senmut had watched as, in full view of both armies, the soldiers picked out by the King had their heads smashed in by an officer wielding a stone mace. His Majesty personally dispatched an officer as an example to all that rank was no protection from the King's anger. No one could explain why the Hittite king failed to push his advantage by rejoining the battle with his fresh spearmen, but all were everlastingly thankful that he did not. Instead, as if by mutual agreement, the two kings sent teams of men to collect their dead from the battlefield before breaking camp and turning for home. The Battle of Kadesh was over.

Senmut's spirit had been revived but the boy who had run away to war had gone for ever. The young man who had returned in his place was altogether more serious, thoughtful and considerate. His romantic ideas about army life had been shattered beyond repair and, to his father's delight, he asked Amenmose whether it might be possible for him to return to school. Senmut had seen at first hand the truth of those teaching texts which compared the life of a soldier with that of a scribe. Even the scribes who, like Abau, went to war were unlikely to suffer the same deprivations as common soldiers. Senmut, who had witnessed the deaths of many officers, including his own master, knew that high military rank was no protection against the spear or the mace. Life with the army on campaign was dirty, degrading and dispiriting, as well as being deadly dangerous. Two months with the army had taught him that the education of a scribe could be his greatest asset and his most powerful protection.

Senmut's old tutor, however, needed to be persuaded that the lad had mended his ways. He put the boy through a rigorous interview, reminding him of all the complaints about his behaviour in the past and his attitude towards authority in general, and making it clear that only a serious commitment to improvement in both areas would suffice. Senmut had given up his training a matter of a few months before he might have expected to graduate to more serious studies. Now, most of his former classmates had already chosen their future paths. Some were content with no more than the basic scribal education, as Abau had been several years before. This was perfectly adequate for army scribes, or clerks in local government, or letter-writers in private service, perhaps with a wealthy businessman. Others, usually those from professional backgrounds, were encouraged to specialize in a particular discipline, often in order to follow their fathers' professions, just as Amenmose had done.

Occasionally a student who showed a real aptitude for one particular area of study, even though it was not a traditional family calling, would be taken on as a special apprentice to a master. That was what had happened to Young Amenmose when Master Hori had acknowledged his talent as an artist. Pakhred, together with his master and the other artists at Ipet Esut, was now engaged in planning the pictorial record of the King's campaign that was to decorate the gateways and walls of the Temple. His Majesty had decreed that the Battle of Kadesh should be commemorated at all his most prestigious monuments. Clearly he considered the engagement his finest moment and worthy of being remembered for all time, though some of the participants in the campaign were trying hard to forget the whole experience.

The conscientious Pakhred wanted to be able to picture the scene of the battle for himself, so that he might portray events faithfully, but he knew better than to ask Senmut to relive those terrifying days. He also found that the description to which Hori insisted they should work was somewhat different from the reality as told by Senmut. But the King, as Guardian of Maat, decreed what was true and once that had been put into the script of the god's words it became indisputable truth. As had to be expected, the official report drawn from the campaign diaries was a sanitized version of the real story, and the pictures that were to accompany it would have to paint Kemet and the Lord of the Two Lands in the very best of lights.

Knowing this and accepting the King's divine right to glorify himself before the gods was of no comfort to Senmut. He would never, until the end of his days, be able to look at those brilliantly painted battle scenes without suffering a mixture of strong emotions, predominantly anger and sorrow.

Senmut had fallen behind in his studies long before he left school and then he had missed out on the advice given to his fellow students as to what further education might offer by way of career choice. His tutor was not convinced that his motivation would last and was understandably reluctant to make up the lost study time without a firm undertaking on Senmut's part to complete the course. When it was suggested that Senmut should re-enter the school in a class of younger students, Nebet was sure that he would refuse. She could imagine the disruption that would be caused by his presence in a class of young, impressionable boys. She had seen it demonstrated in Senmut's own misplaced hero-worship of Abau and his cronies. He had grown up so rapidly that she could not imagine him having anything in common with boys two or three years his junior. Even Amenmose doubted the tutor's wisdom in suggesting this course of action, but Senmut seemed so relieved to be taken back into the school that he would accept any conditions set upon him.

On the first morning of his return to school there was hardly a dry eye in the house as everyone queued up to wish him well.

As Tia handed over his basket of food for the day she said, 'There's a date cake in there. For the next few days at least I'll be putting in a little something extra like that. Be sure and eat it all yourself, and don't go giving it away or trading it for beer. You still need feeding up.'

Senmut hugged her, the first time he had done so in a long while. 'Thank you, Tia. I wouldn't dream of giving away your wonderful cakes.' Then he turned to his mother and said, 'And I want to keep a clear head for my studies this time, so I'll be avoiding the strong liquor.'

Nebet nodded, not trusting herself to speak. She could feel her throat tightening with emotion. It was as if she was sending him off to school for the very first time, all over again. She remembered how, on the first day of school for each of her sons, she had waved them goodbye and then hidden herself away to sob out her sadness. Knowing they would be home again for the rest days was no consolation. Their departure was symbolic of severing the maternal bond, and watching her babies leave home was, for Nebetiunet, the hardest part of being a mother. She could only imagine how much harder it must be for those mothers who had to send their sons to schools far away from home. They would not see their children for a year or more at a time and would have to rely on reports from tutors and servants.

Only the wealthiest families could afford private tutors for their children. Paser's mother, Merytra, had often said how glad she was to have been able to watch him and his brothers flourishing under their teachers' guidance. Nebet was grateful, too, for she had been able to share some of those lessons and had learned to read well enough to cope with the everyday business of running a household. She could not write, but then she had a house full of scribes to do that for her if necessary. Amenmose had taught Mutemwiya to read and Neferti was also keen to learn, but Mymy was a lost cause. She had shown no eagerness to acquire even the most basic of reading skills and was happy to remain ignorant. She said she could always rely on her brothers or, more recently, her husband to read for her. Nebet recognized that Mymy's lack of enthusiasm for education was no handicap. The majority of men and women were illiterate and yet they were happy. Despite what the scribes might say, the inability to read did not necessarily lead to misery and hardship, but they were right in saying that education opened doors. Senmut had at last seen the truth of all those words of wisdom his teachers had forced him to copy. He was determined to succeed.

The River was at its lowest and most sluggish. Everything in Kemet seemed to have slowed down. The heat at midday was oppressive and even the local dogs sought refuge from the sun. Menna and Bak spent much of their time at the domestic gardens, watering the thirsty vegetables. There had been a fine crop of cucumbers this year and Nebet had pickled some of them in vinegar. Now the radishes, leeks and onions were ready for picking. Nebet intended to trade her surplus in the marketplace, though the price she would get for the radishes would be low as there was a local glut of them.

She took an inventory of her stores to assess what she would need to see the family through the winter months. She had run down her stocks of dried pulses in the knowledge that she could replenish them from Amenmose's ration allowance. The last of the fava beans were soaking, ready for making bean patties. Tia would mash them in the kitchen mortar with garlic and herbs, and then small balls of the mixture would be fried in duck grease. Bunches of fresh young melokia leaves were hanging in the relative coolness of the cellar. This year's crop had satisfied even Tia's high standards. Nebet remembered the stores check she had made almost a year ago, on her return from Iunet. In spite of all that had happened since then, especially all the unexpected expenses, the family supplies were still at a very respectable level. She could permit herself a moment of self-congratulation, knowing that she had managed the household efficiently and economically and that no one had lacked for anything.

The holiday season of the Year's End was fast approaching. The weaving-sheds were working to full capacity making length after length of fine linen from the latest flax crop. Most of it would be sent to the royal storehouses, from where it might be distributed as New Year gifts or as part of the monthly rations for higher-ranking civil servants. There were linen-workshops attached to almost every major temple in Kemet. Once, as a courtesy between professionals, Nebet had been shown around the establishment at Hathor's temple in Iunet by one of her sister's friends. She had made polite noises but her compliments had disguised her satisfaction in the knowledge that the weavers of Waset were far better organized and produced a far superior product.

Djehutiemheb would have everyone believe that the weavers of Amen-Ra had no equals but Nebet was not so sure. The very best flax grew in the cooler, damper north so it stood to reason that the temple weavers of Mennefer, or Pe or Per-Bastet, having better materials to work with, could produce the very best cloth. As to the supervision and training of the workshop staff, she was hardly in a position to judge. The weaving sheds at Mennefer were probably the most serious rivals to the precedence of Waset. In the capital the craft came under the direct control of the Royal Household, in particular under the nominal supervision of the King's Wife and the King's Mother. There the business was conducted on a much larger scale and huge quantities of linen were produced every year, much of it being traded for goods imported from foreign lands. Kemet was famous, and rightly so, for the quality of its linen. Nebet liked to think that she had played a small part in the system that acquired the cedar and pine from Retjenu, and the ebony and ivory from Nubia.

As the year drew to a close Nebet found her thoughts turning to all that had happened in the previous twelve months. New Year was always a time for reflection and she had more to reflect upon than she had ever had before. Khay came first to her mind. Satra had been as good as her word and had offered him a home. When Amenmose gave up his temporary lodgings at the Mansion to return to his own home, Khay had been glad to accept Satra's offer. He was still, after all, a young boy and Nebet would not have people thinking that she had abandoned her baby to fend for himself. Satra's solution, as well as being generous, was perfectly respectable and, more to the point, Khaemwase was happy.

The opening of the Tjaty's offices at the Mansion meant that Amenmose travelled across the River more frequently than in the past, but Paser's principal base was still in the eastern city close to Ipet Esut, so Ameny had come home to stay. When he had quitted the Mansion, Montmose's old cook, Kheti, had chosen to go with Khay to live with Satra and Nedjemger. As her own house had filled up again Nebet had begun to think about replacing Iset. Idle as the girl had been, she had relieved the burden on Tia and her presence was missed, not that Tia herself would admit as much. Tia was noticeably stiffer and slower than she had been only a year ago. She needed reliable help in the kitchen, preferably from a resident housemaid. Neither Hotepu nor Didet was prepared to commit to live in, since both had aspirations to marriage.

Nebet had also noticed a difference in Meryt since she had spent that extended period living with her parents. Despite the difference in their ages, Meryt had become a friend as well as a trusted servant and Nebet would be sorry to lose her. She suspected that there was a man involved, and she would understand if Meryt left her employ in order to marry and set up a home of her own. If that happened, the household complement of servants would be even further depleted. Nebet was beginning to think seriously about looking for more help. Could she face the idea of training another maid up to Meryt's standard? Could Tia face the prospect of breaking in another Iset? These were matters that would have to be dealt with in the New Year.

Meanwhile the news from the Place of Truth was that there was no news. Wiya was not pregnant despite having been married for nearly four years. At Wiya's age Nebetiunet had already had two children and another on the way. Could Mutemwiya reconcile herself to being barren? Was it possible that Ramose would set her aside in favour of a woman who could give him children? Nebet hoped she knew Ramose's character well enough to put that worry out of her mind. The greatest challenge to his and Wiya's marriage would be the rattling tongues of the gossips of the Village. Nebet could only pray that their obvious love for each other would put paid to any malicious rumours. Mutemwiya was strong and her husband was a well-respected and influential man. His position and his reputation for fairness would provide powerful protection for Nebet's daughter. And, if children of her own seemed an impossible dream, Wiya had already declared her intention to adopt.

Nubnefert had developed into a delightful young woman who demonstrated a pleasing talent for her mother's craft. Djehutiemheb had been more than willing to accept her as a full apprentice in the linen workshops. This made Nebet very happy because it meant she was able to remain close to at least one of her children. While Neferti was gainfully employed in the weaving-sheds she was both content and proud to be seen to be following her mother's path. Inevitably one day Neferti would marry but, though she had been a woman for a whole year now, she was still immature in body. She had a lot of growing yet to do and her mother was in no hurry to find her a husband.

Plans for the holiday festivities were complicated by the family having been scattered in so many directions. Quite naturally Ramose felt it was his duty to preside over the celebrations in the Place of Truth, which meant that Wiya might not be able to spend more than a single day with her family in Waset. Satra, wanting to show how completely she had changed, offered to host one of the holiday gatherings at her new house and Nebet, after all she had said in the past about her sister's lack of generosity, knew they could not refuse. Consequently she had to scale down her own plans for a five-day party. She had sent an invitation to her sister in Iunet but she knew Nubnefert would not come, because the City of the Sycomore had more attractions than Waset at New Year. So it would be just the immediate family, but a small party could be just as much fun and Nebet was determined that they would see the year out in style.

Chapter Thirteen

The Five Days
upon the Year

NEBETIUNET WAS WOKEN GENTLY BY AMENMOSE'S KISS. 'GET DRESSED quickly,' he said. 'We have surprises for you downstairs.'

It was the day of the end-of-year holiday season that was recognized as the feast day of the goddess Isis, mother of Horus. Nebet was aware that the Five Days upon the Year were commemorated differently throughout Kemet, but here in Waset Amenmose's family had always celebrated the feast of Isis as a mothers' day. When his own mother was alive, Amenmose had paid her a visit early on the morning of Isis Day, taking her a gift of fruit or flowers, a custom Nebet had not known of until she came to live in Waset. Now she loved this time of year because it brought her children together. Pakhred and Senmut had come home from school the night before and both Wiya and Khay had promised to visit their mother today. Mymy would make the effort, though Nebet was not expecting to see her before noon.

Nebet pulled her shift dress over her head and struggled to tie the cords at the back of the bodice. She had a moment's regret that she had given Meryt leave to go home for the holidays. The maid's fingers were so much nimbler than hers. She ran her wooden comb through her hair and determinedly ignored the glistening white hairs caught in the comb's teeth. A light smudge of kohl on each eyelid was sufficient for the moment. She would save the more elaborate make-up and her carefully dressed wig for the evening, when Amenmose and she had been invited to a smart dinner party at the Tjaty's house. Now was a time for family. Downstairs there would be presents and hugs and kisses waiting for her. Neferti had been conspiring with her father for the last few days over something, but Nebet had pretended not to notice. The knowledge that her children and husband cared enough to go to such trouble was, in a way, worth more than any gifts that they might give her. Honeyed fruits would be eaten, flowers would fade, but the love that came with the gifts was unconditional and indestructible.

Neferti was waiting for her at the foot of the stairs and insisted that she cover her eyes, then hustled her quickly through the house to the garden. There, a tray of food had been set between two chairs brought from the reception room and placed beside the tiny pool. Foot-stools and some leather-covered cushions provided seats for the younger family members. Amenmose took her hand, led her to her chair and made sure she was comfortable before clapping his hands to summon the children. Pakhred came first, carrying a small, linen-wrapped bundle, which proved to contain a delightful little perfume bottle in blue glazed ware. Senmut's gift was a new needle-case fashioned out of bone and bearing her name in his own careful handwriting. Then Khaemwase appeared from where he had been hiding in the basement. He had caught the ferry at dawn to be with his mother for the morning meal. His gift was a wooden garden trough planted with tuberous lilies. It was so heavy that all three of her sons together had difficulty lifting it and she wondered how Khay had managed to carry it all the way from the Mansion where, she imagined, it had been planted to Nedjemger's orders. All was made clear when Mutemwiya and Ramose entered next, closely followed by Satra and Nedjemger himself.

Mutemwiya kissed her mother and said, 'Ramose said we couldn't let Khay drag that here all by himself as it's so heavy even when empty. I hope you like it. Khay and I chose it between us.'

Satra took up the tale. 'We all came across together and Nedjem planted the lilies this morning when we arrived. The flowers are a mothers' day gift from me, Nebetiunet, since you have been as a mother to me.' She bent to kiss Nebet's cheek.

Nebet could hardly believe her good fortune. Her eyes sparkled with tears of happiness as she gazed from one member of her family to the next, unable to find words to express her thanks. As Ramose poured beer for everyone, Neferti, watched over anxiously by her father, came forward with the last gift. She presented her mother with a small lidded basket that had seen better days, but as soon as Nebet felt its weight she knew that the basket was not the principal gift.

'You'd better open it carefully,' Amenmose said. 'I'm not sure how it'll react to all these people.'

Neferti threw a stern glance at her father and hissed, 'Don't give away the surprise.'

But Nebetiunet had already felt movement in the basket. The gift was alive. She settled the basket in her lap before slowly lifting the lid. Up popped a small, furry head. The green eyes, full of intelligent curiosity, looked straight at her and then the kitten mewed. Nebet laughed, picked up the tawny bundle of fluff and held it up for everyone to see. Her hand under the kitten's chin caused its fur to stand in a ruff round its neck, making it look like a miniature lion.

Neferti knelt at her mother's side and said, 'Do you really like her?'

'She's adorable. This is a wonderful surprise,' Nebet said, kissing her daughter's brow. 'What made you think of getting a kitten?'

'You have to admit,' Amenmose said, 'that Tamiu's a bit past it now. We need a decent mouser in this house and this one's mother is a champion.'

'The little one is the best of the litter,' Neferti assured her. 'I chose her myself.'

'She's just perfect, and I'm sure she'll be the scourge of the rodent population for the whole district, won't you, my pet?' She turned the kitten to face her and smiled as the little creature mewed again, then yawned, its tiny jaws opening impossibly wide. 'What a lovely present. What lovely presents you've all given me. Thank you all so very much.'

'What are you going to call her?' Neferti asked, scratching the kitten's neck until the creature, now sitting in Nebet's lap, was purring loudly.

'She must be Mati,' Nebet said, inspired by the leonine appearance of the young cat.

'Oh, how clever. "My Lioness" is just right,' Neferti laughed.

'But no spoiling her now,' Amenmose warned his daughter. 'She'll have to earn her keep.'

'Of course, Ameny,' Nebet said, 'but she's hardly of a size to face up to a mouse yet, let alone a rat.' Mati yawned again and began kneading with her paws as a prelude to settling down for a nap. Nebet caressed the

kitten's head as the green eyes closed and the purring became almost a warble. 'She'll learn quickly but for now let me enjoy her.'

'As you say, dear,' Amenmose softened. 'It's your day.'

'And the day of the Goddess,' Nebet reminded him. She accepted a cup of beer from Ramose and raised it saying, 'To your spirits, everyone, and may the Goddess look kindly upon you all.'

'To your spirits,' they all replied.

Mymy arrived in the afternoon with Abau and the baby. Wadjet had started to smile and in her dark-grey eyes Nebet saw a definite twinkle. The child was so contented that, as she was passed from one doting relative to another, she smiled and cooed and won everyone's heart. Mymy's gift to her mother was a rather bedraggled bunch of wild flowers which had clearly been picked along the field boundaries that morning. Nebet told herself it was the thought that counted, and thanked Mymy warmly. When Wadjet became hungry, Mymy took her into the shade of the pomegranate tree to feed her, making sure, first of all, to make her peace with the Lady, whose serpent manifestation might be lurking in the corner of the garden wall.

There had been no sighting of the cobra since Wadjet's birth. Saucers of milk left for her had gone sour and no tell-tale patterns were seen in the dust to show where a snake had slithered across the courtyard or been hunting around the grain bins. Tia said these were all signs that the snake had been sent by the Goddess to watch over the young mother and her child and that, once Mymy had returned to her own home, there was no reason for the Lady to stay. Nebet felt a little disloyal in her relief that the snake had gone, but was confident that she had done nothing to upset it and its departure was not a sign of the Lady's displeasure; simply, her presence was no longer needed. Wadjet's flourishing health was most certainly the gift of the Lady. Few children could hope for such an auspicious start to life.

Thoughts were now turned towards preparing for Paser's party. The Tjaty had not been in Waset for the Year's End holidays since His Majesty's accession. He had always accompanied the King to one of the festivals held at the major southern shrines, at Suan as last year, or Behdet or Abdu. This year, however, the King was celebrating in the North, unwilling perhaps to be separated from his family again so soon after the Battle of Kadesh. Paser's decision to hold the party in his private house on the outskirts of the City announced to all the party-goers that this was a time for celebration and enjoyment, and formal business and politics would have no place. The guests included high-ranking officials like the High Priest, Nebwenenef, as well as more humble folk such as his secretary, Amenmose, but all had one thing in common: Paser considered them his friends.

Mutemwiya was thrilled to have been invited with Ramose, and could still hardly believe that she was to rub shoulders with some of the most important people in Waset. She told her mother so while they were making the final preparations for their party attire.

'Why shouldn't you be invited?' Nebet asked. 'The Tjaty thinks very highly of Ramose and respects his intelligence. Paser has always enjoyed intelligent conversation.'

So rarely did Nebetiunet use the Tjaty's given name that Wiya had all but forgotten her family connection with the King's principal adviser. She felt a warm glow of pride as she realized she could hold her head up high in this gathering of the great, for she was daughter to the Tjaty's sister and her husband was the Tjaty's valued servant.

Neferti had offered to take Meryt's place and was enjoying the role of lady's maid. 'Do you know who else will be there?' she asked, as she used a bone pin to tease out the curls in her sister's festival wig.

'I think one of Paser's brothers will be there, and probably his sister too. Their families are all very close. I know Senetnay and Ahmose have been invited but I don't know whether they'll accept,' Nebet said. She was grinding ochre to a fine powder on her slate palette. Mixed with a little grease it would become lip paint and blusher for her cheeks.

'Surely it would be an insult to the Tjaty to turn down such an invitation?' Wiya said, surprised at the suggestion.

'In ordinary circumstances, yes, I'd agree with you. But Senetnay has been through such a lot that she's still not up to company. A formal party like this might be too much for her. The Tjaty will understand.'

The tragedies of child and infant death were not confined to the peasant farmers and the poor city-dwellers. Paser's wife had given stillbirth to their first child. They had mourned that loss for years, long after they had other children to love. They would understand only too well what Ahmose and Senetnay had suffered and would take no insult at the absence of the Chief Architect and his wife.

'Who else, then?' Wiya asked. She pulled the wig on over her short hair and tugged and twisted at it, looking at herself in the Hathor mirror her sister held up for her.

Satra, reaching over to pick up a pair of tweezers, said, 'Meryra and several of the lesser officials from the Mansion have been asked, though Lord Tjia let it be known that he would not be attending. I think he may think himself too far above the rest of us to be seen to be enjoying himself.'

'I suppose the King's brother can't really mix with ordinary people,' Neferti said wisely.

'He was married to the King's Sister,' Satra said, 'but that doesn't make him any better than us. Father knew him when he was a boy.'

'Who else, Muti?' Wiya asked, to steer the conversation away from dangerous ground.

'I'm not entirely sure but your father will know because he wrote out the invitations.'

'And he hasn't told you?' Wiya was astonished.

'I didn't ask,' Nebet smiled. 'I'd like it to be a surprise.'

'Muti, how can you stay so calm?' Neferti asked. 'I can hardly wait to know. I shan't be able to sleep until you come back and tell me all about it.'

'We'll be very late, dear,' Nebet warned, 'so you'd be better going to bed and hearing about it in the morning.' She knew, of course, that Neferti would take no notice of this typical motherly advice.

'How does this look?' Wiya asked, giving the wig one last tug.

'Very becoming, dear,' Nebet said, 'but you'll have to take it off again before you put on your gown.'

Wiya said a very rude word and they all had a fit of giggles.

The litters arrived in time to allow the guests to reach Paser's house before sunset. The party was to be held in the beautiful garden in front of the house where hundreds of saucer lamps placed along the top of the garden wall twinkled in the twilight. As the guests passed through the gate, servants presented them with the traditional floral collars and headbands before ushering them into the presence of their host, Paser, who greeted everyone warmly, making no distinction between family, friends and colleagues.

Nebetiunet, usually so shy and diffident, was emboldened by having lived for a short while in her youth in this very house. Being the senior female member of her family present, she took upon herself the responsibility for making introductions. She was almost overwhelmed by the welcome she received from Paser's sister, whom she had not seen since her own marriage. Their reunion included the wife of Paser's brother, and both ladies were eager to be introduced to Nebet's family and to introduce them to other guests. Soon Nebet, Satra and Wiya were chatting amiably with women whom they had never met before but who all seemed perfectly friendly and approachable.

There were chairs and stools set out in the colonnade round the pool, which was lit by tall alabaster lamps. Reed torches burned in stands between the trees and huge quantities of food and drink were to be found in every corner. The food was delectable. Paser had spared no expense. From the kitchen area wafted the smell of a whole ox cooking over the roasting pit. Plump spit-roasted ducks and geese were torn into portions and distributed with flatbread to catch the tasty grease. Small birds, such as pigeons and quail, were offered whole. The baskets of loaves and the dishes of fruit and vegetables, cooked and fresh, seemed never to be emptied, as servants were quick to replenish them. Nebet could not resist the first figs of the season, so much sweeter and juicier than the fruit of the sycomore. Wine was flowing abundantly. At first, faced with a bewildering choice of fine grape wines, Nebet felt that admitting a preference for pomegranate wine might make her seem unsophisticated. But when she saw her companions sampling their choice of all that Paser had to offer, she felt more at ease.

Musicians, dancers, acrobats and jugglers entertained the guests well into the night. The young children of Paser's sons, allowed to stay up late for once, at last had to admit their tiredness and came to wish the Tjaty good night. People continued to mingle, forming and reforming conversational groups, exchanging pleasantries, commenting on the food, the drink, the entertainment and, above all, the Tjaty's generosity. Satra swelled with pride when Nedjemger was taken on a tour of the gardens by his host. Time passed all too quickly. Guests, feeling they had imposed on Paser's hospitality for long enough, began to take their leave. The party dwindled to his closest friends, among them Nebetiunet and her family.

Someone found a *senet* board and Amenmose and Ramose became engrossed in a highly tactical game, watched by their wives.

'You'll not be able to tear him away from that in a hurry,' said a voice over her shoulder. Nebet turned to see Paser standing behind her.

'You know it's always been Ameny's weakness,' she said.

'Yes, he's always been a good player, or so he tells me,' Paser grinned, 'but I think he may have met his match in Ramose.'

'Thank you so much for inviting us all,' Nebet said, remembering her manners.

'Not at all,' Paser said, pulling up a chair to sit down beside her. 'The pleasure is mine, and it's all the greater now that the party has been reduced to my dearest friends. Look over there.' He pointed across the *senet* players to where Nebwenenef was sprawled, inelegantly, in a chair set against a persea tree. The First Servant of Amen-Ra was fast asleep and snoring loudly. 'Weni never could take his drink.'

In other surroundings, in the company of other people, Nebet might have gasped at this disrespectful comment. Here and now she was freed from the bonds of social etiquette, so she giggled and said, 'I remember one New Year at Iunet . . .'

One reminiscence led to another until she had quite forgotten that she was a humble temple weaver and her companion was the Tjaty of the South. They laughed until they cried over their shared memories.

Eventually Paser said, 'I do so love talking with you Nebetiunet. You bring me back to the real world. I spend so much of my time being diplomatic and saying what people want to hear instead of what they need to hear that I forget what it is to really talk. You're like a cool breeze from the north, refreshing and invigorating.'

'You'd better not let Ameny hear you talking like that,' Nebet said, wagging her finger at him. 'He might get jealous.' Later, when she recalled this conversation, she blushed to think of what she had dared to imply. Of course the Tjaty had meant nothing improper and, though Nebet had worshipped him when she was a little girl, it was always Amenmose who had occupied her heart. It must have been the wine talking.

Paser smiled indulgently. There had been a time, when Nebetiunet had been flowering into womanhood, that he had felt something more than brotherly affection for her, but as soon as she set eyes on Amenmose it was obvious that no other man would ever have her love. 'He's a lucky man, as I have always said. I hope he knows how lucky he is.'

Amenmose triumphantly raised his last piece as he completed the move from the board. 'There! My game, I think.'

Ramose good-naturedly applauded his opponent. 'A good game, too. Thank you for the lesson.'

From her place behind her husband Wiya yawned loudly.

'Tired, dear?' Ramose asked.

'Almost too tired to stay awake,' she said, then glanced guiltily at Paser, worried that he might think her yawn one of boredom.

The Tjaty stood up and said, 'Me too. It's been a delightful party but I fear this body is not as young as it used to be and is longing for its bed.'

Their protestations denying Paser's age and decrepitude woke Nebwenenef. 'I must have dozed off for a moment. Have I missed something?' he asked innocently. The whole party roared with laughter.

They reached home before dawn. With the holidays only half over, there was no need for early rising. They crept to their beds, trying not to disturb the sleeping children. Nebet had arranged that Satra and Wiya would share her room, while Amenmose, Ramose and Nedjemger took the boys' room. Pakhred, Senmut and Khay had joined Gemni on the roof where, to judge by the empty dishes and jars at the foot of the ladder, they had had their own party. Nebet was suddenly very tired, too tired to do more than wipe off the heaviest of her make-up with a damp cloth. When the sun was up there would be a queue for the shower stall in the basement, and Bak and Menna would be kept busy bringing water from the well for the family's ablutions. For the moment all she wanted was her bed and, even though she had to share it with her daughter and her husband's sister she fell asleep almost instantly.

It seemed that she had only just closed her eyes when she was awoken by someone hurriedly rising from the bed. It was hardly surprising after so much wine and beer had been drunk at the party that the need to pass water had become urgent. Nebet thought that, as she was awake, she might as well do the same. As she sat up, the shadowy figure outlined in the half-light through the open door bent double and Nebet heard retching. She was suddenly wide awake. It was early morning and a woman was being violently sick. Wiya was pregnant!

Nebet snatched up her shawl from the clothes chest and went to throw it over her daughter's shoulders. Behind her the third sleeper awoke and sat up, saying, 'What's the matter, Muti?' Nebet's heart skipped a beat as she realized the truth.

Nebetiunet wrapped the shawl about the heaving shoulders of her husband's sister, and said, 'There's nothing to worry about, dear. Satra's not feeling very well.'

'Is it the food? Are we all going to be ill?' Wiya worried.

'No, dear,' Nebet sighed, wondering how her daughter would take the news.

Before she could think how to explain, Satra turned and said, 'I'm sorry to wake you, Mutemwiya. I should have warned you both. This has been happening for a few days now.' Another bout of retching prevented her from saying more but Wiya needed no words to tell her what this meant.

'Is Satra pregnant, Muti?' she asked in a whisper.

'It would seem so, yes,' Nebet said, biting back her inner voice which screamed at the unfairness of the world.

Mutemwiya burst into tears.